Mission Life in Cree-Ojibwe Country

Our Lives: Diary, Memoir, and Letters

Social history contests the construction of the past as the story of elites — a grand narrative dedicated to the actions of those in power. Our Lives seeks instead to make available voices from the past that might otherwise remain unheard. By foregrounding the experience of ordinary individuals, the series aims to demonstrate that history is ultimately the story of our lives, lives constituted in part by our response to the issues and events of the era into which we are born. Many of the voices in the series thus speak in the context of political and social events of the sort about which historians have traditionally written. What they have to say fills in the details, creating a richly varied portrait that celebrates the concrete, allowing broader historical settings to emerge between the lines. The series invites materials that are engagingly written and that contribute in some way to our understanding of the relationship between the individual and the collective. Manuscripts that include an introduction or epilogue that contextualizes the primary materials and reflects on their significance will be preferred.

MISSION LIFE IN CREE-OJIBWE COUNTRY

Memories of a Mother and Son

Elizabeth Bingham Young
AND E. Ryerson Young

EDITED AND WITH INTRODUCTIONS BY
Jennifer S. H. Brown

AU PRESS

Copyright © 2014 Jennifer S. H. Brown
Published by AU Press, Athabasca University
1200, 10011 – 109 Street, Edmonton, ab t5j 3s8

Cover map © Marzolino / Shutterstock.com
Printed and bound in Canada by Friesens
doi: 10.15215/aupress/9781771990035.01

Library and Archives Canada Cataloguing in Publication

Mission life in Cree-Ojibwe country : memories of a mother and son /
Elizabeth Bingham Young and E. Ryerson Young ; edited and with introductions by
Jennifer S.H. Brown.

(Our lives: diary, memoir, and letters) Includes bibliographical references and index.
Issued in print and electronic formats. isbn 978-1-77199-003-5 (pbk.).—
isbn 978-1-77199-004-2 (pdf).—isbn 978-1-77199-005-9 (epub)

1. Young, Elizabeth Bingham.   2. Young, E. Ryerson (Egerton Ryerson), 1869–1962.
3. Missionaries—Manitoba—Biography.   4. Methodists—Manitoba—Biography.
5. Methodist Church—Missions—Manitoba.   6. Mothers and sons—Manitoba—
Biography.   7. Cree Indians—Missions—Manitoba.   8. Ojibwa Indians—Missions—
Manitoba.   i. Brown, Jennifer S.H., 1940–, editor ii. Series: Our lives (Edmonton, Alta.)

BV2815.M3M58 2014   266'.7092   c2014-905549-8
                                               c2014-905550-1

We acknowledge the financial support of the Government of Canada through
the Canada Book Fund (cbf) for our publishing activities.

Assistance provided by the Government of Alberta, Alberta Multimedia
Development Fund.

Canada Council   Conseil des Arts   Alberta
for the Arts   du Canada   Government

The Indian Story-teller, J. E. Laughlin, watercolour on paper. The painting shows the
Ojibwe leader Zhaawanaash ("Souwanas") with E. Ryerson (Eddie) and Lillian Young,
the two eldest children of Egerton R. Young and Elizabeth Bingham Young, at Berens
River. rom 2008.10.1, with permission of the Royal Ontario Museum (photograph
copyright rom). Laughlin illustrated several of Egerton R. Young's books; this image
appears opposite page 222 in Young's Algonquin Indian Tales (1903). Eddie's jacket,
doubtless made by "Little Mary" Robinson, is now in the Royal Ontario Museum
(see figure 7 in this volume).

J. E. Laughlin.

Contents

PART II "A Missionary and His Son" and Subsequent Reminiscences, by E. Ryerson Young

PART III Supplementary Documents and Excerpts

Abbreviations

HBC	Hudson's Bay Company
HBCA	Hudson's Bay Company Archives
JSHB collection	Young family materials in possession of Jennifer S. H. Brown
Norway House baptismal register	Wesleyan Methodist Register of Baptisms, Norway House, 1840–89. Baptisms solemnized in the Wesleyan-Methodist Chapel, Rossville, deposited in the UCA, Conference of Manitoba and Northwestern Ontario. Copy in Jennifer S. H. Brown collection.
OED	*Oxford English Dictionary*
ROM	Royal Ontario Museum
UCA, Winnipeg	United Church Archives, Conference of Manitoba and North-western Ontario, Winnipeg
UCCA, Toronto	United Church of Canada Archives, Toronto
UCCA, Young fonds	Egerton Ryerson Young Fonds, no. 3607, accession no. 94.030c, United Church of Canada Archives, Toronto

Foreword

The Reverend Egerton Ryerson Young, a prolific writer on Methodist mission work, and his wife, Elizabeth Bingham Young, lived in what is now northern Manitoba from 1868 to 1876, first at Rossville, the Methodist mission at Norway House, and then at the newly founded mission station at Berens River. *Mission Life in Cree-Ojibwe Country* combines a memoir by Elizabeth, written in 1927, and the reminiscences of her son, Eddie, also recorded many years after the events described, in 1935 and 1962. Supplementary documents serve to deepen our understanding of the two main texts, as do the introductory materials, editorial annotations and documentation, and extended commentaries, all expertly prepared by Jennifer Brown.

The writings of Elizabeth Bingham Young introduce us to a female dimension totally lacking in most missionary accounts. She had just married and was only twenty-four years old when she travelled from Ontario to Norway House. Despite what must have been a very jarring transition, she contributed to the missionary outreach in ways that her husband could not, or would not, himself. She learned Cree and associated closely with the local women. While at Norway House and Berens River, she acted as a nurse and doctor, as well as giving birth to four children of her own. Her reminiscences appear in all their immediacy.

The second family member showcased in the volume, Eddie, is in many ways even more intriguing than his mother. Born at Norway House in June 1869, Eddie was raised to the age of seven among the Cree at Norway House and the Ojibwe at Berens River. He soon became immersed in the local culture, which he absorbed without the preconceptions and value judgments brought by an adult. He grew up speaking Cree and, by the time he reached the age of five, had become, in the opinion of his father, "the best interpreter he had."

The primary source of Eddie's acclimatization was his Cree nurse, Mary Robinson, whom the Youngs had taken into their household after her husband abandoned her. Little Mary, as she was affectionately known, cared for Eddie during his years at Norway House and Berens River. The descriptions of Mary's efforts to save Eddie from a whipping at the hands of his father are among the most moving in the account. Eddie learned from Mary control, self-restraint, and a sense of independence. Vividly he recalled the culture shock he later felt on his arrival in a rural Ontario school, where other boys teased him and called him "Indian" names. At all times, Brown rigorously calls attention to points at which Eddie's memories deviate from other recorded observations closer to the events in time. She is very careful.

Mission Life in Cree-Ojibwe Country also tells us a great deal about Egerton Ryerson Young, pater familias. The last twenty or so years of his life he devoted to writing and lecturing about his family's years in the mission field, producing a total of twelve books. As did many of his Christian missionary contemporaries, he adopted a patronizing attitude toward the beliefs and customs of First Nations. Thanks to the recollections of his wife and son, he now becomes more three-dimensional. Despite all the bravado of his books, Young was a complex figure. Although he spent the better part of eight years of his life trying to convince the Cree and Ojibwe to abandon their traditions, he developed a keen interest in Native legends and, as Brown notes, seemed able to earn the respect and confidence of local elders. He evidently had no objection to Eddie's friendship with Sandy Harte, the Cree boy who lived with the Youngs at Norway House and taught Eddie how to trap, or to his son's association with the Ojibwe leader Zhaawanaash at Berens River, who often entertained both Eddie and his younger sister Lillian with traditional stories. In his final year at Berens River, he was nonetheless furious and upset to discover Eddie's participation in an Ojibwe dance ceremony, possibly fearing (as Eddie later conjectured) that his son was becoming too closely entangled in Ojibwe ways.

One senses in Young a certain frustration and disappointment. He and Elizabeth, despite her ill health, spent seven physically and mentally demanding years together in the "North West." Why did his advance in the Methodist Church subsequently stall—merely because he chose to leave Berens River after only two years of the expected three-year term? Following his return from the mission field, he earned only a series of poorly paid pastoral appointments in southern Ontario. What, then, did he finally obtain in exchange for his "Indian work"? Perhaps seeking a larger stage, the gifted public speaker and writer embarked in 1888 on what proved to be a very successful lecturing and writing career.

Historians depend on documents that can be studied, analyzed, and placed in a larger historical context. Thanks to this volume, we now have a clearer, more intimate understanding of the life of a mid-nineteenth-century family in the Canadian mission field. Elizabeth Bingham Young's memoirs provide invaluable insight into the experience of mission wives, as well as allowing us a new perspective on the character and writings of her husband. And Eddie's reminiscences offer a first-hand account of a young boy's acculturation to Native ways. Their memories are thoughtfully framed—Jennifer Brown is a superb editor—and a fascination to read.

Donald B. Smith
Calgary, Alberta
June 2014

Acknowledgements

The memoirs, correspondence, and other writings of Egerton R. and Elizabeth Bingham Young and their son, E. Ryerson, which their descendants have preserved and curated over the past 140 years, offer a unique record of life in a Methodist mission household at Norway House and Berens River, Manitoba, in the years 1868 to 1876, and also provide unusual glimpses of a returned missionary family's parsonage life in Ontario. When Elizabeth Young and her son, "Eddie" as he was known in youth, undertook, in later life, the substantial projects of recording experiences in the North that profoundly influenced them and whose details remained sharply etched in memory, they created remarkable documents for which we may all be grateful.

In turn, two grandsons of the Youngs, the Reverend Harold Egerton Young and Harcourt Brown, always appreciated and took interest in the documentary materials that they received from Elizabeth ("Grandma") Young and E. Ryerson Young in the years after Egerton R. Young died, in 1909. In the 1970s, once retired, they worked with siblings and cousins to locate and gather records that were at risk of being separated and scattered down the generations. Although they each retained documents and copies of items of particular importance to them, they arranged for the bulk of Young papers to be donated to the Archives of Ontario in 1978. Later, in 1994, H. Egerton Young and I agreed that the United Church of Canada Archives in Toronto would be a more appropriate home, and the papers were transferred there. I owe special thanks to H. Egerton Young for sharing with me the writings of his father, E. Ryerson, and grandmother Elizabeth Young, and for granting me permission to use them in my research, writing, and teaching, in tandem with the materials held by my father, Harcourt Brown (d. 1990).

In my generation, David J. E. and William C. Young, grandsons of E. Ryerson Young, generously donated to the Royal Ontario Museum in Toronto the Cree artifacts that their (and my) great-grandparents brought home from the North, and a few of those treasured items are pictured in this book. Their cousin and mine, the Reverend Dale Young, has shared with me a number of stories she heard from her grandfather about his early life in Cree country, adding some oral history to his invaluable writings.

Much of my research in the years from 2004 to 2011 was supported while holding a Canada Research Chair in Aboriginal Peoples and Histories at the University of Winnipeg. Based with me at the university's Centre for Rupert's Land Studies, several former students (who became friends and colleagues) contributed to this project. My CRC research associate, Susan Elaine Gray, collaborated with me on two books bringing forth the Berens River field research of anthropologist A. Irving Hallowell (see citations in Part II). Master's student Mallory Richard transcribed the typescripts of E. Ryerson Young's memoirs as a base for my editing of the texts appearing here. Anne Lindsay, during her student years and ever since, has been a pillar of research support, remarkably skilled at finding and helping to interpret no end of obscure sources and references. Also at the University of Winnipeg, Diane Haglund, archivist of the United Church Archives, Conference of Manitoba and Northwestern Ontario, was always happy to assist in finding sources and responding to research questions.

At the Royal Ontario Museum, Kenneth Lister, assistant curator, Arctic and Subarctic, was most helpful in providing information on and access to the Egerton R. Young collection donated by David and William Young. Thanks also to Nicola Woods for her assistance in arranging for photographs of selected items and to the ROM for permission to reproduce some of them here. Also in Toronto, Nichole Vonk, General Council archivist at the United Church of Canada Archives and her associate, Elizabeth Mathew, helped greatly in locating and securing copies of needed materials, answering queries, and providing permission to publish documents in the Young fonds. My warm thanks also to two linguist colleagues: Saskatchewan Cree linguist and historian Keith Goulet, who helped with numerous questions concerning Cree terms and names, and Jeffrey Muehlbauer, who assisted on many linguistic points and took on the challenge of interpreting Sandy Harte's Cree-syllabics letter to Egerton Young (see Part III, sec. 7). And, not least, my appreciation to Google, the search engine that amid its flotsam and jetsam comes up with data and answers I could never otherwise find.

A special thanks to Pamela MacFarland Holway, senior editor at Athabasca University Press, who took keen interest in this project from the outset and shepherded it through the many phases leading to publication. My gratitude also to Renée Fossett, professional indexer, who has once again worked her magic on a challenging book in need of the best possible index. And, finally, particular warm sentiments for Wilson B. Brown, who started hearing about the Young family in the 1960s and took on, among other things, the digital compiling of their genealogy and the copying and enhancing of old photographs and other documents; he has been the best of research companions throughout. Not least, his interest in pursuing Young antecedents led us into co-authoring another book linked to this one—a biography of Egerton R. Young's great-grandfather, *Col. William Marsh: Vermont Patriot and Loyalist* (2013). There, as here, stories, perspectives, and insights have come from carefully held memories and old documents to shed light, not only on family histories and dynamics, but on their larger historical contexts as refracted through the actions and responses of individuals living through events and situations largely beyond our ken.

Jennifer S. H. Brown
Denver, Colorado
February 2014

Mission Life in Cree-Ojibwe Country

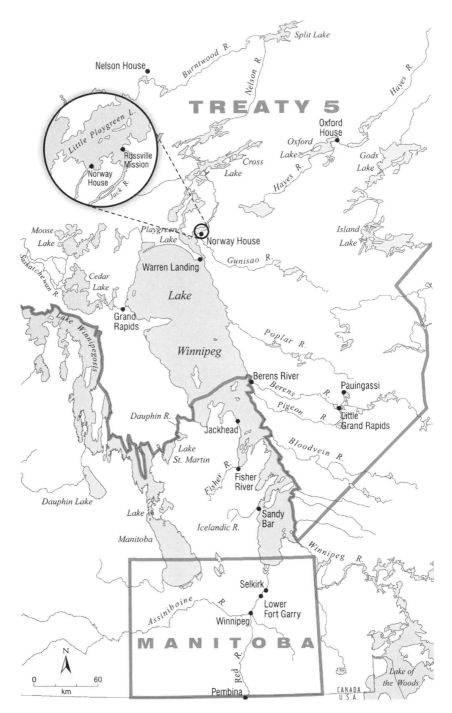

The Norway House and Lake Winnipeg region as of the end of 1875, showing the area covered by Treaty 5, signed in late September, and various settlements to which the Youngs refer in their writings. Map by Weldon Hiebert.

Introduction

In May of 1868, Elizabeth Bingham Young and her new husband, Egerton Ryerson Young, began a long journey from Hamilton, Ontario, to the Methodist mission of Rossville, located near Norway House in the Hudson's Bay Company territories known until 1870 as Rupert's Land. Egerton Young had been ordained in Hamilton as a Wesleyan minister in June 1867 and had settled there as pastor of its First Methodist Church, an impressive appointment for the newly minted clergyman. In January 1868, however, much to his surprise, he received a letter from his superiors, Enoch Wood and Lachlan Taylor at the Methodist Mission Rooms, Toronto, telling him that the church missionary committee had "unanimously decided to ask you to go as a missionary to the Indian tribes at Norway House, and in the North-West Territories north of Lake Winnipeg."[1]

Egerton and Elizabeth had been married less than a month. His pastorate was meeting with great success, and his parishioners very much wanted him and his new wife to stay. The request was disconcerting but strongly worded, and the decision was a difficult one. Twenty-two years later, in his first book (1890), Egerton recalled how Elizabeth and he prayed together for wisdom and guidance in the matter and reached a resolution:

> As we arose from our knees, I quietly said to Mrs. Young, "Have you any impression on your mind as to our duty in this matter?"
>
> Her eyes were suffused in tears, but the voice, though low, was firm, as she replied, "The call has come very unexpectedly, but I think it is from God, and we will go."[2]

---

1 Egerton R. Young, *By Canoe and Dog-Train Among the Cree and Salteaux Indians* (London: Charles H. Kelly, 1890), 27.

2 Ibid., 28. In the language of the time, Young was received "into full connection" in the

The young couple surely assessed the possible costs to Egerton's career if he declined his superiors' request. But, in her husband's memory, Elizabeth took hold of the issue, relying on her genuine sense of spiritual guidance while providing him with strong support. During the next years, their life and work at the Norway House Methodist mission of Rossville, and then at Berens River, was a collaborative enterprise in which Elizabeth's ability to take initiatives, to build relationships, and to deal with problems often unexpected and always challenging was critical. The experience changed the family's lives for good, exerting strong influences on them long after their return to Ontario in 1876. Egerton's work became well known over the next three decades through his lectures, books, and other writings. The mission memoirs of Elizabeth, however, and of their son, E. Ryerson Young ("Eddie"), add dimensions otherwise lacking. Long hidden away, they provide remarkable insights into the family's life during and after their mission years, in voices rather different from that of the husband and father. They also shed light on the close relationships that mother and son formed with certain Cree and Ojibwe individuals whom they came to know well and who were instrumental in drawing Eddie deeply into their own social and linguistic universe for as long as the experience lasted.[3]

Methodist Missions in Upper Canada and Rupert's Land

Canadian Methodist missionary work began in Upper Canada (later Ontario) in the 1820s and received a strong impulse from the conversion of its first notable Aboriginal adherent and later missionary, Peter Jones. Within a decade, Methodism was spreading among the Ojibwe people of the region "with astonishing rapidity," encouraged by circuit preachers both white and Native, and its adherents began to look toward new fields to the northwest.[4]

church at the Methodists' annual conference in Hamilton in June 1867: J. E. Sanderson, *The First Century of Methodism in Canada*, vol. 2 (Toronto: William Briggs, 1910), 217.

3 See Jennifer S. H. Brown, "Growing Up Algonquian: A Missionary's Son in Cree-Ojibwe Country, 1869–1876," in *Papers of the Thirty-Ninth Algonquian Conference*, ed. Karl S. Hele and Regna Darnell (London: University of Western Ontario, 2008), 72–93.

4 John Webster Grant, *Moon of Wintertime: Missionaries and the Indians of Canada in Encounter Since 1534* (Toronto: University of Toronto Press, 1984), 75–78. On

By 1840, the Methodists, through their parent Wesleyan Missionary Society in England, had received an invitation from the Hudson's Bay Company to establish a series of missions in Rupert's Land—carefully placed at posts where they would not confront Anglican or Roman Catholic clergy, who were being permitted to work in other locales.[5] The English-born Reverend James Evans, who already had substantial experience with Ojibwe missions in Upper Canada, was to be stationed at Norway House. Under his leadership were Robert Rundle (sent to Fort Edmonton), George Barnley (sent to Moose Factory), and William Mason, all English born, and Ojibwe preachers Peter Jacobs and Henry Bird Steinhauer, born in Upper Canada. Evans soon had troubles with the Hudson's Bay Company, exacerbated by accusations about his personal conduct, and left for England in 1846. By 1850, the others had withdrawn for various reasons, except for Steinhauer, who established a mission at Oxford House (Manitoba) in 1851, and Mason, who remained at Rossville until 1854, when he joined the Church of England.[6]

In 1854, the Wesleyan Methodist Church in Canada was formed from various existing Canadian and British groups.[7] The Canadian Methodists took over the charge of the Indian missions in the northwest and sent out a second contingent to revive the work. Thomas Hurlburt, who had previously worked with James Evans in Upper Canada, became chairman of the Hudson's Bay District missions, based at Rossville. English-born Robert Brooking, who had preached in Africa for six years and then in Upper Canada, went to Oxford House.[8] Ojibwe preacher Allen Salt was sent to

Peter Jones, see Donald B. Smith, *Sacred Feathers: The Reverend Peter Jones (Kahke-waquonaby) and the Mississauga Indians* (Toronto: University of Toronto Press, 1987).

5 Neil Semple, *The Lord's Dominion: The History of Canadian Methodism* (Montréal and Kingston: McGill-Queen's University Press, 1996), 174, explains the political and tactical reasons for the company's invitation.

6 Grant, *Moon of Wintertime*, 101–2.

7 See Semple, *The Lord's Dominion*, 5, for a chart showing successive Methodist reorganizations in Canada.

8 See the biographies of Hurlburt (by Arthur G. Reynolds) and Brooking (by Anthony J. Hall) in the *Dictionary of Canadian Biography* online. While the first western Methodists fostered the use of Native languages through support for translating and printing the scriptures and teaching James Evans's Cree syllabics, Hurlburt was the only non-Native Methodist missionary in his times who could preach without an interpreter.

Lac la Pluie (Rainy Lake), while Henry Steinhauer began a new mission at Whitefish Lake, Alberta.[9]

Hurlburt and Salt, however, soon had to leave their postings, for reasons that signalled an issue common for missionary couples of the time. In 1857, Hurlburt was obliged to depart "on account of Mrs. Hurlburt's precarious health," and Allen Salt similarly returned to Upper Canada on account of his wife's ill health.[10] Charles Stringfellow and his wife (mentioned in Elizabeth's memoir), who had lately arrived at Oxford House, were moved to Rossville in the Hurlburts' stead, but by the time the Youngs replaced them there in 1868, Mrs. Stringfellow was described as an invalid. Other instances of mission wives' illnesses are not hard to find; indeed, when the Youngs left Berens River for Ontario in 1876, after only two years there, the reason cited was Elizabeth's poor health. In their case, other factors also influenced their leaving — as may have been true with the other wives; details are often lacking. But mission life and work could take a heavy toll on the women who were "volunteered" into their husbands' religious vocations. Such assignments required stamina and qualities beyond their undoubted zeal and devotion.

The Youngs in 1868 were part of a third small wave of Methodist missionaries sent to the Northwest from Canada. Their years of service, 1868 to 1876, were among the most eventful of that century — a period of great transitions in the Northwest and of developments that presented challenges for all involved. Married late in the year of Canada's confederation, 1867, Elizabeth and Egerton were almost immediately called upon to serve at the Rossville mission north of Lake Winnipeg. From May through July of 1868, they journeyed from Hamilton, Ontario, by ship and train to St. Paul, Minnesota Territory, and then by Red River cart to the Red River Settlement in what was still Rupert's Land of the Hudson's Bay Company's territories, in a party led by the experienced western missionary, the Reverend George McDougall. The trip across the American plains, aside from its physical challenges, occasioned anxiety because of hostilities between the Sioux and the American military following the Minnesota Sioux Uprising of 1862; the party made sure to display conspicuously a British Union Jack, useful when

9 Grant, *Moon of Wintertime*, 146; Young, *By Canoe and Dog-Train*, 10.

10 "Stations and Missionaries, 1857–58," in *32nd Annual Report, Canada Conference* (Methodist), Toronto, 1857.

accosted by some Sioux checking on their identity. They reached Red River just in time for a terrible storm, and to find the settlement much afflicted by a plague of locusts, and then continued their journey north on Lake Winnipeg, by HBC York boat, to the Rossville mission at Norway House. The prairie trip, in particular, was both memorable and not to be replicated, as by 1873, when they travelled on furlough, they could make use of expanded rail and steamship travel in Minnesota and on Lake Superior.

In 1869–70 came the Red River Resistance led by Louis Riel and other Métis greatly concerned about the annexation of Rupert's Land to Canada and the losses of lands under the new grid survey regime that cut across their old established river lots. Norway House, four hundred miles to the north, was not caught up in the political strife, but the transport of mail and sup-plies and the prices and availability of goods were all affected. As Red River became Winnipeg, the new postage-stamp province of Manitoba acquired a Canadian-based governing structure. Then the summer of 1870 saw the spread of a serious smallpox epidemic on the western plains. Although Norway House was largely spared, the outbreak caused much anxiety and disruption.

Finally, the years from 1871 to 1875 saw a major shift in Hudson's Bay Company operations and transport. The dominance of York Factory on Hudson Bay and of Norway House as the nexus of inland travel began to fade, with serious consequences for the Cree who relied on Company employment.[11] Across the region, new economic and land pressures impelled the negotiations of the first five numbered Indian treaties in western Canada. Egerton Young, in trying to help secure the future of the Aboriginal communities at Norway House and, later, Berens River, was drawn into advocacy and letter writing on their behalf as plans for Treaty 5 developed in 1874–75. At Berens River, Egerton and Elizabeth Young were both enlisted as witnesses when the treaty was signed there in September 1875.

The Youngs left mission work in the summer of 1876, before the political and social impacts of the new Canadian regime and the new Indian Affairs policies and legislation were fully felt. During their tenure, the region still

---

11 For background, see Frank Tough, *"As Their Natural Resources Fail": Native Peoples and the Economic History of Northern Manitoba, 1870–1930* (Montréal and Kingston: McGill-Queen's University Press, 1996), chaps. 1–7.

lacked residential schools, Indian agents, reserves, government-appointed schoolteachers, medical personnel, resident police forces, a cash economy, and rail and steam transport. They were largely on their own, playing many roles with limited resources, in times of great changes whose consequences and ramifications for Aboriginal people, for the churches and fur traders, and for the land itself, could not yet be seen. They witnessed the foreshadowing of a new era, but they were still living, as it were, in older times — which lends particular interest to their records. They also served in a time when Indian missions in Canada still had a high profile and standing among the public. By the 1880s and 1890s, many believed that Aboriginal peoples were disappearing or would soon be assimilated, and the churches turned their attention increasingly to China and Japan, with their large populations and their promise of growth.

The Youngs also served in an era when there was as yet no place for women in the mission field except as missionary wives, or sometimes schoolteachers. In the late 1870s, efforts to organize women as missionaries began, but only in 1881, with the founding of the Woman's Missionary Society of the Methodist Church of Canada, did real opportunities open for women to become professional missionaries — that is, until they got married. In the next decades, more than three hundred single women served the WMS in Canada, West China, and Japan until 1925 when the United Church of Canada brought Methodists and other denominations into a new structure.[12] Many of those women had advanced their education at such institutions as the Hamilton Ladies' College — an option not open to Elizabeth Young.[13] Some features of her upbringing and experience in Bradford, Ontario, were, however, probably of more practical use than the colleges as preparation for mission work.

12 Rosemary R. Gagan, *A Sensitive Independence: Canadian Methodist Women Missionaries in Canada and the Orient, 1881–1925* (Montréal and Kingston: McGill-Queen's University Press, 1992), 4–5. Many did not serve long, as marriage (commonly to male missionaries) intervened.

13 On the mixed record of Methodist women's education in the late 1800s, see Johanna M. Selles, *Methodists and Women's Education in Ontario, 1836–1925* (Montréal and Kingston: McGill-Queen's University Press, 1996), chaps. 4 and 5.

The Father's Books and the Mother's and Son's Recollections

The most visible and best-known outcomes of the Youngs' mission years are the dozen books that Egerton Young wrote and published from the 1890s until his death in 1909, contributing to an expanding genre of missionary literature.[14] In 1887, a decade after he left the Northwest, he began to realize that the telling and writing of his mission stories could open a new career. In May of that year, Mark Guy Pearse, a distinguished English Methodist on tour to raise funds for missions, paid a visit to Young at his parsonage in Meaford, Ontario. In an introduction to Young's first book, *By Canoe and Dog-Train*, Pearse wrote that during his visit, he "sat entranced" by Young's vivid stories of his mission experiences. He secured from his host "a promise that Mr. Young would come to England and tell the people 'at home' the story of his Mission."[15] Young was already disappointed with the small pastorates that he had been assigned since his return from the field. In March of 1887, he made a short lecturing trip to New York, and, in 1888, he undertook an extended lecture tour in the eastern United States.[16] Its success led him to take up Pearse's invitation to England, in 1889, and launched his career as a much sought travelling speaker and advocate for missions in North America, England — and, in 1904–5, Australia. His speaking tours not only encouraged him to write but also fostered a demand for his books, some of which went through several editions and were translated into French, Swedish, and German, and he attained some international fame in church circles.[17]

14 See, for example, Myra Rutherdale's discussion of the genre in *Women and the White Man's God: Gender and Race in the Canadian Mission Field* (Vancouver: University of British Columbia Press, 2002), xxi.

15 Mark Guy Pearse, "Introduction," in Young, *By Canoe and Dog-Train*, 1, 3.

16 Young's scrapbook and diaries document his lecture travels. On 21 March 1887, his first lecturing venture brought a letter from the Methodist Episcopal Church on Broadway in New York thanking him for "his tender thrilling and evangelical discourse" to the Preachers' Meeting held there on 7 March. JSHB collection.

17 Jennifer S. H. Brown, "Young, Egerton R.," *Dictionary of Canadian Biography* online. The full texts of six of Young's twelve books are available on the University of Alberta's Peel's Prairie Provinces site (www.peel.library.ualberta.ca); Google searches locate copies or reprints of most of the other six books.

The Youngs left as legacies other substantial records besides the books and other writings of the missionary himself. This book sets forth, in Part I, the memoirs that Elizabeth Bingham Young wrote in 1927, and, in Part II, the recollections of her son, Egerton Ryerson Young Jr., born at Norway House in 1869. Part III then presents a number of important and revealing documents that they or others wrote, which add to and complement the two main narratives. Deeply affected by their years among the Cree and Ojibwe (Salteaux in Young's usage), mother and son both set down vivid memories of those times. Their records are rich in stories and details, some of which were also recounted by their husband and father. But they each retold some stories differently and added others, along with their own vivid personal impressions. Their voices also speak from different angles. Elizabeth went to Norway House as a new wife, aged twenty-four, leaving her family home and a rural small town that stood in great contrast to her northern destination. Her son, E. Ryerson, known in his boyhood as "Eddie," was born at Norway House and became immersed in Cree and Ojibwe life, culture, and language around his parents' mission. The young mother and her small son shared their life at Norway House and Berens River, and they later recollected that life powerfully moved by strong impulses to record their memories as best they could. Their respective genders and ages, however, gave a distinctive cast to the writings of each.

The mother's writings focus mainly on the years from 1868 to 1873 at Norway House, where she had to find her way, learn quickly, and adapt: "culture shock" is a fair description. There she learned Cree, worked closely with the Rossville women and their families, acted as nurse and doctor as best she could, and gave birth to three children. Her memoirs say less about her more difficult years at Berens River, 1874 to 1876. By comparison, Eddie was barely four years old when he left Norway House. He had some distinct memories of it, reinforced by family stories. But his most memorable experiences were at Berens River — and later, as he went through the trials of adapting to rural Ontario school life after the family left Cree and Ojibwe country, when he was seven.

As a missionary's wife, Elizabeth of course had no salary of her own; the church expected such wives to be immersed in their husbands' endeavours. In May of 1868, at a valedictory service for Young and two other missionaries who, with their wives, were going off to new postings in the

Northwest, the Reverend W. Morley Punshon — an Englishman and the incoming president of Conference of the Wesleyan Methodist Church — gave expression to this sentiment while crediting the wives' sacrifices. The church, he said, was "really sending out six missionaries," not three, "and these had to be maintained. These are women who hazard their lives as well as the men — women who make our manhood cheap, because they are privileged to go forth without a murmur to the sustentation of those whose name they bear." All should pray "that they, with frailer organizations, though perhaps a well-knit network of nerves — for there is not so much of the robust muscular strength — may be preserved for the trial. . . . They go out with their lives in their hands and offer up their ease, social status, and all the other comforts of the well-regulated Christian city home; they go out as the heralds."[18] Elizabeth, many times, was to draw upon her "well-knit network of nerves" and other qualities as well.

As for Eddie, he began life as the firstborn son of the respected "praying master" of Rossville. He was said to be the first white child born at Norway House, but, more importantly, the Cree people of the mission adopted him as one of their own. They gave him a Cree name, and a Cree woman, Mary Robinson (or "Little Mary," as the Youngs knew her), became his nurse for his entire time at Norway House and Berens River. His relations with her and the other Aboriginal people whom he got to know in those years stayed in his mind and shaped his outlook and interests for the rest of his long life.

Elizabeth Bingham and Egerton Ryerson Young: Early Lives

Elizabeth Bingham was born in Bradford, Canada West (later Ontario), on 10 April 1843. Her father, Joseph Bingham, born in 1819 in Somerset, England, came to Canada with his parents and younger siblings in about 1830. When his father died soon thereafter, Joseph was apprenticed to a tanner and took up that trade and boot making in Bradford. He married Clarissa Vanderburgh on Christmas Day, 1841. Clarissa's maternal grandfather, Peter Vanderburgh, was a loyalist from New York. In 1816, Peter's

18 Punshon's remarks, originally reported in the *Globe*, are quoted in George Young, *Manitoba Memories: Leaves from My Life in the Prairie Province, 1868–1884* (Toronto: William Briggs, 1897), 45.

son Richard Vanderburgh, a farmer, married Elizabeth Fulton, daughter of Captain James Fulton, also a loyalist. Clarissa, born in 1819, was their eldest daughter. We know little about her early life, but Clarissa's granddaughter, Winnifred Young Watson, later recalled hearing that, before her marriage to Joseph, Clarissa "as a girl used to drive her pony and small rig to Toronto Market," from the Vanderburgh farm near Richmond Hill, north of Toronto. Later, from her home in Bradford, she reportedly would "drive her cart or wagon into Toronto to attend the market."[19]

Clarissa's husband, Joseph, died in August 1867, four months before her eldest daughter, Elizabeth, married Egerton Young. A widow for nearly forty years, Clarissa died in 1906.[20] A number of her letters to Elizabeth and Egerton survive, written to their distant mission post of Rossville in 1868–69. (See Part III, sec. 4, for excerpts.) They reflect her enterprise and her trials, supporting her younger children and trying to keep them in school while running a boarding house with seven or eight boarders who needed meals served, washing done, and fires kept burning in the cold winters of that epoch — and wishing and hoping that her daughter and son-in-law would come home sometime soon.

Joseph and Clarissa Bingham had eight children, six daughters and two sons. Elizabeth's position as the first born made a difference. In her 1927 reminiscences, she recalled that "being the eldest the right to superintend was hers and she took the position." It proved good training for the large responsibilities she was to assume at the Methodist missions at Rossville and Berens River.

Elizabeth attended the Bradford grammar school and then "a private school for ladies" (unidentified) in Barrie, some miles to the north. Bradford, she later recalled, was a growing centre in her youth. She saw her

19 Harcourt Brown, notes and typescript, "Clarissa Vanderburgh Bingham," based on a 1961 conversation with Winnifred Watson and written ca. 1985 for Ruth Coan Fulton, the compiler of *Fulton Genealogy, 1751–1986* (Portsmouth, NH: Peter E. Randall, Publisher, 1986). JSHB collection.

20 On the Binghams and Vanderburghs, see Loretta Skidmore and Richard Rawson, compilers, *History of Our Heritage Past and Present* (California: Privately printed, 2012), 72–87; Fulton, compiler, *Fulton Genealogy, 1751–1986*, 202–8; and Wallace McLeod, compiler, "Vanderburgh Family Tree" (1962) and "Supplement" (1964), typescripts distributed under the auspices of the Vanderburgh Reunion Association.

first train at the age of ten, when the railway arrived there, and hotels, banks, trades, and churches were flourishing. Her father was a trustee of the town's Methodist church and held an important role as leader of two class meetings — an institution central to early Canadian Methodism. Class leaders were, as Neil Semple explains, "sub-pastors," who recommended people for membership, promoted the faith, helped with administration, and made pastoral visits. Respected and trusted, they were expected to hold "spotless reputations, practical intelligence, and an abiding devotion to the task."[21]

Elizabeth sang in the choir; the Bradford church choirs, she remembered in a *Globe* interview, "were noted for their excellent music."[22] She had a fine singing voice, and, in his mother's obituary, E. Ryerson noted that "she became the proud possessor of one of the first organs brought into Bradford."[23] Music and hymns played a central role in Methodist observances, and at Rossville, and later at Ontario church gatherings, Elizabeth was remembered for her singing of Cree hymns.[24]

In the years 1853 to 1855, Elizabeth formed an acquaintance that proved significant. During those years, the Reverend William Young served a three-year term as itinerant minister at the Bradford Methodist church and brought his family to live nearby.[25] His third son, born in 1840, was Egerton Ryerson Young, and he and Elizabeth met both at church and probably in

---

21 Semple, *The Lord's Dominion*, 228. Classes ideally had about twelve members and met once a week, attendance being required. Elizabeth's memoir records the honour and affection accorded to her father on his death.

22 "Bradford Rather Fancied Herself in the Early Days of Mrs. E. R. Young," *The Globe* (Toronto), 10 April 1929, noting Elizabeth Young's eighty-sixth birthday.

23 E. Ryerson Young, "Elizabeth Bingham Young," obituary, *Missionary Monthly*, August 1934, 340–43. The "organ" was probably the melodeon that Elizabeth managed to take to Rossville; it appears from a letter that Egerton wrote to Elizabeth on 8 September 1873 (see Part III, sec. 11) that the melodeon remained there when the Youngs left in 1873.

24 Semple, in *The Lord's Dominion*, 63, observed of hymns, "It is difficult to exaggerate their importance in the spiritual lives of Methodists." In his mother's obituary for *The Missionary Monthly*, E. Ryerson Young wrote that, when possible, "Mrs. Young accompanied Mr. Young on his lecture tours and added not a little to the attractiveness of his lectures by singing a song or two in Cree" ("Elizabeth Bingham Young," 342).

25 George H. Cornish, *Handbook of Canadian Methodism* (Toronto: Wesleyan Printing Establishment, 1867), 70. Three-year assignments to serve in specific places were typical of Methodist practice through most of the 1800s.

school until Egerton began to attend high school in Bond Head, the town just to the north. In a letter to her nephew Harcourt Brown, written in 1958, the Youngs' youngest daughter, Winnifred Watson, recounted her parents' early mutual attraction: "Talk about children going together early. Father left Bond Head high school when he was fifteen and Mother was 12 and they waited all that 15 years for each other. The kids nowadays have nothing on that!!"[26]

Egerton's father, William, was born in 1808 in the township of Murray, on the Bay of Quinte, which lies on the northern shore of Lake Ontario. His father was Stephen Young, who migrated from Vermont in about 1801. In Vermont, Stephen had married Lucy, daughter of Matthias Marsh, who, with his father (Colonel William Marsh) and siblings, had sided with the British in the American Revolution and had acquired loyalist land grants in the Quinte area. William began his Wesleyan Methodist ministry in 1835, serving a dozen circuits and church charges over the next decades. In 1834, he married Amanda Waldron (1812–42), daughter of New York–born Philip Schuyler Waldron, who had settled at the Bay of Quinte with his family in about 1790. Amanda's older brother, Solomon (1795–1878), became a respected Methodist preacher — one of the first to be born in Canada — in the 1820s and surely influenced the path of William Young's career. In the early 1830s, Solomon and his family were living at his mission posting at Muncey, on the Thames River, Upper Canada, as was his sister Amanda, who taught at the mission school for a couple of years before her marriage.[27]

These interconnected families reveal a pattern shared by many in the period. Coming from New York and Vermont, some were loyalists, while

26 Winnifred Watson to Harcourt Brown, 21 January 1958. If Winnifred had her father's age correct, then Egerton left school in 1855, and the pair waited twelve years, not fifteen: Elizabeth and Egerton were married in 1867. In her letter, Winnifred added: "Mother was the prettiest girl in the whole district and she won a beauty contest over in Queensville [a village to the east of Bradford] — which I didn't know they had in those days." The flyleaf of a schoolbook that Elizabeth received as a prize in 1860 is inscribed, in another hand, "This was a Prize given for the best-looking Girl in Bradford." See also Part III, sec. 16, "An Unusual Ballad," a poem written in 1925 by E. Ryerson Young commemorating his parents' early attachment.

27 See Egerton R. Young, *The Apostle of the North: Rev. James Evans* (New York: Fleming H. Revell, 1899), 43–45, where Young also tells of his mother being attacked in her schoolroom by a drunken chief and having to escape out the window — an incident that helped confirm the Youngs in their strong temperance stance. The mission served Delaware, Ojibwe, and Oneida people.

others arrived after the American Revolution, attracted by the liberal land-granting policies that the otherwise arch-conservative lieutenant governor of Upper Canada, John Graves Simcoe, instituted to attract American settlers and build the population of the region. While the newcomers welcomed access to inexpensive land, they did not share Simcoe's allegiance to the Church of England as it became entrenched under his regime, nor were they sympathetic to the elitism and the hierarchical social order that he fostered.[28] Some were already Methodists; others were drawn to Methodism after they moved north. In 1790, the New York Methodist Conference appointed William Losee as the first preacher to establish circuits, form classes, and found Methodist meeting houses in the Bay of Quinte region. He "effectively laid the groundwork" for Methodism in Canada and set the stage, so to speak, for denominational rivalry in Upper Canada.[29] Tensions between the Methodists and the Anglicans under their respective advocates, the Reverend Egerton Ryerson (Egerton Young's namesake and himself of a loyalist family) and Bishop John Strachan, were endemic from the 1820s onward in the region that became Ontario.

Egerton Young was born in Crosby, Upper Canada, on 7 April 1840. His mother, Amanda Waldron, died on 5 April 1842. Six months later, William Young, left with four children under the age of ten, married again. His second wife, Maria Theresa Farley, became the only mother Egerton knew. A former teacher, she emphasized Egerton's education "especially in Scriptural knowledge, helping him to memorise large sections of the Bible."[30] When he finished school at Bond Head, he was one of eight siblings and needed a livelihood. At the age of sixteen he received a teacher's certificate from the Bond Head Grammar School and began teaching in Emily Township, west of Peterborough.[31] In June 1860, the Board of Public

28 For in-depth discussion of these issues, see Alan Taylor, "The Late Loyalists: Northern Reflections of the Early American Republic." *Journal of the Early Republic* 27 (2007): 1–34.

29 J. William Lamb, "Losee, William," *Dictionary of Canadian Biography* online.

30 Methodism, as Neil Semple observes in *The Lord's Dominion*, 62, "was founded on a deep personal knowledge of the Bible. Its members were enjoined to read parts of the Bible daily and to ponder and discuss its important message."

31 E. Ryerson Young, "Egerton Ryerson Young," typescript biography, n.d., 1–2. JSHB collection.

Instruction examined him in "the several branches of study" required to teach grammar school and issued him a certificate of qualification. The next year, he applied his teacher's salary to a strenuous teacher training program at the Toronto Normal School, during which time he became acquainted with his namesake, Egerton Ryerson, by then both a pillar of the church and a leading educator.

In 1861, aged twenty-one, Egerton was appointed to the school at Madoc, a town to the north of Trenton, where, as sole teacher, he had charge of 105 students. The huge workload took away his pleasure in teaching, and as he wrote to his parents in March 1863, "I care not how soon a change is made for something else."[32] The change came when, in May of that year, he was received on probation in the Wesleyan Methodist Church; taking up his father's calling, he became a circuit-riding preacher. His evident success led to his ordination on 9 June 1867 and to his appointment as pastor to the First Methodist Church in Hamilton, Ontario — an advancement that made it possible for him to contemplate marriage, although his resources were still slim.[33] On 26 August, he wrote to his older brother James,

> What do you think of the step I am taking? Can you blame me for it? I think it is the right course I am pursuing. I have a pleasant parlor and another nice large room here and I think we can be as happy as it is right for mortals to be. . . . If you have a hundred dollars or so for which you want good interest for a year or two I wish you would lend it to me. I had some cash on hand but have been paying of[f] my liabilities at the Book Room, and elsewhere and now I am about ashore. We expect to have a very quiet wedding owing to their late afflictions: but I should like to be able to appear well and to have some funds on hand. . . . When the time for our marriage is arranged I will send you word. We hope to have Dr Ryerson to perform the ceremony.[34]

32 Young's letters are in the United Church of Canada Archives (UCCA), Toronto, Young fonds, series 1, box 1, file 2. The letter to his parents is dated 9 March.

33 Brown, "Young, Egerton R.," *Dictionary of Canadian Biography* online.

34 UCCA, Young fonds, series 1, box 1, file 2, Young to James Young, 26 August 1867. Here and throughout, ellipses in quotations from primary sources were not present in the original but indicate omissions on my part.

The "late afflictions" were the deaths, earlier in August, of both Elizabeth Bingham's father, Joseph, and her brother John. Despite her family's recent bereavement, the marriage took place on Christmas Day, 1867, but it was indeed a quiet ceremony: Egerton's parents could not be there, nor was there time for a honeymoon. As Egerton wrote to his stepmother five days before the wedding,

> Dear Ma, I think you will have to wait a few weeks longer ere you see *us* in Trenton. There are so many barriers in the way that we have given up the idea of being with you during the holidays. . . . We have a great many sick just now. I dare not leave them. The scarlet and typhoid fevers are hard at work. . . . I would feel anxious if away from the sick ones; so we have decided to return to Hamilton the day after Christmas."

He wrote with great pleasure, however, of his new personal circumstances:

> "I have a very cosy home here, and with the lady of my own heart, expect to be very happy and contented. My people are very kind and will welcome my help-meet very warmly. . . . Lizzie sends her love to you and wishes much to see you all, a wish which I hope will soon be gratified.[35]

Egerton and Elizabeth could not have anticipated the new direction that their lives would take within the next month, on receiving their church's request for distant mission service.

Setting Down Memories: Elizabeth Bingham Young's Writings

Egerton R. Young died in 1909 in Bradford, Ontario, at the age of sixty-nine. Elizabeth, aged sixty-six, was to survive him as a widow for twenty-five years. His loss brought major change to her life. From the 1890s onward, Young

---

35 UCCA, Young fonds, series 1, box 1, file 2, Young to Maria Farley Young, 20 December 1867. In writing "help-meet," Young used the biblical term from Genesis 2:18, in which God said, "It is not good that the man should be alone; I will make him an help meet for him." Eugene Ehrlich and David H. Scott note in *Mene, Mene, Tekel: A Lively Lexicon of Words and Phrases from the Bible* (New York: HarperCollins, 1990) that during in the 1600s a hyphen crept into the term (104).

had travelled widely on his lecture tours, often with Elizabeth; in 1904–5, they voyaged around the world, making an extended stay in Australia. In about 1904, Young acquired, with the help of his daughter Lillian's prosperous English husband, Robert Helme, a fine large house in Bradford, the town where Elizabeth had grown up, and "Algonquin Lodge," as the Youngs named it, became the much loved centre of family life.[36] When Egerton died, the house had to be sold, and Elizabeth subsequently lived in various places, spending time with her daughter in England and with her children and grandchildren in the Toronto area. For most of her last decade, she resided with her youngest daughter and husband, Winnifred and Herbert Watson, and it was there, after almost twenty years of widowhood, that she evidently found the peace and felt the urgency to begin, in her mid-eighties, to record her recollections of her mission life.

Elizabeth Young set down her reminiscences in two sets of handwritten texts. She began writing the first and more organized memoir, which is presented here, in 1927. It fills about sixty lined pages (119 and 122–80) of a daybook printed for the year 1909 but put to different uses later.[37] An entry on page 118, just before the text begins, dates the start of the memoir and also explains why Elizabeth began to compose it at this point in time: "July 3 [1927] Sunday we spent in Hamilton, at the First United Church. Having accepted an Invitation to the Diamond Jubilee Service . . . to be there as their guest as the Wife of their Pastor of sixty years ago that was there in 1867." On 27 June 1927, the Reverend J. E. Hughson had written from Hamilton expressing "great pleasure" that she had consented to come: "no words that I can write will express to you the appreciation of our people that, at your advanced age, you should undertake this journey, in your love for the old church where you began your life in the parsonage." Elizabeth was introduced at the Sunday morning "Double Diamond Jubilee Communion Service," as the pastor told of Egerton Young's service in 1867–68 and gave recognition to elderly church members "who are still

36 Harcourt Brown (b. 1900) described his memories of Algonquin Lodge in a letter of 21 June 1986 to his brother, Egerton Brown. Debbie Blair described the house in "The Grand Old Dame of Bradford," *Topix* (Newmarket-Aurora), 21 May 1986, A5. The house was demolished not long after.

37 The original document is in the UCCA, Young fonds, series 5, box 11, file 1. The pages in the daybook were numbered by the printer, and earlier pages had at some point been removed, whether by Elizabeth or someone else.

with us to greet Mrs. Young today with the same affection."[38] The power of the occasion must have moved her to start writing, probably soon after Herbert and Winnifred Watson drove her back to their home.

These untitled reminiscences were not Elizabeth's only efforts to create records of her mission life. From March to November 1868, she had kept a diary describing life in Hamilton and during the journey to Norway House, with occasional entries thereafter. A good many days were left blank, however, and some pencilled entries are almost illegible. More substantial is a group of thirty-three pages in the Egerton Ryerson Young fonds in the United Church of Canada Archives, filed under the title that appears on the first page: "The Bride of 1868."[39] These pages are largely unnumbered and not in chronological order, sometimes repeating descriptions of events covered elsewhere and sometimes including new details. Elizabeth also penned a set of twelve pages of memories, some of which appear in Part III, and added details on a few other single pages of text. Her son, E. Ryerson Young, also recorded on several loose pages various stories and memories that he heard from her, and these are cited on occasion.

Elizabeth Young in Print and in Private

A few notes suggest that Elizabeth sometimes gave talks to church groups; her papers also include a fifteen-page text titled, "Reminiscences of My Missionary Life," promotional in tone and perhaps written for some public presentation. Her only known publication is "The Transformed Indian Woman," a short article, in two parts, that appeared in *The Indian's Friend*, the organ of the Women's National Indian Association, based in Philadelphia.[40] The association, founded in 1879, campaigned for the honouring of Indian treaties and for Native rights, while supporting missions, assimilation, and the implementing of the 1887 Dawes (or General

---

38 Copies of Hughson's letter and the church's diamond jubilee program of 3 July 1927 are in the JSHB collection.

39 UCCA, Young fonds, series 5, box 10, file 8.

40 Mrs. Egerton R. Young, "The Transformed Indian Woman," *The Indian's Friend*, vol. 10, no. 6 (February 1898), 9–10, and no. 7 (March 1898), 9–10.

Allotment) Act, which was intended to foster individual ownership of land on reservations. Elizabeth's article was suited to their readership, laying out a simple dichotomy between the deplorable lot of Native women, oppressed and abused by tyrannical men before the Gospel came, and the wonderful transformations wrought in the men's behaviour and attitudes and in women's situations once Christianity took root.[41] But its prose did not resemble her usual voice — except in her telling of a Berens River story from her own experience (which is included here in the Berens River section of her narrative, under the heading "A Mother's Crisis").

As Myra Rutherdale points out, "Public missionary accounts and actual experiences in the mission field were often disparate. . . . It is precisely because the published letters and texts were designed to capture the attention of British and southern Canadian audiences that they presented the most extreme discourse of colonization generated by missionaries in northern Canada." Mission women's (and men's) personal letters and memoirs, in contrast, convey direct observations and perceptions not written for public, promotional purposes. Taken together, the sources cast light on "the ambiguities of the mission experience."[42] Mission service brought new personal ties, learning, and perspectives. Mission women's daily work, more than men's, entailed "intimate relations, especially with Aboriginal women." The result, however, was "closeness but not equality" as mission women began "to define themselves in relation to others. They did not recognize that both the others and their White selves were being changed by cultural interaction. Rather there was a tendency to reify moral and cultural differences."[43]

The writings of both missionary women and men show, unsurprisingly, that they were not versed in Boasian anthropology, discourse analysis, or postcolonial critique. The value of their personal, private writings lies in their immediacy and their empathy with their subject matter (although, in fact, such empathy often shows through in Egerton Young's published

41 For an overview of this recurring theme in missionary and other colonial rhetoric, see David D. Smits, 'The 'Squaw Drudge': A Prime Index of Savagism," *Ethnohistory* 29, no. 4 (1982): 281–306.

42 Rutherdale, *Women and the White Man's God*, xxii.

43 Ibid., 154, 155.

books even though he was writing for the consumption of broad church audiences in Canada and England, with all their stereotypes and imperial and ethnocentric assumptions).[44] The lesson that Myra Rutherdale draws from her studies of Anglican mission women in western Canada is the need to listen closely to all the available sources, to tolerate ambiguity, and attend to the ways in which the women themselves were changed and to varying degrees lived the rest of their lives between cultures, even after leaving the mission field.[45]

Preserving the Documents

After Egerton Young died in October 1909, his wife Elizabeth and her daughter Lillian Helme, visiting from England, immediately faced difficult decisions about his papers.[46] Elizabeth kept many of them but passed much of the collection to her son, E. Ryerson Young. The other eventual recipient was Harcourt Brown, eldest son of her daughter Grace Amanda Young Brown and nephew to E. Ryerson, or "Uncle Ed," as he knew him. Brown, although never a church-goer himself, had respect and affection for his grandmother (see Part III, sec. 16, for his memories of her) and was embarking on a professorial career that involved using documents and libraries. The family knew that he appreciated the importance of the papers, and, around the time of Elizabeth's death in May of 1934, he received a substantial collection kept in a small pine trunk — a "cassette" made for Egerton Young by a Hudson's Bay Company carpenter. In mid-1934, he brought a large collection of Young's books, periodicals, and pamphlets to

44 Among various examples, see his discussion in *By Canoe and Dog-Train*, 223–29, regarding his Christian obligation to end polygamy. He and Elizabeth dealt together with some difficult cases, trying to work out which wife might best remain and how the others could be supported, and by whom.

45 Rutherford, *Women and the White Man's God*, 95.

46 On 17 October 1909, Lillian wrote to her son, Egerton Helme, "We are having a very trying time now looking through father's letters of 1867 & up. Dear grandma finds it very hard to destroy them but there are boxes accumulated for years. We are having sad hours. They are splendid letters full of vim [?] all the way through." JSHB collection.

Victoria College Library in Toronto — works largely focused on missions and church histories but also including publications of the Bureau of American Ethnology and other documents.[47]

In the 1970s, Harcourt Brown (my father) became concerned about the disposition of the papers and engaged in correspondence and conversations with the Reverend H. Egerton Young, the son of E. Ryerson, and with other grandchildren of the Youngs. As they were all ageing and now somewhat scattered, they reached a consensus about preserving the papers and finding them a safe home. The Archives of Ontario staff expressed much interest in acquiring the collection, and Harcourt Brown and H. Egerton Young agreed in the late 1970s to deposit at the archives the papers that they had located by that time, along with a few further items contributed by cousins. Some materials were retained for Brown's and my study and research, and some were found later. The archives also provided us with photocopies of the documents of most interest to us. After the death of Harcourt Brown in 1990, H. Egerton Young facilitated and encouraged my study of the family papers, entrusting to me his father's remarkable memoir, "A Missionary and His Son," recalling his boyhood at Norway House and Berens River, and other writings. In the early 1990s, he and I agreed that the United Church of Canada Archives (UCCA) in Toronto would be a more suitable repository, and in 1994 the collection was transferred there where it resides as the Egerton Ryerson Young Fonds (no. 3607, aaccession no. 94.030C).[48] Those of Harcourt Brown's and H. Egerton Young's holdings that are now in my hands will eventually join the Young fonds. Further information on E. Ryerson Young and his writings is provided in the introduction to Part II of this volume.

47 On HBC cassettes, see www.furtradestories.ca/details.cfm?content_id=273&cat_id=3&sub_cat_id=1. The Youngs' cassette, painted black, has the typical dovetailing but its lid is slightly curved rather than flat, an unusual feature. Norway House HBC journals of the time mention cassettes being made there. The Egerton Ryerson Young book collection was donated in the name of "Mrs. Young and family" (inventory list in the JSHB collection). In 1969, Harcourt Brown visited to see whether the collection still survived and was referred to the theological library; the contents had evidently been dispersed (Brown to Jennifer S. H. Brown, 13 December 1969).

48 Letter from Ian Forsyth, deputy archivist, Archives of Ontario, to the Reverend H. Egerton Young, 15 February 1994.

The originals of several documents published here are housed in the UCCA, and they or excerpts from them are published here by permission. Their archival references are listed below.

Series 1: Correspondence. Box 1, file 9: Correspondence from the Bingham family, 1868–69. Excerpts of letters from Clarissa and Sarah Bingham.

Series 2: Notebooks and Diaries. Box 1, file 14: Diary, 1868. Excerpts. Box 2, file 3: Notebook, Berens River (187[?]). Miscellaneous notes. Excerpts.

Series 4: Literary Manuscripts. Box 10, file 4: First trip (of Egerton Young) to Oxford Mission, September 1868. Excerpts.

Series 5: Records of Elizabeth Bingham Young. Box 10, file 3: "Daily Reminiscences of Norway House's Living" (manuscript), excerpts. (Moved from series 4 when her authorship was discovered.) Box 10, files 5 to 7: Correspondence. Letters from Egerton R. Young to Elizabeth Young from Norway House and Berens River, 1873, 1874. Box 10, file 8: "The Bride of 1868," by Elizabeth Young, ca. 1930–32 (miscellaneous manuscript pages, most unnumbered), excerpts. Box 10, file 10: Diary, 1868, excerpts. Box 11, file 1: Notebook/Diary, reminiscences 1850s on, untitled. Pages 119 and 122–80 are published here.

Series 6: Records of Egerton Ryerson Young Jr. Box 11, file 6: Reminiscences of his life and times. This memoir (untitled) was composed in 1962. The portion beginning with the Young family's departure from Berens River, in 1876, and extending through to the end of the narrative (Young's outline of his church career) is published here, along with a few earlier excerpts recounting childhood memories that supplement his first memoir.

A Note on Memory

Elizabeth and E. Ryerson Young wrote their memoirs from six to more than eight decades after the events and circumstances that they record, and their accuracy and reliability call for some comment. Their texts effectively "speak for themselves," but contextual research has also helped me to situate them and to evaluate their contents. Substantial church, mission, and fur trade records, along with contemporaneous family correspondence and other writings and documentary sources, are available from the period. They have served to confirm a great deal of the substance of these texts, indicating that Elizabeth and her son had, on the whole, remarkable powers of recall. Occasional slippages of names, dates, and sequences occur as indicated in the footnotes, but a great many memories and details are clear and sharp.

Some recent studies of memory help us to understand certain factors that may have aided the Youngs' powers of recollection. Valerie Raleigh Yow cites psychologists' findings that older people retain more memories from childhood and young adulthood than from recent years. Such autobiographical memory is "personal, long-lasting, and (usually) of significance to the self-system." She adds that "we also remember as a group; that is, we listen to people who have shared the same experience with us, and we gain a feeling of identity with them."[49] Elizabeth and Eddie were both young in their mission years, and were part of a family that talked about and reinforced their northern experiences as significant and life-changing. Yow writes that "people choose memories important to them; they repeat them over the years as they seek to reinforce meanings in their lives." As she notes, some research points to gender differences in memory: "Women tend to remember details of personal experience more often than men," and their "memories of feelings surrounding events are articulated in more detail." But, for both genders, "events in which there were high levels of mental activity and emotional involvement will be remembered."[50] These features were certainly present in the Youngs' mission life at both Norway House and Berens River. They had strong reasons for remembering, both orally and when they took up pen or typewriter. Elizabeth (d. 1934) never got to read Eddie's memoirs, and we can't tell to what extent her son read her various writings as his eyesight failed in the 1930s (although he wrote down a few of her memories and stories). But their accounts dovetail in many respects. Together they provide an enormously rich and detailed portrait of their mission experiences — and also of the Youngs' lives as a returned missionary family after 1876. They and the contextual sources around them also make possible a kind of triangulation in situating their histories; we are able to envisage their lives and listen to their stories from various angles without having to rely on a sole text or a single voice in isolation.

49 Valerie Raleigh Yow, *Recording Oral History: A Guide for the Humanities and Social Sciences*, 2nd ed. (Washington, DC: Rowman AltaMira, 2005), 35–36.

50 Ibid., 50–51.

Terms and Editorial Practices

The Youngs' writings used ethnic and other terms of reference that were commonplace in eastern Canada in the mid-1800s. "Indian" was standard at the time; modern Canadian terms such as "Aboriginal" and "First Nations" were, of course, not in their vocabulary. As Elizabeth recalled her interactions with the Cree women and children around her, she also drew upon terms that English-speakers in eastern North America had begun using two centuries earlier. In 1643, in New England, Roger Williams recorded from the Narragansett language the words "squaw" (woman) and "papoos" (a child),[51] and both began turning up in dictionaries without the derogatory connotations that "squaw," in particular, acquired in the past century. Context is critical in assessing terminology and its baggage. Elizabeth certainly thought of the "Indians" as other, as different. But she wrote of them with sympathy and an effort at understanding, and not to denigrate them, looking, within her frame of reference, for means of helping them and improving their circumstances.

As she learned Cree, the words she was hearing probably reinforced her use of "squaw" and "papoose." The Cree word for woman, *iskwew*, is related to the root word that Roger Williams originally recorded and is not greatly different in sound. As for "papoose," fluent Cree speaker Keith Goulet, of Cumberland House, Saskatchewan, points out that a Cree term for baby, *bebeesis*, is a "Creeicized English word" that is still in use; if the *b* is unvoiced, the word becomes *peepeesis*, "a form of endearment."[52] Elizabeth, finding these words somewhat familiar, would naturally have kept using the terms that she knew.

A number of Cree words and expressions recur in Elizabeth's memoir and occasionally in her husband's writings (his efforts at Cree occur mainly in one notebook of Cree word lists and phrases that he and others at Rossville compiled).[53] It is striking that five decades after she left the

51 Roger Williams, *A Key into the Language of America* (London, 1643; reprinted Providence, RI, 1827), 44. Thanks to Keith Goulet for providing this reference.

52 Keith Goulet, e-mail of 25 February 2013.

53 On this document, housed in the University of Manitoba Archives, see David H. Pentland, "The Rossville Mission Dialect of Cree: Egerton Ryerson Young's 1872 Vocabulary," in *Essays in Algonquian Bibliography in Honour of V. M. Dechene*, ed. H. C. Wolfart (Winnipeg: University of Manitoba, 1984), 23–45. This vocabulary and

Northwest, she could still transcribe from memory numbers of Cree words well enough that they can readily be identified. In the text published here, her Cree terms are glossed (inside square brackets) with orthography provided by linguist Jeffrey Muehlbauer. He and Keith Goulet have been unfailingly helpful in assisting with the transcription and interpretation of her words and also with some terms occurring in Egerton's writings. One example from Egerton's book, *By Canoe and Dog-Train*, documents how his efforts to use Cree terms posed challenges for him, his interpreters, and his audiences as they sought mutual understanding. In September 1869, he was preaching to Cree speakers at Nelson River, north of Norway House. He was trying to convey the Christian concept of God as "our Father," with "our" in the inclusive sense of "everyone's." However, not knowing the nuances of Cree, he quoted himself as using the term "'*N*otawenan' (*our* Father)." As Muehlbauer explains, Young erred in employing the exclusive *nohtâwinân*, 'Our father [not yours],' when his intended meaning was the inclusive *kohtâwinaw*, 'Our father [including yours].' An old man asked him for clarification, wondering, was God then the missionary's Father? Young answered yes. The man then asked, "Does it mean He is my Father [Muehlbauer: *nohtâwiy*] — poor Indian's Father?" (He seemed to realize that Young had used the wrong term for what he meant.) Young assured him that was so. "'Then we are brothers?' he almost shouted out. "'Yes, we are brothers,' I replied."[54]

Apart from borrowings from Cree, several other English words merit comment. Although the Youngs often mention deer, there were no deer as such at Norway House. When Anglophone traders and missionaries spoke of deer (or what they sometimes called reindeer) and of deerskin, they were referring to caribou, a term that was still working its way into English from French Canadian usage in those times. The Youngs did not, however, use the Scottish term "bannock," which was to become a common name for the unleavened bread cooked on the trail. Instead, they occasionally refer to

Elizabeth's texts made no use of the (Plains) Cree syllabic system that James Evans had developed for scriptural translations, but they do document some features of the local dialect.

54 Young, *By Canoe and Dog-Train*, 121. The assertion stirred a "wonderful" audience response but also a reproof, as the man then asked why his white brother had been so long in coming to tell the wonderful story of the "great Book" to "your red brothers in the woods."

"dough dogs" or "beavers' tails" (described by E. Ryerson as "hard as ship's bannocks").

The personal names used for family members in the records vary somewhat and require some comment. As this volume refers to several Youngs, first names are used to identify them wherever use of the surname could cause ambiguity. Elizabeth was addressed by her mother and siblings and by Egerton as "Libbie" or, more rarely, "Lizzie," but in later life she signed herself as Elizabeth — the name chosen here. Her son wrote and published under the name E. Ryerson Young to distinguish himself from his father; "Jr." was almost never used. As a child, he was "Eddie," and that name is used here in reference to his youth. Although no one ever seemed to call him "Ryerson," in his adult years he was best known by the name E. Ryerson Young, which has been adopted here. The spellings of two of his sisters' names varied over time but are standardized in these texts. Lillian, the eldest daughter, was sometimes known as "Lilian," but the former spelling was more commonly used. The name of a younger daughter, Winnifred, usually carried the double n, which is preserved here although it is a less standard spelling than "Winifred."

The texts have been lightly edited. Commas and other punctuation, as well as the occasional word missing in the original, have been supplied, and some paragraph breaks added to aid readability. Subheads have also been supplied to orient readers. Spelling errors, which were few in the Youngs' writings, have been silently corrected unless they indicate idiosyncratic usages of possible interest; the use of [sic] is avoided. Obscure names and terms are footnoted. Some of Elizabeth's writings from the pages collectively titled "The Bride of 1868," as well as certain entries from Elizabeth's and Egerton's 1868 diaries, provide added information. Quotations from these sources, if brief, have been inserted in square brackets within the text. The diary texts are identified as such, with dates; bracketed insertions not otherwise identified are from the pages collected under the heading "The Bride of 1868." In addition, longer extracts from these sources have occasionally been included under subheads of their own, with the source clearly indicated. Complementary information from Egerton R. Young's books and letters and from the writings of others is provided in footnotes, along with other source materials.

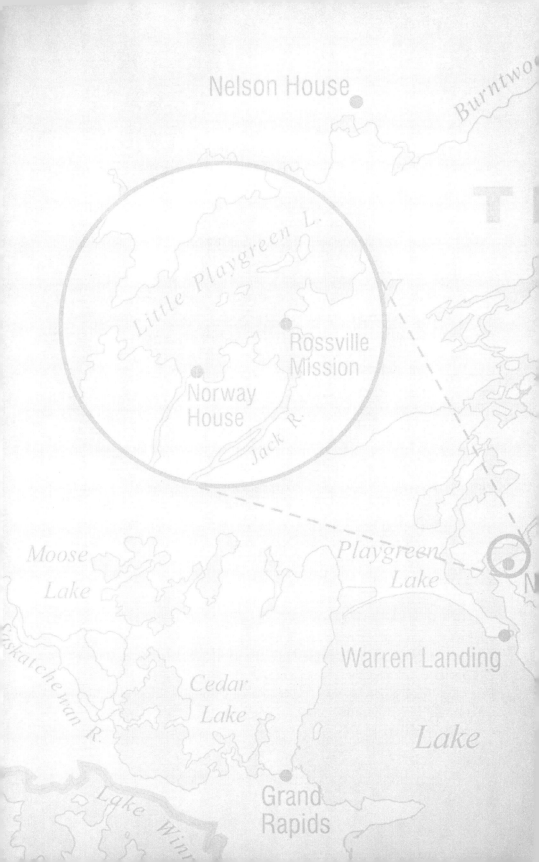

I

Untitled Memoir of
Elizabeth Bingham Young,
1927

The text that follows is transcribed from pages 119 to 180 of Elizabeth Young's daybook, with added inserts as described in the introduction. Headings in quotation marks are Elizabeth's own; others are my own. Daily diary entries that immediately precede and follow her memoir date from 1927, and a diary entry written on pages 120 and 121 is dated 9 July 1927, suggesting that Elizabeth began to compose the text at that time. A statement on page 123 implies a date of 1928: it reads, "July 29, 1868. Just sixty years ago, we arrived at Norway House & Rossville mission, where we were appointed to be missionaries to the Cree Indians." Page 173, however, reinforces the memoir's date as 1927; there, Elizabeth noted that she had just attended her sister Clara's fiftieth wedding anniversary, and Clara was married on 18 September 1877.

"1859 & Sixtys"

In the fiftys and sixtys there was a happy & joyous little girl filling the hearts of home, & making melody. Sisters and brothers came, but being the eldest the right to superintend was hers, & she took the position; we had many friends many visitors some agreeable.

We had a black mammy and her Neddie who came yearly to visit us. They would take all we could give them & ask for more. Where they came from we could not tell, but they were most interesting.

Indians came with their baskets for sale, they came from Rama & Rice Lake, they were easy & happy go lucky people.[1]

---

1 The Ojibwe reserves of Rama and Rice Lake were established on the eastern shore of Lake Couchiching and the north side of Rice Lake, Ontario, respectively. Both had

In winter time, sleigh riding all kinds of sliding, skating, evening parties games, puzzles, guessing games, Forf[e]it games, phillip[i]ne game, interesting.[2]

All through the sixties my young life was very happy, making home happy & summer time picnics. Visiting in the country, often making neighbours happy, in many ways, in sickness, soothing & comforting the dying. In Church work, so happy, in choir singing, in school work, in temperance work, in whatever work interested our Town. Concerts, Tea parties, I was interested beyond measure. It seemed a real pleasure, to be useful, and appreciated by our neighbours & friends.[3]

Leaving Home

On December 25, 1867, I left my dear Mother & my home, in the Town of Bradford, Simcoe Co., Ontario, Canada, for Toronto where my dear Egerton & I were married in the old Methodist Church on Adelaide Street, which is now the Metropolitan Church. We were married by the Rev. Egerton Ryerson. We took dinner in the old Ros[s]in House & then went to Hamilton, where we were very kindly received.[4] It was a wonderful change for me, from a sad home, for the same year in August my Father & Brother passed away leaving us prostrate with grief. But all this of my going away

active Methodist missions. The making and selling of basketry were important to the livelihood of Ojibwe women for many decades.

2 Forfeit, or Forfeits, is an old game in which each player puts a personal item in a pile behind a judge. One player standing behind the judge holds up each item and says, "Heavy, heavy hangs over thy head. What shall the owner do to redeem the forfeit?" The judge, without looking up, then directs the owner to do an act or stunt to redeem the item (www.childrenparty.com/partygames/printversion/forfeits.html, accessed 27 January 2013). Philippine, or Philippina, was another amusement: a person finding a nut with two kernels eats one and gives the other to a person of the opposite sex; when they next meet, the first one to say "Good morning Philippine" is entitled to a present from the other (*OED*).

3 Elizabeth's memoir is interrupted at this point by a diary entry dated 9 July 1927, describing a country excursion that took place that day.

4 The Rossin House Hotel was an elegant five-story hotel at the corner of King and York streets in Toronto. Opened in 1857, it suffered a serious fire in 1862. It reopened in August 1867, four months before the Young's marriage.

was arranged while my Father was still alive. Yet to have put it off would only complicate matters. Mother was not alone, for three Sisters and one Brother were with her.[5]

We were not blessed with earthly goods, for my dear Father was a very hard working man but met with misfortune, not through carelessness. My Father was a good Christian had a responsible place in the Methodist Church & the full respect of all especially the young people, who loved & had the greatest respect for him, for his goodness, his kindness; for his church classes he had two one in the town, one a little way out of the town. If any were sick & not able to attend they were immediately visited, & if in need at once looked after his love & care was appreciated. The love of his people was shown when he passed away when they looked after his funeral & put up a monument in memory of him.[6]

Although leaving home I could not forget the love & care of both my Father & Mother and many times the heart & thoughts would recall the past, & thank God for his care & love, & leadings in the good and true way & now I can look back with nothing but a true & thankful heart that my way was so lovingly guarded & pleasantly and sweetly cared for. For now I can only see & feel that God for Christ's sake had me in His special keeping. Many proffers of more than friendship came to me, but the unseen hand kept watch until the right one came, then there was no diffidence or trouble, & I am today full of thankfulness to my loving & Heavenly Father for His watchfulness care over one so unworthy. I can sing truly "Praise God from whom all blessings flow."

---

5 The siblings were Sarah, aged fifteen, Joseph, aged thirteen, Clarissa, aged ten, and Charlotte, aged nine (Bingham family tree, in Wilson Brown, family history files). Their widowed mother took in boarders to maintain the family; excerpts from her letters appear in Part III, sec. 4.

6 The first Wesleyan Methodist church was built in Bradford in 1857, Joseph Bingham being named as one of its four trustees. He and his son John, aged eighteen, died of typhoid on 19 and 21 August 1867, respectively, and were buried in Mount Pleasant Cemetery, Bradford. His monument, a tall column mounted on pedestals, is inscribed, "Erected by the Members of Mt. Pleasant Class to the memory of our late leader Joseph Bingham who departed this life August 19, 1867, aged 47 years 10 months." Loretta Skidmore and Richard Rawson, compilers, *History of Our Heritage Past and Present* (California: Privately printed, 2012), 75, with photograph of the monument (supplied by Wilson Brown). Skidmore and Rawson cite the work of several researchers on the Bingham family.

The Invitation to the North West
From "The Bride of 1868":

> Little did I dream when I left my home that as a missionary
> would I be counted worthy to go, for in my young days I had been
> nursed in a Christian home, and now the fulfillment of my early
> wishes and desires I was willing to leave home, friends & with my
> newly found treasure go to the "West." . . . This was December,
> we got the New Years over and was settling down when a written
> Invitation came for us to go to the N.W. as missionaries, which very
> much unsettled us for the moment, for we must decide quickly.
> So we began to think & decide, my beloved's church were all very
> much opposed to losing their much loved Pastor, for they had
> just had some very interesting Revival meetings and many new
> members were added to the church. The President of the Ladies
> [Wesleyan Female] College was the only one who gave my beloved
> any encouragement, he thought it was just the climate for his
> Constitution, but he was the only one.[7] But with a good deal of
> serious thought & prayer we decided to go, so from that moment we
> were getting ready and seemingly up-set & divided in our thought
> and work. We had many invitations here & there, the friends could
> not show us too much kindness and attention.

From Hamilton to Detroit

> July 29, 1868. Just sixty years ago, we arrived at Norway House
> & Rossville mission, where we were appointed to be missionaries
> to the Cree Indians.

---

7 Young, in *By Canoe and Dog-Train* (London: Charles H. Kelly, 1890), 29, also tells of
the sole fellow minister, presumably the same man, who supported his going — having
abruptly turned down a mission request years before with dismal consequences. On the
college and its role in educating another mission wife, see Jan Hare and Jean Barman,
*Good Intentions Gone Awry: Emma Crosby and the Methodist Mission on the Northwest
Coast* (Vancouver: University of British Columbia Press, 2006), 3–6. The school's name
varied between "Ladies" and "Female" College.

On May the tenth 1868, having everything arranged, settled, and farewells all said we parted from our Hamilton friends. [In her diary, 9 May 1868, Elizabeth wrote: "We have alreddy bid adieu to my dear *Ma* and sisters in *Canada* and my own dear brother Joey, and also those dear brothers by marriage, we have yet to say goodbye to Pa Young. . . . We meet so many friends who were or seemed very anxious for our special welfare, this we thank *God* for."]⁸

My beloved had first closed a very successful term of years and all were happy with a large number of members added to the church who were grieved at his departure, yet all wished us well.

We embarked at Thorolds. [Thorold, on the Welland Canal. According to Elzabeth's diary (13 and 14 May), they traversed the Welland Canal and Lake Erie on 13 May, reaching Detroit around midnight.]

The Officials of the Hamilton First Church were very much surprised & grieved at their official meeting, at the close of the year of 1867. My husband announced his intention of devoting his life to mission work among the Indians of the Hudson Bay district.

The Board expressed its appreciation of him in the following resolution: "We the members of the quarterly board of Hamilton City East Circuit, cannot allow our beloved Pastor & his wife to depart without an expression of our high appreciation of their services amongst us. His faithfulness, zeal and affection have endeared him to all our hearts, and we pray that he may be equally successful in winning souls for Christ, in the land to which he journeys."⁹

---

8 The "brothers by marriage" were James Strong and William Sibley, to whom Elizabeth's sisters Mary Anne and Eleanor (Nelly) were married, respectively; "Pa Young" was William Young, Egerton's father. In his diary entry for 11 May, Egerton also described their departure: "Our last day in Hamilton. Spent the day in packing up for our journey. Paid up Bills. Made a few visits and said goodby to many dear friends and last of all to my dear aged father Rev. W. Young, loaded up my democrat." (A democrat is "a light four-wheeled cart with several seats, one behind the other": *OED*.)

9 For the full text, see Part III, sec. 1.

The Travelling Party

Elizabeth's diary, 14 May, reads: "The rest of our party joined us. Now our Missionary company is complete." The members of the party, some of whom had joined the group in Detroit by rail, were the following:

> Rev. Geo. Young age 46. Occupation Wes[leyan] Missionary. Mrs Young 45. Their Son George 16. [To establish the Methodist Church in Red River (Winnipeg).]
>
> Rev. Geo. McDougall. Occupation Wes Missionary. Georgina McD his daughter.[10]
>
> Rev. Peter Campbell age 30 Wes Miss. Mrs [N?] Campbell age 30. Two children Annie 3, Ella ½.
>
> Rev E. R. Young age 27 Wes. Miss. Mrs. Young age 24.
>
> Matthew Snyder age 22. Teacher. Ira Snyder age 18. Teacher.[11]
>
> John Day [aged] 24 Carpenter. Margaret Day 23.
>
> Geo. A Caswell Age 25 farmer
>
> Enoch Skinner 12.[12]

10 Georgina McDougall had been attending the ladies college and was returning with her father to the family's mission home at Victoria, in Saskatchewan. She died of small-pox on 1 November 1870, aged eighteen. John Maclean, *The Hero of the Saskatchewan: Life Among the Ojibway and Cree Indians in Canada* (Barrie, ON: Barrie Examiner Printing and Publishing House, 1891), 25.

11 According to Young, the Snyders, younger brothers of Mrs. Campbell, "had consecrated themselves to the work as teachers among the distant Indian tribes" in Saskatchewan. See *By Canoe and Dog-Train*, 32.

12 Egerton Young's diary, on a page dated 20 April 1868, listed everyone's names and most of their ages and occupations; the Youngs were the most junior missionaries in the group. At least half of the party was bound for Saskatchewan with the Reverend George McDougall: he and his daughter Georgina, the Campbells, the Snyder brothers, and Enoch Skinner. Enoch Wood Skinner spent several years with the McDougall family, learned Cree, returned to Ontario, then was sent back to Saskatchewan as assistant to the Reverend John McDougall, but died in a gun accident on the way. See Maclean, *Hero of the Saskatchewan*, 25.

Detroit to Milwaukee, St. Paul, and Red River

The journey from Detroit to Milwaukee took the Youngs across Lake Michigan. In her diary, Elizabeth wrote on 16 May: "Had a violent attack of sea sickness. Neptune demands an offering. Allmost too indisposed to rise, however mustered up courage to leave my birth, food repugnent. Mr. George Young kindly came in and gave me a little port which made me feel very much better." The following day, the lake was quite rough, and both Elizabeth and Mrs. George Young were too sick to leave their staterooms: "we had to lie right down and lay there all day pretty near." Her husband evidently fared better. His diary entry for 17 May reads: "That disagreeable disease sea sickness has prostrated many. . . . I am kept in perfect health as well upon the sea as upon land."

In her memoir, Elizabeth continued:

> When we reached Milwaukee we were detained by the Customs, on account of the horses.[13] So several days were lost on our journey. However my husband had a wedding,[14] & as Mr McDougal's Daughter Georgenia was troubled with Rheumatism ["That is why she left Hamilton College and nothing would do but she must come with her Father, home"], and had no flannel under clothes, the Ladies of the partie improved the opportunity & secured some flannel & insisted on my doing the cutting out, & very soon we had the dear girl comfortable in nice warm flannels.[15] [Elizabeth's diary, 18 May: "I cut out two pairs of drawers and partly made one pair."]

13 Young, *By Canoe and Dog-Train*, 33, noted delays over the horses (they had fourteen) and other goods; a telegraph to Washington was required to persuade "the over-officious officials" to let them pass. In *Manitoba Memories: Leaves from My Life in the Prairie Province, 1868–1884* (Toronto: William Briggs, 1897), 55, George Young wrote that despite prior letters from the us consul in Toronto, the Milwaukee officials "demanded duty on the entire outfit ere we could be allowed to proceed."

14 In his diary, Young noted on 18 May: "Had the felicity of uniting in connubial bliss two young people who came in search of a parson. Happiness to them!"

15 The Hamilton college was the Wesleyan Female or Ladies College mentioned above. Flannel was "an open woollen stuff of various degrees of fineness," which was "highly recommended by medical men as a clothing, both in hot and cold climates, from its properties of promoting insensible perspiration." See "Flannel," *Encyclopedia Britannica*, vol. 9 (1878), 292, which also noted the enormous quantity of flannel manufactured in and exported from England in the period.

We took the train on the Lacross[e] Railroad [19–20 May] to the Miss[iss]ippi boats up to St Pauls; here we were at the point where we had to prepare for the Prairies, by procuring such things as dried fruits, Bacon, sugar, tea, flour, and all necessaries, for after leaving this point it would be impossible to be able to get anything in the way of food. We were advised not to forget anything, even salt ["as it is the last of stores or shops we will see for days weeks yea months. The H.B.C. Stores will be all we will see and those are only to exchange for the furs of the Indians. I remember when very much in need of some special article, and asked them for it; that was there answer, 'We are not here to serve Whites.' That answer was not needed twice, I did without."]

We had to prepare against mosquitoes, black flies, sand flies, bull dog flies. The women folks got some Quaker poke bonnets, mosquitoe Skreening, made long veils & weighted them down with shot.[16] This done & many other little necessaries accomplished, horses ready, wagons ready, Carts ready, harness all in good shape. It was wonderful to see what a wonderful procession we made. Now [27 May] we were off and our first night on the Prairie.

The party next stopped near Clearwater, Minnesota, on the west side of the Mississippi River not far from its headwaters. Some of them stayed at the "Linden Hotel," where Elizabeth was able to bake bread for the trip (diary entry, 30 May). On 1 June, Elizabeth wrote in her diary: "Through the blessing of God we were enabled to make another start on our journey. Our poney is very sick and almost unable to draw us let alone much of a load. About ½ past 4 you might have seen us starting, a small stove hanging to the top of the waggon also a tea kettle and a yeast pail" (whereupon the Youngs caught up with the rest of the party).

Just as we were busy getting ready for the night our carts & wagons arranged in horse shoe fashion & tied together & our

---

16 Poke bonnets had a distinctive cylindrical shape protruding around the face. As they resembled an inverted coal scuttle, they were sometimes called coal-scuttle bonnets (OED). Elizabeth also mentioned this sewing session in a diary entry for 22 May. There, she referred to the bonnets as "shakers," evidently equating Shaker with Quaker: "We are busy. I am trimming some shakers & Mrs [George] Young's making a pair of drawers for Miss McDougal." (Elizabeth often spelled "McDougall" without its final *l*.)

horses hobbled for fear of there wandering away, we were very much surprised excited & perplexed to see flying towards us men on horseback coming. Soon [we] found out that they were Indians who thought we were Americans & were on the war path. They had lately had some misunderstanding and were very much imbittered and very angry. They, the Indians, called the Americans Keche-mookimen (long-knives) and if it had not been for our "British flag," the Union Jack, we would have been badly treated. That is [our] no. 1, Introduction to the Indian Country.[17]

Day in and day out we had peculiar incidents, interruptions, such as the breaking of wooden [Red River] carts that were constructed without a bit of iron in any point whatsoever, consequently you could hear them as far as we could see them. There were days we had to carry water from one point to another, and our firewood was Buffalo chips. Narrow escapes from accidents occurred very often as our companions carried fire arms, so as to assist in our menues. One day our Leader [George McDougall] shot a goose, and divided it amongst the party, my part was a leg. It must have descended from the Ark, for tough was no name for it.

We camped early, and in the morning struck our tents early, preparing the night before as far as we could our lunch for the next day, so that there would be no midday delay. Sunday was sacredly kept. We had service in the morning, and the after part of the day was spent in resting.[18]

17 Egerton Young's diary ends on 26 May and so omits this incident, and Elizabeth's diary entries are sporadic after 2 June, but see Young, *By Canoe and Dog-Train*, 38–39: When settlers warned the party about dangers of Sioux attacks, George McDougall told them, "We have a little flag that will carry us in safety through any Indian tribe in America." When the Sioux horsemen approached a few days later, "our Union Jack fluttering from the whip stalk [a stick or staff to which the lash of a whip is attached: *OED*] caused them to fling their guns in the grass and come crowding around us with extended hands. . . . At Mr. McDougall's orders we stowed away our rifles and revolvers . . . and met them as friends, unarmed and fearless." American relations with the Sioux were at a low point following the Minnesota Sioux uprising of 1862 and the government's reneging on treaty commitments; Young detailed the dismal treatment that had been accorded to the Dakota chief, Little Crow, and his people.

18 On 17 June, Elizabeth wrote in her diary: "We are near Fort Abercrombie [North Dakota] . . . the glorious sun shining brightly upon us and plenty of wildflowers, Indians,

Excitement and experience often occurred. One day as we crossed from American Territory we threw out [hoisted] our Union Jack and our American horses ran away. Our guide said, "Let them run; they will soon get tired" as they were loaded down with Missionary Luggage.[19]

One other day it took nearly all our horses to pull one heavy ladened wagon out of a deep revine & those that were left, were being so stung with bull dog flies, that one of [our] sympathetic women made a smudge fire and before we were aware of it, the prairie grass was on fire. Now our leader who had just reached the top of the revine with the other members of the party called out, every man to his place, and away we went with the wind blowing the fire away from us, so for days we were exposed to a Prairie fire.

We were glad if we found a farmers home so that we might get some milk or eggs or butter, but alas these commodities were all too scarce.

Fierce wind storms came and unless our things were tied securely they would fly from us, never to be seen again. On the Prairies we were exposed to hot sun, wind storms, rain storms, thunder storms.

I made yeast, mixed bread, put it to rise as we were journeying along, and when we camped for the night, I borrowed the Frenchmans sheet iron stove & baked some bread & buns. This was a new experience travelling on the Prairies, but a very acceptable one, for all enjoyed the agreeable change.

and from the Fort we can hear the bugle sounding which makes it feel quite civilized again. . . . We have been drinking whisky . . . I mean drinking water from a stream called Whiskey Creek." In *Manitoba Memories*, 58–59, George Young described this fort, which had been besieged by the Sioux in 1862, as "a few log-houses and long stables, and one miserable store . . . and a sort of wooden structure called a 'fort.'" Whiskey Creek was "a miserable mire-hole and unbridged," so his party had to fill it with bushes and brush, "and then dash our tired horses across the abominable place and up a steep bank, as best we could."

19 George Young recalled that, on passing from Pembina "into our good and beloved Victoria's dominions," all "joined heartily in singing the national anthem," and "our loyal brother, E. R. Young, hoisted the Union Jack, a beautiful flag with which he was presented in Canada" (*Manitoba Memories*, 62).

Even Mr George McDougal came without invitation as soon as he heard of the home made bread.[20]

Prairie chickens was another pleasant & agreeable change. While I drove the horse Egerton used the *gun*.

Our days were long. We struck our tents early in the morning & only rested at noon long enough for the horses & ourselves to lunch, & then we camped early, which was a good & sensible thing to do.

Sojourn at Red River

After many days of wonderful experiences, & dangerous adventures, we camped on the shores of "Lake Assinioboine" [the Assiniboine River, swollen by spring flooding]. The smoke from our camp fires went down and curled on the lake. When Egerton saw this, he assured us that we were going to have a storm, and immediately prepared for it by using long laid up *rope* that was given to him by one of his Parishiners, as we were leaving Hamilton. This rope he used by tying up Dr George's & our tents. The storm came in the night and we were up & busy holding our tent from blowing away, tents & wagons carts were more or less blown down & much confusion.[21] Georgenia McDougal who was ill with Rheumatism her tent was down, Egerton went for her & put her in our tent making her comfortable. This was our farewell to our long tedious journey of marvellous experiences. We certainly were Pioneers to the lone land of the North West Territory.

20 In "The Bride of 1868," Elizabeth quoted McDougall as saying: "I do not wait for an invitation when there is anything good I come."

21 Elizabeth also made note of the storm in her diary entry for 3 July: "a dreadful hurricane of wind came up throwing down tents . . . and those of us that had tents up we had to hold onto them with all our strength." See Part III, sec. 2, for Egerton's story of "the rope from Hamilton" and his detailed account of the storm, described there as a "cyclone." In *Red River* (Montréal: John Lovell, 1871), 440–41, J.J. Hargrave wrote that the storm did great damage in Red River, especially to churches. George Young also gave a dramatic account of the storm and added that muddy Winnipeg left him "with a strong tendency to discouragement." Further, "a locust plague was on all the land," fields and farms "swept clean," causing great scarcity of flour and feed, and rising prices (*Manitoba Memories*, 62–63). Indeed, Elizabeth noted in her diary entry for 4 July 1868: "The grasshoppers have completely destroyed the vegetation around here for some distance."

The next day after gathering our things together we crossed over the River to Old Fort Garry. Here we were under the necessity of waiting for days for some mode of conveyance, by which we could go northward. The longest delays end sometime. Soon came the call to get ready, and we were not sorry, for two weeks of expectation and experience at a Mrs Gowlers farm was not a very pleasant one, although we could almost accept of anything coming off of the Prairies after weeks & weeks of most wonderful experiences there.[22]

Here we separated from our friends, some to stay at Fort Garry and others to go farther west, and we Egerton & I to go to Rossville mission — near Norway House, Hudson Bay fort. The days spent on the great lakes, rivers, and Prairies were full of adventures & strange experiences.

From Red River to Norway House

On 17 July, Elizabeth wrote in her diary: "We are leaving the Widow Gowlers this morning. . . . After a very comfortable stay and rest we can hardly pull up stakes to go, [but] the Lord helping us we will go. At 4 this morning we were up. Arrived at the lower fort about 9:00." In an entry dated 20 July, she described the subsequent preparations at Lower Fort Garry: "We again commenced packing our things again for the last part of our journey. . . . Mrs Campbell gave me two Buffalo tongues to boil for our journey. Mrs [??] boiled one and [??] ham. She sent for butter and made cakes for us for which we are very thankful for. After dinner we got started with some of our young men from Norway House. They are fine fellows. I promised Mrs Campbell my photograph when convenient."

> So we gladly accepted the call to continue our journey, in one [of the] H.B. Companys Inland boats [a York boat]. It had neither deck, awning, nor cabin. Its crew consisted of eight Indians, one of these men was called our guide whose duty was to act as Steersman.[23]

22 It appears that Elizabeth had been staying at the farm since 7 July. That day, she wrote in her diary: "Mr McDougal took Georgenia and I to Mrs Gowlers for which I was very thankful. . . . They got supper for us. It felt so good to sit upon a chair and yet if it was nothing else but bread and butter and tea we enjoyed it."

23 The steersman was Thomas Mamanowatum, who, Egerton R. Young later wrote, "was familiarly known as 'Big Tom' on account of his almost gigantic size" (*By Canoe and*

Into this little boat our outfit was thrown & a snug little place was assigned to us in the stern near the guide.

At the lower Fort-Garry, we stopped for mail for the northern H. Bay Co posts, and also supplies for the Indians. Lo & behold to our astonishment a big ox was being consigned to our boat, & unfortunately just near our part of the boat, you may be quite sure we did not appreciate such company. [Elizabeth's diary, 21 July: "Here we sit this morning with a[n] ox in front of us. Pemekin bags."] However when we reached the end of our journey we were told a nice roast for Christmas would be very acceptable. Here we were for more than ten days with this animal in front of us, through storm sunshine & shadow, through rough sea & smooth sea, and when we were forced to camp on shore, over this animal we had to climb. There was no alternative, submit was our constant *theme*.

This new start we hoped was & would be the end of our long & joyless "Honey-Moon." We were starting on a three hundred sixty mile trip of Winnipeg Lake & Jackfish River, & our ship was driven by sails when we had a good wind, and when calm by *oars* with good strong men at one end of them.

Elizabeth described the outset of their journey in her diary, writing on 24 July: "This morning we were aroused about 3 o'clock, in about 18 minutes we were all on board and scudding along with a favouring breeze. . . . About half past 7 we boiled our kettles for our second breakfast. We past several beautiful islands on the way and instead of our getting off for dinner the boys of our boat set up the little stove on a bag of Pemekan and boiled their kettles. . . . Slept on the boat tonight." The following day, she wrote: "This morning Egerton came three times and tried to get me up, and succeeded the third telling me that William had a pigeon nearly cooked for me that he had shot early in the morning, got up and got my breakfast then did some

Dog-Train, 42). Young paid tribute to his qualities and abilities on this voyage and as a leader at Rossville in *On the Indian Trail and Other Stories of Missionary Work Among the Cree and Saulteaux Indians* (London: Religious Tract Society, [1897]), 219–30, noting that his name meant "O be joyful." Keith Goulet (e-mail, 1 March 2013) writes that "*minowatum*' is to look upon other or something in a positive, cheerful and joyous light. The *ma* in *maminowatum* signifies that it is a recurring state and characteristic of such a person."

baking, remained here till dinner time then started for Pigeon Point. The waves appeared to me very rough, but got to land safely. Egerton took his gun went off shooting, got enough berries for tea tonight and tomorrow night."

> We were always glad to go on shore however long it might make our journey. Why? Because of our objectionable company. ["If to go on shore, we had to get up, walk along the sides of the boat, in the meantime carefully walk over the beast, and feel sorry for the poor beast. If we were forced to leave the boat in a rough place a Stalwart Indian would place his back at my disposal and carry me ashore of course I took it in good grace & thanked him."][24]
>
> When it was impossible to proceed on our journey, our Indians would go on a hunting expedition, perhaps find some duck eggs. When fortunate they would come back delighted & at once put them in the pot, eggs & all, the ducks simply minus feathers. Then when the weather was fine they were ready to call, *How, How,* & off we would go again.[25]
>
> Now we are nearing the end of July and also our long journey. A few more experiences & we are at Norway House Fort, on the evening of the twenty-ninth of July.

On Sunday, 26 July, in her last diary entry before they reached Norway House, Elizabeth wrote: "It is a very rough morning raining and very windy. William had breakfast ready for us but could not have worship on account of the storm. After dinner it cleared up so we had worship. Everything seems so strange to me. We feel that the Lord is the same to us here as elsewhere he takes care of us here. We are enjoying good health and we are thankful to God for it."

24 Young, in *Indian Life in the Great North-West* (Toronto: Musson Book Company, [1899?]), 95, wrote that when the boat got stuck in shallows offshore, "a good-natured, genial Indian, named Soquatum, would quickly jump into the water and, coming round to the side of the boat next to Mrs. Young, would take her on his back, and, holding to his head with her hands and arms, thus she would be safely carried ashore." This may be the same person as So-qua-a-tum whose conversion Young described on pp. 104–14.

25 Elizabeth misremembered the wake-up call: in *By Canoe and Dog-Train,* 48, Egerton gave it as *koos koos kwa!* "Wake up!" Jeffrey Muehlbauer suggests the transcription, *koskoskwê!* 'shake! move!' from the root *koskoskw-* 'shake/move' but adds, "Different than any modern form, also not exactly in the Watkins dictionary either."

Settling in at Rossville Mission

The H.B. Officers were good enough to row us over to the mission, & when nearing our destination we heard singing.[26] It was a pleasant greeting although it was not for us, it was praises to God our Heavenly Father [during a service at the church] & we were happy, happy to be at the end of our *Long, tedious, tiresome, Venturesome* journey. We were rejoiced to at last be in a house, & delighted to see a bed let alone sleep in it, for we had been two months & nineteen days roughing it. Even the Heavens greeted us, that night we had a fearful thunder storm. It shook the house so that the picture over where we slept fell down, we were glad to escape being hurt.

The next day our Predecessor [Charles Stringfellow] & Egerton went out to take a survey of the mission premises, and while [they were] casually walking through a field a bull lowered his head & steered straight for them. Fortunately seeing him in good time they were almost able to escape him, not without getting part of Egerton's trowsers torn down. So our greetings were out of the ordinary.[27]

The next performance was to assist Mrs Stringfellow to get ready to leave for civilization, as they were to leave for Winnipeg in the boats we came in. The dear little woman asked me to make them cakes for the journey. I was very happy and pleased to do it. That is if I had not forgotten how. ["They had been there for ten years without any change and as Mr Stringfellow said, he was glad to go; he would now get some Roast and Yorkshire pudding. They

---

26 "The Chief Factor was most kind and entertained us to tea, and then piloted us over two & a half miles to what was to be our mission home," Elizabeth recalled in "The Bride of 1868." The "Chief Factor" was HBC Chief Trader James Green Stewart, who was in charge of Norway House from 1867 to 1871: C. S. MacKinnon, "Stewart, James Green," *Dictionary of Canadian Biography* online. See also Young, *By Canoe and Dog-Train*, 54–55.

27 The bull was more dangerous than Elizabeth knew. Egerton later wrote a graphic account, which he never published: "Adventure with a Bull at Norway Ho[use]" (see Part III, sec. 3). The Stringfellows had served at the Oxford mission from 1857 to 1863 and had been at Norway House for five years. Charles Stringfellow was born about 1832 in England and came to Canada in 1855. Ordained in 1857, he married Ann Taylor in Québec in May of that year immediately before their trip to Oxford. From 1868 to 1896 he served various churches in southern Ontario. Thanks to Anne Lindsay for compiling this information from census and other data.

had had sorrow, lost a dear little child by pulling a tea pot of hot tea over itself, while the mother was ill in bed.[28] These troubles are hard to bear where you have friends who sympathise & Drs to Prescribe for you, but when you have to bear all alone it makes quite a difference, as we found out to our sorrow."]

As soon as we got them off happily, we at once began arranging our things, cleaned up the house and tried to settle our things.[29] Our parishners were human beings, glad to see us, & in their peculiar welcome, of course we did not understand their *How, How.* We kept our Interpreter [Timothy Bear] near us, so as to quite understand them.

The First Cree Visitors
In "The Bride of 1868," Elizabeth recounted a story about the Youngs' initial lesson in Cree hospitality:

The first introduction we had to our Indian visitors was an Indian woman coming in, and by her sign language for neither of us knew one word of the language, we knew she wanted something to eat so I went to work and put before her, placed the food on the table as I would before ourselves, and seated her there. She certainly was hungry and when through she said nenaskomooanan [Muehlbauer: *ninanaskomonân*] which means thank you, & picking up her skirts

28 This child, likely an infant, was not named. A daughter, Sarah Elizabeth, was born 18 February 1866 and baptized 27 May by her father (Norway House baptismal register, no. 1262), and census data also list an older sister, Jane. In *The Battle of the Bears: Life in the North Land* (Boston: W.A. Wilde, 1907), Young described Mrs. Stringfellow as an "invalid" at the time of her leaving (57).

29 In a short manuscript titled "In the Land of Fur and Frost," E. Ryerson Young recorded his mother telling him that the Stringfellows had been keeping hens in the upper storey of their house. "E.B.Y. soon had the chickens out of the house and the terribly dirty place cleaned up. Kept the hens outdoors too long — froze to death. 'Didn't expect the cold to come down so soon and so severely.'" (In fact, the hens in the attic initially gave way to rabbits, who likewise met an untimely end: see Part III, sec. 16, in relation to Young's "Unusual Ballad.") "In the Land of Fur and Frost" consists of eight half-page sheets containing mission recollections typed by E. Ryerson Young on the basis of notes or stories from his mother. JSHB collection.

she put what was left in the pouch which she had made and backed
out so we looked at each other in utter dismay.[30]

In her memoir, she continued:

We began at once making broths, soups, for the sick, & feeding
the hungry. We quickly found out what we were there for. The sick
needed medicine. We were glad and happy to do what we could
for the poor people in every way we could, and began at once.

Our first Sunday there we were pleased to see the Indians
coming in so orderly, and delighted to see the officers & their
help from the fort taking their accustomed places in the church.
This was Sunday morning. The evening service was wholly the
Indian service.

We very soon became acquainted with our duties and what
was expected of us. Although we were young and inexperienced,
there certainly seemed to be a Guiding hand leading us, directing
us, and helping us, getting to understand the ways of the Indians
& the H.B. Companys ways.

September 1868: A Brief Separation

Shortly after the Youngs settled in at the Rossville mission, Egerton was
called away to Oxford House. Although not in her 1927 memoir, on one of the
pages in "The Bride of 1868," Elizabeth described coping with his absence:

But ere we get unpacked and our things in order, Mr Young has
to leave for Oxford mission many miles away ere I know the
language or even get acquainted with the Indians. So now the work

---

30 In *By Canoe and Dog-Train*, Egerton R. Young dated this story to the day after the
Stringfellows left. Elizabeth had laid out a loaf of bread, corned beef, and vegetables left
over from their trip, and "the food . . . was to have been our principal support for two
or three days, until our supplies should have arrived." It was a lesson in Cree etiquette.
If a generous host lays out a quantity of food, "the invited guest," Young observed,
"is expected to eat all he can, and then to carry the rest away" (58–59). In a small
way, this recalls Cree "eat-all feasts," at which it was unpropitious and disrespectful
not to consume all the food offered. See Jennifer S. H. Brown and Robert Brightman,
*The Orders of the Dreamed: George Nelson on Cree and Northern Ojibwa Religion and
Myth, 1823* (Winnipeg: University of Manitoba Press, 1988), 100–101.

of getting ready has to be attended to, but it is summer and not too taxing as in Winter; this we learn as time goes on, changes of clothing, & presents for the missionary and guns to secure food as they go along, of course a supply of 'tea & sugar,' flour, the Indian Guide will be cook and will make what Indians call 'dough dogs,' mixed flour & water made flat, like a Beavers tail pressed on a stick & one end pressed in the ground in front of the fire.

August [actually 8–19 September 1868], my good husband is on his mission of good will to the Oxford Mission and missionary. And my work is to look after this mission in his absence. The D[ay] School,[31] the church services, and answer the many and varied Calls that are constantly made on the mission and now this is the beginning, and what we pray for most is Wisdom, patience, & desire to please and win the people of this mission. Squaws with their Papooses come in without knocking and squat down on the floor of the Kitchen the most comfortable room in the house, when rested and gather their thoughts and find out what they came for. It may be muskuki [Muehlbauer: *maskihkiy*] medicine, or food, or clothing. Of course they know they will get a cup of tea & a piece of Bread; fancy perhaps a half Dozen [women] at the same time. It is quite a tax on your Larder, especially when you are some hundreds of miles away from fresh 'Supplies,' that come to you once a year. You try not to think of this when you try to win, try to make the poor half starved, famished, unkempt creatures happy. So if we impoverish ourselves to build up the poor creatures. . . .

Soon after Mr Young went away I took ill, was unable to wait on myself and could not make the old Indian Woman [helping me] understand what I wanted, there happened to be a Free Trader in the Village & she went out and found him & brought him with her, then things were soon made right & I was helped as I prescribed for myself and was understood, & restored to comfort, peace &

31 The schoolmaster deserted his post, so Egerton found, on returning, that Elizabeth "had taken the charge in the interim, and succeeded in keeping the children together" (Young, letter dated 5 October 1868 to *Wesleyan Missionary Notices*, n.s., no. 2 [February 1869], 31). Peter Badger was the teacher and continued as such till mid-1875; perhaps he had a temporary dispute or misunderstanding with the newcomers.

sleep came to my rescue. . . . we soon got things going fire & hot water was all that was needed. We were thankful. This is only the beginning of my lonely times. . . . Sometimes the absence would be greater and the anxiety would be increased as the Winters are intensely severe. . . . The absence may be three, four or five weeks, no letters from, nor to the absent one. The Chief Factor Mr Stewart used to ask me if the glass of the windows were getting thin looking longing for the absent one. The distance to Oxford 200 Miles. . . .

In such a situation you need courage, Wisdom, patience and Faith in the Giver of all things.[32]

Fortunately, Egerton returned safely on 19 September, a Saturday, and the week following their reunion was a happy one, marked by good news from home. Elizabeth's diary entry for 22 September 1868 — the first since 3 August — reads: "Felt happy all day, worked hard. In the evening Mr Young went to the Fort to preach, did clean myself all day so while waiting for Mr Young, read part of the life of Peter Jacobs — 9 ocl[ock] came and no Mr Y — in a little while I heard voices, and was not disappointed. Mr Stewart & Mr McTavish brought my darling and with him a Scotch boy to live with us. I am not to spoil him, that he knows, I hope the good Lord will help me spoil him thus far that we may be the means of bringing him to Christ."[33] The following day, she wrote: "Patience is my motto today. Today [I] have been pretty busy. I am trying every day to live nearer the cross and to lay my all on the alter. I am afraid I am displeasing my Father in Heaven in laying in the morning. I hope the Lord will assist me to rise earlier so that I may devote more of my time to his glory." And, on 24 September, she added: "I feel truly thankful this morning that the knews [news] from home are so favourable, and that dear Ma enjoys good health. God bless her, I feel wonderfully sustained."[34]

32 Egerton Young recorded this trip day by day (UCCA, Young fonds, series 4, box 10, file 4, "First trip to Oxford Mission, September 1868"), as well as in the letter of 5 October 1868 cited in the preceding note.

33 The book was *Journal of the Reverend Peter Jacobs, Indian Wesleyan Missionary, from Rice Lake to the Hudson's Bay Territory and Returning . . . with a Brief Account of His Life* (Toronto, 1853). The "Scotch boy" was not mentioned further.

34 It must have been during this period that Elizabeth became pregnant with her first child, "Eddie," born 11 June 1869. On letters from home, see Part III, sec. 4, for excerpts of letters that Elizabeth received from Clarissa Bingham in 1868–69.

The Chief Factor's Cariole Ride

> We often exchanged visits to & from the Fort, and enjoyed the
> exchange very much. It was a delightful change & pleasure to
> have them pop in and see us. Chief Factor [Robert] Hamilton &
> Mrs Hamilton were delightful friends, and our visits were mutual.[35]
>
> The Chief Factors positions were something like the Methodist
> ministers itinerary, constantly changing. At one time we [had] Chief
> Factor Roderick Ross, at another time Chief Factor Fortescue, at
> another time Chief Factor [James] Stewart. The officers were Mr Alex
> McTavish, his brother Donald McTavish.[36] These gentlemen were
> exceedingly kind to us, & made us happy, helping us get acquainted
> & acclimatized. We appreciated their kindness very much.

On at least one occasion, the kindness of the chief factors — in this
case, probably Hamilton's predecessor, James Stewart — evidently extended
to offers of transportation. Elizabeth elsewhere recalled a trip that she and
her husband made from the Rossville mission to Norway House, which
culminated in a memorable ride back home:

> I remember once very distinctly on one short trip to the Fort —
> [we] found the Chief Factor very much the worse of liquor.
> He informed me that he was going to give me a cariole run with
> his train of half-wolf dogs, & he did. Fortunately I had been told
> that if ever p[?] are left alone with these special dogs not to speak
> or they might turn on you. Mission House 2½ miles away — we
> were not more than half way across when my friend lost his grip
> on the Cariole (standing on tail end of boards & holding by rope).

35 Robert Hamilton was chief factor at Norway House from 1870 to 1872. The Reverend
George Young wrote to Egerton on 10 February 1871 that "Mr Hamilton regards you as
a sort of Prince among missionaries" (JSHB collection). Elizabeth passed to descendants
a book that Annie Miles Hamilton inscribed to her on 20 July 1872: Isabella Beeton's
Book of Household Management (London, 1872). During this time, Elizabeth recalled in
"The Bride of 1868," "We found out many things that were & would be expected of us."

36 Roderick Ross served as clerk and then chief trader at Norway House from 1869 to
1875 and later as chief factor. James G. Stewart served at Norway House from 1867 to
1871. Joseph Fortescue was a chief trader in the district in 1870–71 (HBCA biographical
sheets); he and the McTavish brothers were not mentioned further in Elizabeth's memoirs.

So I simply snuggled down under the beaver robes that were most luxurious & kept my mouth closed scarcely breathing, as the dogs knew just where to go when on [the] trail to the Mission House — going there every Sunday taking the officers to the morning service. So when they came to their stopping place, I quickly rolled out of the Cariole & ran into the house, & glad to! Father [Egerton] & other officer in the other dog train — rode up to see that all was right.

The dogs were four beautiful fellows, silver bells arched over backs — blue velvet saddle cloths — embroidered with bead work. Twas the Chief Officer's special train of dogs, cariole, robes — highly honored *but fearful!*[37]

"Giving Out Medicines"

Many were the calls, many were the visits, many were the wants, many were the cries of hunger, many were the cries of misery of the Indians. And gradually we became fully acquainted with all the different varieties of ailments.

The men stand around, the women with their Papooses squat around the wall, & chatter amongst themselves, & finally in time ask for what they want. If medicine I have to enquire what is the matter. Oh metunee akesuee [Muehlbauer: *mitoni âhkosiw*, 'She/he is very sick'], Very Sick, perhaps they all bound tight around their Stomach from eating some wild berries. So just give them something very simple such as castor oil. When we went from Ontario we took with us a number of bottles of No. Six, very hot.[38]

---

37 This account appears on a single page of handwritten text transcribed by E. Ryerson Young from his mother's recollections (JSHB collection). The incident is undated, but it most likely occurred while James Stewart was the chief factor. Robert Hamilton, who arrived in 1870, seemed more highly respected and, as noted later in this volume, favoured temperance (at least for Indians).

38 Number Six was the most popular of a series of medicines created by Samuel Thomson, a New England doctor. The concoction was made of one pound of myrrh (a gum resin used also in perfumes and incense), one ounce of capsicum (cayenne, or red pepper) and a gallon of brandy — evidently unbeknownst to the temperance-minded Youngs. John S. Haller, *The People's Doctors: Samuel Thomson and the American Botanical Movement* (Carbondale, IL: Southern Illinois University Press, 2000); thanks to Anne Lindsay for this reference.

Sometimes the men would come in and complain of a bad pain, putting their hands over their stomachs, and I would take a good teaspoon full of No. Six and with sugar & hot water give them to drink. It seemed to just touch the spot & this was often called for. One old Co-cum [Muehlbauer: *kohkom* 'your grandmother' (2nd person prefix)] wished me to keep the tea grounds from every meal, in a dish, and put the dish in a corner so she could help herself every time she came in. An Indian woman came in one day who was expecting any moment wanting some particular thing; she had put up for herself a little wigwam & here by herself was going to take care of herself all alone, that was the forepart of the week & on Sunday she was in the Church to have her Papoose christened. They seem so *hardy.* They say white women lace [referring to corsets] too much.

Elsewhere, Elizabeth further described some of her early experiences as a mission doctor:

Most fortunately I had a Dr's book, and as I had daily reference to it, I became very Proficient & able to deal out simple medicines, and perform, such as treating cuts. For instance a big tall Indian [was] cutting wood in yard and caught the axe in the clothes line & it threw the axe on his head and gave him a very nasty gash. The poor man came in to me bleeding terribly & as quick as I could [I] got some warm water, scissors, court plaster.[39] I sat him down, cleaned the bleeding then cut the hair away from the sides of the cut, & then strapped the cut, criss-cross, leaving little spaces for the pus to pass out. . . .

A little Indian boy came in one day with a fish bone in his throat, I stood him up turned him partly over & opened his mouth as far as possible & made a hook of my finger and went hunting for the bone & soon got it out — these are some of my medical experiences which were happening very often.

39 Court plaster is a sticking plaster made of linen or silk, spread with an adhesive such as isinglass (*OED*).

My advice to missionaries going out would be to take a course of lessons in nursing & caring for the sick. Unfortunately I was minus all this, the very thing I needed most. Being the eldest of a large family I had some little idea of some sickness, colds, yes colds, mumps, & all childrens diseases. This of course was a help. And with a good mother's care & loving attention on all our little wants God [had] blessed us with good Parents for which no children can be too thankful.

So with my good Dr Book of which I made good use of, and the very fact of being kind, attentive to their individual wants following the teachings of our blessed master, we made and gained friends, that were kind and helpful to us when we needed their help. "Cocum Mary Murdoo" was really helpful to me in learning the Language not that she understood English but when I would pronounce the Indian words and made sentences & [if] they were right she would tell me; so in a very short time I could talk Indian & understand the language. It made a great difference to the success of the days work & the pleasure of understanding them at first hand.[40]

---

40 "So in less than one year," Elizabeth wrote to her grandson, Egerton Helme, "I mastered the language well enough to speak, to talk, consult, in fact, to enter into conversation with them and not to be left to their tender mercies again, altogether": handwritten transcription by E. Ryerson Young from pages labelled "From Mother's letter to Egerton Helme — August 15, 1927." Egerton Helme, born in England, was the son of the Youngs' daughter Lillian. JSHB collection.

"Cocum" Mary Murdo was, according to Egerton, "an old widowed woman" to whom the Youngs "became very much attached." She shared their York boat trip to Norway House, and Egerton praised her as "bright, clever . . . and a most devout and consistent Christian" (*The Battle of the Bears*, 55). Her husband, Murdo, a skilled steersman and guide, had drowned in the Hell's Gates Rapids in the Nelson River. In *The Field and the Work: Sketches of Missionary Life in the Far North* (Toronto: Methodist Mission Rooms, 1884), 96–97, John Semmens told of the incident in some detail but dated it to 1877, an evident error.

More on the Women
Reminiscences from "The Bride of 1868"

Then too they [the Indian women] are always in the open air, in the
Summer in their canoes, hunting for rabbits, fish, and then hunting
for fire-wood, busy making moccasins, sometimes bring them to
sell. In the Winter, their clothes are very poor, from the ankle to the
knee any old cloth to make a legging, wound around and fastened.
Some kind of a Jacket & then a Skirt, over all this A Tartan shawel
or blanket, sometimes both. And if a papoose it is strapped on a
board and with strap attached to the board and made into a loop
put the loop around her head and throws the blanket right over
the babe, and marches off any distance in the coldest of winter and
the little fellow will come out pipping hot. On this board there is
a cloth shaped like a shoe & laced up, but ere it is laced up a layer
of moss is put on the board then the papoose placed on it & a layer
of moss placed on top of the child then it is laced up. This moss is
gathered by the women & spread out to dry after picking pieces of
sticks & rubbish out, this does in place of clothing. . . .[41]

Our Callers were many, varied in wants, varied in appearance.
Some a little Paquasican [Muehlbauer: *pahkwêsikan*], Flour, others
medicine, something to eat, one poor old woman with nothing on
but a skirt and an old blanket over her Shoulders & it cold winter
weather. They often carry their moccasins under their arms until
they reach the mission & then they put them on they walk threw
Snow & Ice in their bare feet. . . .

It is well if the missionary has plenty of provisions especially
tea. It would simply injure our work. To refuse to help them &
give them a cup of tea would be disasterous & we might shut the
door & lock it. So even if we went without ourselves it would pay
us to rob ourselves, some of our friends say do not be so generous.
A very old woman comes in seemingly weak and although we do
not understand one word, we know perfectly well what she wants
and we cannot nor will not refuse her, when you are asked to even

---

41 For Elizabeth Young's further remarks on the virtues of moss, see Part III, sec. 5.

save the tea leaves that are already had been drawn in a dish so she can have it for a drink when she comes in. Sometimes the kitchen is full of callers, and as my dear husband would say, 'It is the most comfortable place & they enjoy it.' Then the work must wait, another time. They simply come in without knocking, they think if the[y] knock they are not welcome.[42] So let them come, they simply sit squat on the floor, they much prefer that mode for comfort.

The Visit of Tapastanum

Indians that had no permanent home & made the woods their home were called Wood Indians.[43] An old Wood Indian [Tapastanum] came into the mission one day, with his squaw & made himself perfectly at home with his exclamations of Ha, Ha, Ho, Ho. Mr Young at once made it his business to entertain him by showing him pictures & taking him right through the mission house.[44] We made a cup of tea for him & his wife and now there were more Ha, Ha's, & Ho Ho's. He was most gorgeously gotten up. Down the outsides of his leggings were a string of bells, & in front of his breast, a round looking glass, and opposite in the back another.

42 The Youngs left their outer doors unlocked but found need to assert a degree of privacy. Elizabeth was startled one morning by a man who quietly came into the house looking for Egerton and appeared at her bedroom door, reflected in the mirror where she was combing her hair in her nightdress. She shouted, "A-wus-ta-kena! ('Get out, you!')" [Muehlbauer: *awasita kîna!* 'You, go away!']. The man told Egerton that the usually gentle Ookemasquao had gotten so cross that "it made him jump." Egerton explained that it was best to knock at inner doors before entering (*Stories from Indian Wigwams and Northern Camp-fires* [New York: Eaton and Mains, 1892], 34).

43 "Wood Indians" was a term that Anglophones at Norway House often used for "pagan" Indians who had not settled like those at Rossville — for example, Cree groups around Cross Lake, Split Lake, and the Nelson River.

44 In "The Bride of 1868," Elizabeth recalled Egerton's efforts to both entertain and educate Cree visitors: "My husband took many things out for his own pleasure, and made them of much amusement to them, a Kellidascope, a "magnet" which they called a keche munetoes [great spirits], The Dalby Iron, Picture[s], to interest them." E. Ryerson Young, in "Scientific Evenings" (see Part II, chap. 5), described the kaleidoscope with its "tumbling bits of coloured glass" making patterns when the tube was turned, and the big "horse shoe" magnet that pulled needles to it. The "Dalby Iron" has not been explained.

He was most picturesque in his multitude of paraphernalia & his Ho, Ho, Hi Hi, Ha, Ha. It was almost impossible to satisfy him, & almost impossible to get near the point of saying good-bye.[45]

Very much like the Indian that came, presented two ducks & remained to help us eat them ["and being very much entertained looking at pictures the afternoon passed away & tea time arrived & he enjoyed another meal with us"] & at bed time when asked if he had not better see if his wigwam was where he left it in the morning, he immediately said I am waiting for what you give me for the ducks. Imagine our great surprise, we understood that they were a present. We very quickly gave him all the present was worth and a good deal more. And with it learned our dear bought lesson, never to take a present from an Indian.[46] Three hundred and sixty-five days a year were full of such doings, so day in and day out were very much alike.

Queen Victoria's Picture

In "The Bride of 1868," Elizabeth wrote that the Rossville people showed much interest in Queen Victoria. Accordingly, Egerton, evidently in the spring of 1869, requisitioned a portrait of the Queen, which would have arrived from England the following summer (1870):

We had not been there long and we heard them speak at times about the Mother Queen often. So Mr Young sent by the Packet

45 In "Tapastanum: 'A Noted Conjuror for Many Years, Who Long Resisted the Teachings of Christianity'" (*Papers of the Fortieth Algonquian Conference,* ed. Karl S. Hele and J. Randolph Valentine [Albany: State University of New York Press, 2012], 223–40), Anne Lindsay provides a detailed overview of Tapastanum's missionary and government contacts, notably his unheralded role in bringing the Pimicikamak Cree of Cross Lake into Treaty 5.

46 In "The Bride of 1868," Elizabeth quoted Tapastanum as saying, "I am waiting for the present you are giving me for the present I gave you." As a result of this incident, Elizabeth and Egerton decided to learn how to value "presents," based on HBC trade prices: "So from the H.B.C.," she wrote, "we got a tariff price for everything which was the value of a 'Beaver Skin.'" (The HBC priced each item it sold in terms of the value placed on one "made beaver" pelt, as Elizabeth was trying to explain.) In this way, if they accepted a present, they had an idea of what to give in exchange, since "presents" proved to entail bartering.

that left for England in the next spring, for a Picture of Queen
Victoria in her Coronation Robes. It would take a year to go, and
the same to come, but it came. So my beloved told the Guide of
the boats when he expected the Picture that if he would be very
careful in bringing it over fifteen or more Portages he would pay
him well. These Portages are great rocky places that the H.B.Co's
boats cannot go around. So the men are to carry their loads over
the Portages on their backs, and if they can possibly drag the
boat empty around they will do it but if not they will have to drag
it across the portage. So our Picture of the Queen, made some
journey ere it came to us."[47]

Fish, More Fish, and Household Help

In a single-page text preserved by her son, Elizabeth recalled how people
asked her about the mission diet: "What did you live on [at] Home?" Her
answer was: "Fish, Whitefish, Jack fish, Sturgeon, occasionally deer meat,
Rabbits, moose meat, very few ducks or geese. As for vegetables, none except
watery potatoes." The Norway House diet did indeed revolve around fish.
The dogs — essential to transportation — lived on fish. But people also relied
heavily on fish, there being so little else to eat.

In "The Bride of 1868," she elaborated:

September was coming and as Winter would soon be here in
these northern Latitudes, nets had to be prepared for the Fishing
that takes place to provide for our Winters need, net mending,
net making, occupied the Indians time very much, Fish to the
number of three or four thousand were caught and staged
[put on high outdoor racks] & hung up frozen for our use and
the dogs all through the Winter of eight months. . . .

47 On p. 97 of his 1870 diary, Egerton recorded in theatrical terms the showing of the
"splendid framed picture" at Rossville: "Great was the excitement of the Indians to see
their 'Great Mother across the waters.' There was no peace in the Mission House until
every man of them had been permitted to march in and gaze upon that womanly, motherly
queenly face. With uncovered heads and glittering eyes they looked upon the picture and
then with quiet steps and catlike motion they glided from the room with a grace and
reverence that would not[?] have done honor to a St James drawing room reception."

Through the summer they [dogs] find for themselves. Mr Young had a few dogs he was very careful of, a St Bernard [Jack: see fig. 5], & a Newfoundland dog Cuffie.[48] They were the only dogs allowed in the house, of course there were others that he had special care over. In the Winter time every dog got two fish in the Evening, but before going on a long journey they were fed Extra. In October the Indians with nets went out into the lake and secured some thousands of fish, Stageing for Winter Supply for men, and dogs, women and children. I have often had around my cooking stove fish for Twenty dogs 2 apiece. Throwing them out as they come in from the Stageing, hard frozen. It required some skill to feed some twenty dogs, there was some excitement when two or three trains of dogs were harnessed & Sleds packed up and got ready for a long trip as dogs need feeding by the way. So the sleds are packed to the utmost with fish for dogs, the missionaries Books; presents, for his expectant people, clothing for body & bed, and food.

Fish also provided the topic for another brief reminiscence:

Fish day. Once a month I had the Indian women come in through the cold winter and scale & clean enough fish to do me for a long while. You say, Why? Well the cleaning fish two or three times a day becomes nauseous and tiresome in the extreme, especially when you are compelled to live on this menue day in a[nd] day out.

These women will scale clean & put the fish on a clean board & place them in the fish house, where they will be frozen hard & keep any length of time. It not only helps me, but gives them a little occupation, & in the meantime something to eat, for they are not sent away hungry.

48 See Young, *By Canoe and Dog-Train*, 94–95. Cuffie (or Cuffy) became Elizabeth's special sled dog. She and Jack were gifts from Mr. and Mrs. William E. Sanford, of Hamilton, Ontario: see Young, *My Dogs in the Northland* (New York: Fleming H. Revell, 1902), 125–26. For more about Cuffy, see Part II, chap. 13 ("Dogs").

Eating fish twenty one times a week, no matter how you perform the cooking. Stuffing & baking, making fish balls with bread crumbs, frying, steaming with milk & egg, Sauce. Even babies & [are] fed on the Soup and are fine healthy rosey cheeked babies.[49]

In "The Bride of 1868," Elizabeth also commented on her great need for household assistance, given the living conditions at Rossville and the heavy mission duties that she carried. Finding reliable help, however, was a challenge:

It was hard to keep our Indian made [maid] in the summer; the moment the Ice was cleared away they wanted to fly around in their canoes, but in winter very different, the cold, the snow, & the Wigwam the only place, or with a shawll put around them fly over to the Fort or visit the mission house. The young Indian maidens were scarce. When I had one for a few months and she was able to get a new dress or new shawl, a young Indian would come and plead with the missionary to ask Kitty Cochrane to be his Bride. Mr Young would say to him, 'go and ask her yourself, or go ask some other Village girl. Why do you want Kitty?' His answer was, 'oh Kitty knows how to cook, O-kee-masquaoo [the master's wife] has taught her.'[50] We began to think this was another occupation for us match making, but no, we thought, let them make their own selection. . . .

After a while I found the best help was a widow woman [Little Mary, described later], for it was almost impossible to keep a young

49 "Fish day," which is also the source of the comments at the start of this section, is a one-page text written by Elizabeth and kept by E. Ryerson Young (JSHB collection). On p. 7 of "In the Land of Fur and Frost" (the eight-page typed memoir cited earlier), Elizabeth described the ingenious method by which young children were fed fish broth: "The Indians fed many of their children out of tins that were made for lamps. There was a little spout in which wicks were to be placed that would absorb the oil or grease and the wicks being ignited would give the light required. The wicks would be used in their place but fish soup would be the fuel supplied and the children would suck the wick and be most satisfactorily fed."

50 Elizabeth also mentioned her epithet in her account of Sandy Harte (see Part III, sec. 7), there spelled "Okimasquao" (Muehlbauer: *okimâskwêw*, 'the master's wife').

girl as help. I also thought that their wants were many, that I had
better have them do some Indian work for me, and then pay them,
they would help me & I could do for them, but they not only wanted
the materials but wanted food while doing the work. I found I was
paying in some instance double. They made moccasins, leggings.
There was not much time for resting or reading, looking after the
house and waiting on the frequent callers, visitors.

The Annual Requisition for Supplies
From "The Bride of 1868":

Once a year, and that was about Christmas time we sent our
Requisition to England for some things, as the mission at the time
belonged to the English w m s [Wesleyan Missionary Society], but
in our time the Canadians took it over. While under their control
we had some very valuable Parcels sent out to the mission most
serviceable, & acceptable, and useful. Our Canadian Requisition
for Canada was for Flour, Butter, Flour to last a Twelve Month
and butter for the year, Sugar.[51] Then we had to buy cotton, reels
of thread, print the common things we have to send for so as to
pay the Indians for work done for us, as money is of no use there.
So it means quite an outlay all at once and quite a good deal of
thinking, to make it last all the Twelve Months, as we have so many
calls that are unexpected. Some are cruel enough to say, 'Why do
you give them, why are you so generous, & so on?' What is our
mission there? But to win them for Christ, to refuse them we would
be guilty, & might at once come home. Medicines are among the
things required.

51 Elizabeth also recalled that from England the Youngs got coffee beans, sugar in
cubes, tea in lead-lined chests, and rice. Coal oil came from Canada. "We never dared
send for anything that was not absolutely necessary," she remembered. One time, though,
the Youngs sent in an order "for some tinned goods calling them 'canned' goods — the
big men at the front thought the missionaries were asking for candies and refused
to send them! Missionaries must not have such luxuries" (typed page of memories in
E. Ryerson Young's papers, j s h b collection).

Christmas, a Recent Introduction

Christmas and New Years were a little change from the ordinary routine. We were expected to receive callers & entertain them. It was quite an undertaking to prepare for several hundred Indians more or less, all our Village Indians, all the Fort Indians, and many Wood Indians. ["That meant much for us to learn in preparing & making ready, first what was needed in preparation for Christmas, for it was all new to us, for we were not in Civilization, we were now where there was no Christmas and for New Years, Dog-feasts in the past."] So we had to be satisfied & make plain buns & have plenty of tea, prepare seats for the callers who were many from far and near.

Now the question was what shall we give them? Our supplies were not very plentiful, and our larder quite bare. We had tea, our boxes of tea came from England, but what about cakes. All I could think of was to set some yeast, make a sponge & let it rise, & then busy myself and make some buns plain as I had no sugar nor shortning to put in, no not even currants or raisins.

Now the day has come we are up early. We get our big kettles on, get in some seats from the Church, tea made, the buns arranged on plates. Now they begin to appear; our first callers were or must have had no breakfast as the plate of buns passed to them. They were about to empty the plate, when we were forced to say, *ches-qua* [Muehlbauer: *cêskwa*], that is, stop. If they all emptied every plate, we would not have enough for all, so we were very sorry to have to cry, "be careful."

This was like the Indian partaking of the first Sacrement. When the wine was all in one goblet, instead of only taking a sip, he drank it all, & the rest had to do without.

The New Year's Feast

> That [holiday] in heathen times [was] a Dog Feast. But ever since
> missionaries have come it has been changed. It is now a Christian
> feast.[52] To make this a great success it means much thinking &
> much work, & a good deal of care and thought for the missionaries
> wife. For weeks before the Indians were consulted as to how
> much could they contribute towards the Feast. Some promised
> a little tea when they came in with their Packs of Fur, some a
> little sugar, some venison, a little Flour. All this was brought to
> the missionaries wife. As it was winter and very cold weather,
> anything that could be frozen could be kept nicely. So about five
> days before the first of January, some of the Indian women would
> come in & help me prepare the meat, & make some bread & buns.
> We might make meat pies if we were fortunate enough to get some
> shortning of some kind. If only bears greese, we might make rice
> pudding if we were fortunate to get some milk, & a few plums as
> the H.B.C. called a coarse raisin. If that was the case, we thought
> ourselves very fortunate.
>
> Then when the day was near we would get the Indians to
> fix the tables in the church, and early on the day, although great
> big white buttons [of frost] were on the heads of the nails, even
> before we began to bring our kettles of hot water in, and make
> the tea.[53] As the church was oblong, we made one table across
> the top & one long one down each side. The top table was for
> the missionary and the Chiefs. Everything being ready and
> the Indians gathering, before anything was touched the orders
> were that all that were feeble & unable to come, they were to be
> waited on first with some of everything that was prepared. So

---

52 "Dog Feast" was a simplistic missionary term referring to "pagan" ceremonies at
which dogs were sacrificed and consumed (see, for example, the illustration in Young,
By Canoe and Dog-Train, 213). On the complex roles of dogs in Cree culture and spiritu-
ality, see Robert Brightman, *Grateful Prey: Rock Cree Human-Animal Relationships*
(Berkeley: University of California Press, 1993), 133, 184.

53 Elizabeth added concrete details in "The Bride of 1868": "a large square stove in the
middle of the church was kept hot and the boilers on it for the Tea." Here she also noted
that it was the chief who ordered that food be carried to those who could not attend.

there were several parcels made up & young men were ready to take the parcels. This was a beautiful thought, and it was carried out beautifully.

When this was done, the distribution of the Feast began, and all enjoyed themselves hugely. ["The Blessing asked, all were happy the Fort people, Christian Indians, & Pagan."] When this part was finished, the speeches began. As the time since all this performance occurred my memory cannot possibly retain accurately what was said. One thing I can call to memory [is] Big Chief David Rundel. If he had eaten too much a dose of castor oil would relieve him, and if he told a *lie*, the same or a dose of salts, for the time being would make all right. After the speech making was over, the young men went out & enjoyed a game of football on the Ice. Now the clearing up, & cleaning up.

In "The Bride of 1868," Elizabeth shed further light on the holidays and their aftermath:

There was much 'No-nas-koomoo-win-ah' [*nanâskômowina* 'thankings'] which means 'Thanksgiving,' and there was much Thanksgiving in the missionaries heart for the closing of this most interesting day of the year which is called 'ooch-me-gou-kesigow' [*ocêmikow-kîsikâw*? 'One Is Kissed Day'] which means 'The Kissing day,' as on this day the men claim the right to kiss every woman they meet.[54] The first young man that came to the mission that morning so surprised me by being as I thought rude by imprinting one on my cheek. For peace sake I did not struggle or make a fuss, but that was

54 Kissing the women on New Year's Day was an established fur trade custom, along with other celebrations less decorous than those at Rossville: see Carolyn Podruchny, *Making the Voyageur World: Travelers and Traders in the North American Fur Trade* (Toronto: University of Toronto Press, 2006), 178–80. Henry Ross Helpin, apprentice postmaster at Norway House, 1872–75, wrote a lively account of his first New Year's celebrations at Rossville and Norway House in 1873 and his encounter with the custom of kissing: see David R. Elliott, ed., *Adventures in the West: Henry Halpin, Fur Trader and Indian Agent* (Toronto: Dundurn Press, 2008), 64–65. Jeffrey Muehlbauer notes that the modern Cree term for New Year's Day is still *ocêhtow-kîsikâw*, 'Kissing-Each-Other Day.'

the last, as well as the first. The thought came to me, it will not hurt me. Then I found out the reason. . . .[55]

The holidays are over now, it's hard work keeping the cold out, making ourselves warm and comfortable when the weather is from 30–40 & sometimes 50 below zero. When we have to keep stoking wood in the big box stove at night as well as day, to keep from freezing. The Indians are away hunting trapping they have their wives & families to hunt for rabbits, fish, and find food for themselves, or starve, thus the missionary will help where needed, which is often, more often than not. The days come and go, & at the close of the day the work done seems so little and yet we have been busy. It does seem so unsatisfactory & monotones but every day seems alike. The calls for muskeeke [*maskihkiy*], medicine, food, Tea, sometimes clothing, even clothing for the dead, a Shirt, socks, so day in and day out, the wants are varied and many. To have refused to help would seem cruel, & unchrist-like, so we did our best & in our souls were satisfied that this was our work.

Smallpox and Measles

In another brief reminiscence, Elizabeth remembered the fear that she and Egerton felt "to hear that that terrible disease, the small-pox, had broken out among the Indians on the great plains of the Saskatchewan." In her memoir, she likewise recalled an outbreak of the disease:

> We were terribly frightened at one time, so much so that we immediately procured some lymph from H.B.C. and began vaccinating those of the Indians who had not been vaccinated.[56]

---

55 Young, *By Canoe and Dog-Train*, 66: "It used to amuse me very much to see thirty or forty Indians, dressed up in their finest apparel, come quietly marching into the Mission House, and gravely kiss Mrs. Young on her cheek." She would laugh and retort, "See that crowd of women out there in the yard, expecting you to go out and kiss them!"

56 According to the Norway House post journal (HBCA B.154/a/69, fo. 46), 16 September 1870, a boat arriving from Carlton reported smallpox "all over Saskn and in Peace River. 12 deaths in the Fort at Carlton and Indians dying in every direction on the Plains, no provisions." Lymph here refers to the "middle taken from the cow-pox vesicles, etc., to be used in vaccination" (OED).

We had a busy time & sometimes a very sore time as many were very ill from it. So we had to nurse them & give them medicine. So the mission was more like a *hospital* than a mission home.

["Very soon the Mission was full, some were taken very ill, & others not at all. It was now an anxious and an exciting time for the missionary and people. As there was an urgent call from Winnipeg for the Norway House Christians Indians to take or form a brigade of boats, and take the much needed supplies up the mighty Saskatchewan River where they could be reached by those who needed them so that the boatmen need not be exposed in any way of contagion. This was done, but was extremely hard on the Principal man Samuel Papanakis, a Faithful old General. All came home well but Samuel, he was simply worn out, and to the distress of the Missionary & the Mission he passed away" — leaving his widow, Nancy, destitute and badly in need of aid the next winter."]⁵⁷

At another time somehow the measles found there way into the mission and the beef that Mr Young brought as treat to the mission family was at once put in the pot, and made into broth, & soup for the sick, that was the pleasure of the mission, to see the sick getting better, from the nourishing food.⁵⁸

---

57 The passage in brackets is from a loose page by Elizabeth headed "Memos of my Indian life Sept. 27, [19]28, Small Pox Scare" (JSHB collection), which is also the source of Elizabeth's comment about the "terrible disease." The Norway House post journal (HBCA B.154/a/69), 28 March 1871, recorded "carpenters making a coffin for Samuel Papanakis at the mission who died yesterday." On 22 October 1870, the new lieutenant governor of Manitoba, Adams Archibald, issued an edict forbidding transport of items that could carry infection east of the South Saskatchewan River. Egerton Young recounted how he and Norway House factor Stewart had earlier organized a brigade of twenty York boats to carry much needed supplies to posts on the upper Saskatchewan (*By Canoe and Dog-Train*, chap. 17).

58 In *On the Indian Trail*, 150–57, Young told of bringing by dogsled 150 pounds of meat, rice, butter, canned vegetables, and other supplies to Berens River from Winnipeg; most of the food was soon needed for the sick. The mission Indians recovered, but the disease was deadly among the "pagans" beyond the reach of help.

"At another time" refers to the winter of 1874–75, by which point the Youngs had moved to Berens River. In his 1962 reminiscences, E. Ryerson Young recalled his mother's care of the sick at Berens River:

> When the epidemic started mother took as many as she could into the mission house and then turned the church into a hospital, and when more came, the Indians put up a big buffalo skin-tent for her. All she could do was to go around and keep her patients as clean and warm as she could and feed them twice a day. She kept boilers on the stove in the mission house and also on the big stove in the church in which she boiled whatever food she could get the Indians to bring to her — fish, beaver and deer-meat, etc. Indians in villages all around were suffering and dying, and their friends demanded that mother should come and serve them also, but she could not leave those that were already under her care. If they brought their sick to her she would do what she could for them, but she could not leave all these entrusted to her. And her triumph was, she never lost a patient.

The Arrival of Eddie, June 1869

"A Stranger is expected," Elizabeth recalled in "The Bride of 1868," "and now we must find things to prepare for the reception which will be a very arduous duty, as all absolute necessaries are hundreds of miles distant and communication almost 'Nil,' so we will need much wisdom, patience, perseverence. We send to our English MS [Missonary Society] for our needs. 'But' we know that the requisition will not come for two years." Despite these deprivations, however, the Stranger arrived:

> June '69 our dear little baby Boy was born. That was a very serious time almost a sad time. A kind Providence overruled it, & made us masters of the situation. We thank Him ever & always for His Goodness, Kindness, in helping over & through the difficulty. Unforeseen difficulties occurred over which we had no control, causing the trouble. Our baby Boy was the Idol for the moment.

The Indians rang the bell, & put the Flag up, & came to see the little stranger & white faced boy.[59]

My Indian woman Kitty Doggie who came from the Scotch settlement, the lower Stone Fort, she was a very eccentric and very peculiar old Indian woman, having been more or less in contact with the Scotch & French half-breeds. She became familiar with broken English, & also with their manners. Placed as we were, having no Drs to summon to our aid, we were forced to Dr ourselves & do the best we could. My Dr book was a great help to me, and, at this crisis, it was certainly invaluable, assisting me to prescribe for myself as no Indian woman could do. It was thought at one time both mother & child would pass away; on hearing this, I quickly prescribed for myself, and fortunately in a very short time there was a happy release and new hope, new life, new love, was broadcast, and very soon mother & son were enjoying a new lease of life, and there were many callers, to, see, and welcome, the new comer and an Indian name given to him. Sagastaokemow [Muehlbauer: *sâkâstêw-okimâw*], the sunrise Gentleman.[60]

This was the Indian name for our baby boy, and now without any luxury, or anything but simple fare, yes, very, very plain, fish liquor, rabbit broth. Not being able to nurse him, which I suppose was for want of nourishing food for myself. ["Now increased care,

---

59 Writing of the event in "The Bride of 1868," Elizabeth thanked God "for His love and care over both of us through the past months," adding "and now we are more than happy in each other's embrace & love. The dear little white Face to feast our eyes upon." Young baptized his son Egerton Stewart Ryerson Young in November 1869, no. 1456 in the Norway House baptismal register. The naming recognized the friendship and "great kindness" of Chief Factor James Green Stewart, in charge at Norway House at the time, in sharing the post's "last bag of flour" when the Red River grasshopper plague caused everyone's supplies to run short (see Young's letter of 8 June 1869 in *Wesleyan Missionary Notices*, n.s., no. 4 [August 1869], 60). The name "Stewart" was, however, omitted in later family records.

60 Egerton Young also told of this name, which he spelled "Sagastaookemou" and likewise glossed as "the sunrise gentleman" (*Stories from Indian Wigwams and Northern Camp-fires*, 36). Keith Goulet (e-mail, 12 June 2013) notes that *sagi-* [or *saki-*] is a morpheme meaning "coming out into the open" and *wastew* signifies "to give off light" — in reference to the sun just beginning to appear. For a baby's name, he would expect a diminutive ending, *-masis*: the "little Sunrise Chief"; possibly the name was shortened by English speakers.

now, new thought for food, no cow, no milk, but fish liquor & Rabbit soup. But *soon a cow was found*, and then milk was plentiful.[61]
It was a varied article not only for our little son but for the head of the family. When winter came I used to freeze it in cakes, and when getting Mr Young's food box ready for one of his winter trips I was able to give him an extra luxury for his menu. It seems a small thing to think of, but oh a wonderful luxury added to your food out in the Cold, snow."]

However, he grew, and as it was summer time, we enjoyed the fresh air, dressed accordingly, but as soon as the cold weather and winter came we were forced to remain indoors and made every effort to keep from freezing. . . . Instead of moss I used plenty of flannel, and warm woolens wrapped around and laced up. Thus he was kept warm.[62] This was our first & second winter in that cold climate, and of course [we] had very much to learn in many ways, 1st how to keep ourselves warm in the house as well as outside.
It needed all our injunuity, to clothe and feed ourselves with our scanty fuel, our limited foods, our much less suitable clothing and it being our second winter, and a tender young baby to care for.

61 Egerton, however, in a letter to the *Christian Guardian*, 31 March 1873, recalled the challenge of feeding cow's milk to his infant son in winter: "Liquids, even to coal-oil, still freeze at night as soon as the fires go out. Fancy getting up in the night to give a little babe a drink, and finding the milk frozen solid in the cup, on the table, at the head of your bed."

62 In "The Bride of 1868," Elizabeth wrote: "My bonny Sweet Boy had to be dressed any how, any way, as there were no Stores, or any Conveniences for White Babies. So we must adopt the Indian costume when the weather gets very cold. We must hunt up all the Flannel I can lay my hands on. Cut up my clothes and do some knitting. Fortunately I had some Knitting yarn which I made good use of, Knitting little vests, & adopted the Indian plan of a moss bag without the moss. The bag in the Shape of a Shoe laced up to the chin." Egerton — rebutting John McDougall's criticisms of his comments in *Stories from Indian Wigwams and Northern Camp-fires* about the difficulty of obtaining supplies at HBC posts — recalled "Mrs. Young, at the beginning of a cold winter, asking one of the officials at Norway House if he would be so kind as to sell her six yards of flannel. His answer was, 'Can you not possibly manage to do with four?' and four was all she received." The Company, even if it had items in quantity, would only "sell a little to us *grudgingly*." See Young in John McDougall, *"Indian Wigwams and Northern Camp-fires": A Criticism* (Toronto, 1895), 31.

Little Mary and Eddie

Mary Robinson, known to the family as "Little Mary," was a pivotal figure in the life of young Eddie, as is amply apparent from his own memoir
(Part II). In "The Bride of 1868," Elizabeth recalled:

> My help and nurse for my boy was a poor hunch backed Widow. She
> was a wonderful help, her love & care for the wee one was truely
> marvellous, making his moccasins, sewing for him. She was true and
> faithful, Kind, thoughtful and true; if [he was] out of sorts would
> make her bed beside his bed, and up at the least sound, nothing was
> too much for her to do. This poor woman was cruely treated by her
> Indian husband. One hunting season they picked up their few things
> and went together and when the husband was fortunate in his hunt &
> shot a deer, he left it where it fell, shouldred his gun and stalked into
> camp ordered his squaw to go and bring the deer in, and added —
> Kui-a-peu [Muehlbauer: *kwêyâpêw?*], that is, hurry. And as she was
> leaving he threw his tomahawk after her and it struck her backbone
> lengthwise and the poor woman fell and was injured could not rise.
> When he saw what he had done he picked up his traps and fled and
> never was seen again.[63] She was taken care of by her friends, who
> never thought she would live, poor thing, how she suffered for years
> from the cruel blow, another instance of heathenism & the need of
> the love of Jesus to subdue these haughty men who think the Gospel
> of Jesus Christ is only for the Squaws.
>
> And now Mary is my nurse and a truely devoted one to my
> boy, it is mutual. Now the Indians never correct their children so
> when boy needed correction Mary would be very much put out &
> very much hurt and if only putting him in a corner. She could not

---

63 This story varies from the versions in Egerton R. Young's *Algonquin Indian Tales*
(New York: Fleming H. Revell, 1903), 32–34, and in E. Ryerson Young's "A Missionary
and His Son" (Part II), which are more detailed and cite unscrupulous traders and
alcohol as factors. For Mary's story in broader context, see Jennifer S. H. Brown,
"A Cree Nurse in a Cradle of Methodism: Little Mary and the Egerton R. Young Family
at Norway House and Berens River," in *First Days, Fighting Days: Women in Manitoba
History*, ed. Mary Kinnear (Regina: Canadian Plains Research Centre, University of
Regina, 1987), 19–40.

be found and finally we would find her with arms around the little man cooing some Indian story in his Ear.

Once when so grieved she went away from the house and visited friends until starved and hungry. And Indian-like would come peeking around the dog & cow houses until she saw Eddie, he would go to her, and then come to me pleading for Mary to return. Of course she may come, and Mary would come and begin where she left off. Eddie was the only one who made a fuss, she was glad to come hungry & unkempt.

In her 1927 memoir, Elizabeth continued:

We were so delighted to have little hunch back Mary to help as nurse and care for him. Although she was a poor lame cripple, a more capable person we could not have had. She was so interested in everything that appertained, that belonged to the dear little fellow. She could not do too much for him. If he happened to have a cold or was out of order the least little bit down her bed would be made just beside his. So she could hear and wait on him at once. The dearest little Indian leather moccasins would she made [make] for him, and when needed little leggings, & leather jackets, with Indian silk work [see figs. 2 and 7 for examples of her work]. She was such a good help. We would have brought her to Ontario with us when we came for good, but for fear something might happen to her and we would by her people be blamed and thought careless. We thought it better not to run any risk, & superstition reigned still amongst them. However we kept her long as we remained here, and found her invaluable in many ways, and when the little Boys sister [Lillian] came, while she was fond of her, she did not displace her first love.[64]

64 Egerton Young, in *Hector, My Dog: His Autobiography* (Boston: W. A. Wilde, 1905), 184, cited the Cree word "sakehow" ("beloved") as the term that Eddie used to address Little Mary — one of numerous signs of mutual attachment. Keith Goulet provides the orthography *sagiyaw*, 'one who is loved' (e-mail, 23 March 2013). In his 1962 memoir, "Eddie" wrote that when Lillian was born, "Little Mary felt her carefully all over; then she laid her back in mother's arms saying, 'girl very nice but I like boy better.' Father had some difficulty in making her understand that he could not support a nurse for each child, and if she would take care of the boy she must take care of the little girl too."

Winter Travel and the Home Front

New experiences in every direction, in preparing our food,
preparing clothing, preparing the missionary for his long and cold
journey by making douffle socks, leggings, moccasins, warm under
clothing, and shoe pads for the dogs, snow shoes for themselves, and
as far as we could make biscuits with plenty of fat in them, and as it
was cold weather they would freeze, that is if they could keep them
from the dogs.[65] Now they are nearly ready. Two sleds, well packed
with plenty of bedding, fish for dogs, change of clothing, kettles to
make tea in, tin cups, plates a knife or two, and a few books, and
presents for the Indians.[66] Now the goodbyes, as we will not hear
from them, it may be for two or three weeks, or longer. The cold is
intense, my wonder is how they will really endure it. It was not how
should I get along, the mission to look after, the school, the church,
the sick. The hungry. The home and my baby boy. Every day brought
its work, its care. Its varied duties, & yet out of all the good Lord
brought me safely, and my dear husband home safely.

We were delighted to have a cow, so I not only had the luxury
of having milk for my baby, but was able also to have milk and if in
cold weather could freeze it in cakes so as to add a little comfort for
my husbands menu, when on his long cold journeys to the distant
Indians. Time went on as usual day in & day out. Sickness, hunger,
poverty and want, but somehow you get used to it, going & coming,
with the Hymn ["Abide with Me"], "Change & decay in all around
I see." Perhaps, once or twice a year we hear from our loved ones.
Then there is great excitement when the mail comes. All work is
stopped and everything else for the time being.

65 "Shoe pads for the dogs," also called "duffle dog shoes," were dog shoes "of a firmly
woven warm woolen cloth called duffle," of which Young carried "a large stock" on every
trip to protect against sharp ice and freezing (Young, *My Dogs in the Northland*, 191).
Young, in *Hector, My Dog*, 184–85, described Mary's organizing of women to make a
supply of shoes before winter trips.

66 The books were mainly Cree translations, in syllabics, of one of the Gospels and four
Epistles. The Reverend Thomas Hurlburt, in his 1857 report from Rossville, stated that
three thousand copies of these texts had been printed on the mission's small printing
press, and stitched and bound "by Miss [Charlotte] Adams, the devoted School Teacher"
("Stations and Missionaries, 1857–58," in *32nd Annual Report, Canada Conference*
[Methodist], Toronto, 1857, xxix).

Prayer Meetings and Parcels

It was a pleasure to have every Tuesday afternoon a female prayer meeting. It was well attended ["& the Indian women were very pleased. They have nice sweet voices, & prayed faithfully & very much in earnest"]. It would shame some White friends could they hear their Indian friends pray to the No-Tow-we, our Father [Muehlbauer: *nohtâwiy*, actually, 'My father'].[67] If any bundles or parcels came I would immediately sort them out & arrange something for each one, make a cup of tea, and have a social afternoon much, very much to their delight and happiness, their *Ho, Hos & Ha, Ha's.*

Not only the cup of tea and perhaps a piece of bread, but the garment of whatever size or shape. The mission packages from the English auxiliary in London [and, later, Ontario] were very useful, as for years they had been sending their parcels to Rossville mission.[68] At this particular time I was fortunate to receive a very useful bundle, so that it was a great pleasure to distribute the articles amongst the poor people, and to make them happy. Jackets, big aprons, under garments, small shawls. ["On these special afternoons I made parcels for each woman."] If I had not enough to go around, I would have to resort to my own wardrobe, to make sure that none would be disappointed & made unhappy. But at the close of the meeting felt that all were satisfied having had an enjoyable & profitable afternoon.

["When you see how they live, in tents made of Birch bark, & only large enough to have the very centre of the tent for the fire to keep them warm, to cook their scanty food, & at night to gather around & in their day clothes & a blanket sleep, they have so little, so to teach them cleanliness & thrift is almost impossible. When their husbands kill a deer the women drew the skins, make moccasins & leggings for the men & often when a moose is killed they dress & make the men shirts which are very warm, & most useful."][69]

67 As noted in the introduction, the subtleties of Cree challenged the Youngs; the intended inclusive term, 'our Father,' would properly be *kohtâwînaw* (Muehlbauer).

68 See Part III, sec. 10, Young's letter of October 1873 to the *Christian Guardian,* expressing his and Elizabeth's thanks for items sent, and for their warm reception.

69 For more about tanning and sewing, see Part III, sec. 6.

The Arrival of Lillian

In March 1871, during a bitterly cold winter, the Youngs' second child, Lillian, arrived. Elizabeth made no explicit mention of the event in her 1927 memoir but wrote of it in some detail in "The Bride of 1868":

> March 10, '71. A Sweet little Girl was given to us. The weather was fiercely cold so cold that we had to put blankets up to the windows to keep mother and child from catching cold. The Chief Factor's wife [Annie (Mrs. Robert) Hamilton] and Kitty Doggie were with me, and to our surprise the Indian woman announced that the baby's hip was out of joint. At once she straitened it and bound it up. Of course we were anxious about it, and to know the cause, then I remembered having been standing on a chair that had some nails oozing up and they caught the soul of my shoe and threw me, and I fell and had to crawl to the lounge and lie down and keep quiet as I was all alone in the house. Hence this trouble, but the Indian nurse was equal to the trouble and she pulled the little leg and thigh, and bound them firmly for a little while, so it became firm, but at times weak.[70]
>
> And now we have a pigeon pair, love. A precious boon, what love, what joy, what care, but joy and love covers a multitude of hardships. The day came for Christening came, and as an Anglican minister was passing through Norway House & Rossville Mission and Chief Factor Hamilton and Mrs Hamilton honored us with their presence we had our darling christened with Mrs Hamilton as Lillians God Mother.[71] Egerton Jr & Lillian were great pals, and as Lillian was the Chatter box, they soon made the mission resound

70 Dr. C. Stuart Houston, an expert on developmental dysplasia of the hip, advises that Elizabeth's fall would not have caused the dislocation of Lillian's hip nor would a single such treatment have sufficed to correct it (e-mails, January 2013). A study of Caucasian infants with hip instability found that, in fact, "over 88 per cent recover spontaneously in the first two months of life." C. Stuart Houston and Robert H. Buhr, "Swaddling of Infants in Northern Saskatchewan," *Musk-Ox* 36 (1988): 13.

71 The Norway House baptismal register, no. 1480, no precise date, gives her full name as Clarissa Maria Lillian, E. R. Young officiating. On the Anglican baptism, a typed note in the Young family files states that "Clara Maria Lillian Young" was baptized on 10 August 1871 by the Reverend Mr. [Robert] Phair, "English Missionary" (JSHB collection). Mrs. Hamilton was a daughter of HBC factor Robert S. Miles and Betsey, daughter of Chief Factor William Sinclair and his Cree wife, Nahoway.

with their melodious Voices. And to[o] they were never timid or fearful of the Indians and would sit down and play with them or eat with them and talk with them, the Indian Language came first and was no trouble [for them] to interpret for us.[72]

The garments that should have come for her brother, came in time for the dear little Sister, for which we were so thankful, as the cold weather still reigned in climate. The Indians were not as fond of the dear little pinky faced girlie as they were of her brother, but she was the life & fun of all squaws & papooses. She would sit down eat, play, & amuse all with her quaint sayings, talk Indian to the amusement of all everybody, our good old Mary is busy taking care of two busy bees of two lively children. We had a dolls Indian cradle made for her, & an Indian doll put in it to her delight. The doll was put in laced up and carried around, what a happy time dressing & undressing Lily & Eddie were happy playing Indian, talking Indian, taking dollie out for a paddle in the canoe.[73]

Elizabeth's 1927 memoir continues with recollections of her young children:

The Indians called the little Girls White fish. There was not much respect shown for little girls as for the boys.[74] Yet callers came to see the little pale face girl, & give her a name & this is her Indian name — Minnie-Ha-Ha (Laughing Water).[75] The weather was

72 As Elizabeth noted elsewhere in "The Bride of 1868," the Youngs took pleasure in the children's learning Cree, and Eddie's language skills were useful and esteemed. In contrast, Jan Hare and Jean Barman note that mission wife Emma Crosby, in British Columbia, was unhappy that her daughters, influenced by the Tsimshian girls under the mission's care, "took on similar dress, and even spoke their language. . . . Uneasy with the girls' increasing influence on her young children, Emma's religiosity reached its limits." On 10 March 1880, Emma wrote to her mother, "The want of associates for the children we begin to feel some, for we cannot allow them to associate with the children of the village." Hare and Barman, *Good Intentions Gone Awry*, 160.

73 This vignette pertains to the Berens River years, given that Lillian was less than two and a half on leaving Norway House — although Little Mary probably made the cradle board there.

74 Keith Goulet notes that both boys and girls could be named after fish or other animals (e-mail, 23 March 2013), so "whitefish" would not in itself be derogatory.

75 See Young, *Stories from Indian Wigwams and Northern Camp-fires*, 36, on the children's names. In 1895, the Reverend John McDougall (son of George), in his *"Indian*

cold outside, but with much care, & much making fire, we kept comfortably warm, and with God's blessing we were happy with our dear little baby girl.

While lonely & at times longing for dear ones, to come and relieve the monotony yet we never gave way to disponding. Now time passed away. Our two darlings grew & waxed strong, making the mission ring with their melody. We were thankful for these dear little white-faced cherubs. They were brightness and the joy of loving hearts.

Special Potatoes

In the brief set of recollections titled "In the Land of Fur and Frost," E. Ryerson Young quoted his mother as saying of Norway House, "The potatoes we found there were watery and all but useless. Mr Young had a few potatoes with him, which he planted and after some careful work and protecting the seed, finally gave the Indians a new and valuable supply of food."[76] Her memoir and other writings expand on this comment:

In our unpacking [in August 1868] we found a few special potatoes that Grandpa Young dropped into one of our boxes, and now though late for planting they must be planted. We put them in the last of July, hoping, trusting that they would preserve the seed, as they will have only August, September. Winter in these cold regions comes in early. So they may only have two months.

Wigwams and Northern Camp-fires": A Criticism, lambasted Young for presenting "the Sioux name of 'Menehaha'" as a name given by the Crees when it is in fact a poetical name from Longfellow's "Hiawatha" (7). Young, in rebuttal, noted that he did not claim that the name was Cree and detailed how Lillian received it. When the HBC held its annual council at Norway House, those who attended knew "many Indian languages" (and some had read "Hiawatha," even if the Youngs had not): "They gave the lovely child the beautiful name" (17).

76 To this comment in the typescript, E. Ryerson Young added a note in ink: "The 'Gooderich' [Goodrich] potato — from Rochester, N.Y. Famous in its day." On the origin and advantages of the Goodrich potato, developed around 1850, see Craig Allen Lindquist, "Garnet Chili Potatoes," 25 August 2007, www.vegetablesofinterest. typepad.com/vegetablesofinterest/2007/08/garnet-chili-po.html. Potatoes were grown in quantity at the northern posts and missions, but their quality was poor. On 26 September 1856, for example, the Reverend Robert Brooking wrote from Oxford House, "Good potatoes, here, is merely a relative term. What we call good, here, would only be considered fit for the pigs in Canada" (*Wesleyan Missionary Notices*, no. 12 [15 May 1857], 188). William Young's gift to his son, husbanded through Rossville winters, appeared wonderfully successful.

"Yet they had to go in," Elizabeth wrote in "The Bride of 1868,"

> and as the frost comes fast and hard in this north land, they really
> only had six weeks when we had to take them up, and they were only
> like marrow fat peas, but we put them away wrapt up carefully in
> Cotton wool, and put out of the reach of the frost, as we had to keep
> a fire in a big box stove overnight, fancy no hard wood, no coal,
> *but* with constant refilling we managed to keep warm even if it was
> soft Poplar.
>
> Yet when spring came and we went to look for our seed potatoes
> we found them, but shrunk up to very small potatoes, yet not
> dismayed or discouraged we put them in the Ground, And now they
> had the whole summer to grow and fill up, and to our astonishment
> & surprise, when time to take them up, we had quite a big pailful
> of beautiful potatoes, but alas the verdict, not one could be used,
> all must be kept for seed. As a Birmingham mayor said, Cruel man
> not to let you have one, but I did not think so, when we think of the
> yield and what it did for us in a few years when we were allowed to
> cut off the seed ends, and use the rest, and oh what a luxury, we did
> enjoy them. We did not need to mash and peel, but first cook them
> with their jackets on & what a luxury. Soon we were able to supply
> the H.B.C. and Indians with our seed potatoes.

Elsewhere in "The Bride of 1868," Elizabeth wrote, "The Winters were
eight months long, so cold that our [first] potatoes were only marbles in size
when they were planted, but now to our glad surprise we found several pecks
of marvellous potatoes. Of course they were put away, and were planted summer after summer until we could afford to cut off the seed ends and use the
rest." A story told a few pages later recounted how Elizabeth, at one time,
saved the seed potatoes from being eaten:

> Once in early spring as soon as early frost had gone and the ground
> was thawed out, my beloved got the Ground ready for potatoe
> planting & gave the school boys a holiday to come and help plant
> seed potatoes; now there was great glee & fun. But alas it suddenly
> came to an end, as they were found eating the inside of the seed

potatoes. My beloved came in his distress; "what shall I do, they
are eating the inside of the potatoe and planting the skin." I at once
said, "we will put on some to boil and cook some fish and make
them a good meal." "But where will we seat them?" We put up a
board table out of doors. I never can forget how much they enjoyed
their meal, and when they wanted to drink up the fish soup they
scouped out a potatoe & made a spoon of it; there was no crying for
a spoon. "Necessity is the Mother of invention." So now they went
off to their work happy and no more cheating the potatoe crop.[77]

"Still at Norway House"

In autumn of seventy-one [1872], my blessed husband came home
to me from District Meeting, at Winnipeg, — prostrated with
Typhoid Fever.[78] This was no small trouble. No Dr, no nurse. To our
joy if we could have any just then, Wm Memotas, our local Indian
Preacher, at one time was an Indian Dr., he offered his services as
Dr and nurse.[79] They were speedily accepted, our joy, & sole anxiety
now was to do our utmost for the patient, who was a most willing,
obedient patient, and the nurse too was all that could be desired,
quiet, attentive, day and night, nothing was too much for him to do
for his Aumeookemow [Muehlbauer: *ayamihêw-okimâw*, praying
master]. Fortunately the patient responded readily, and to our *joy*
& *happiness*, was soon on the road to recovery. We had much to be

77 See Egerton R. Young's *The Battle of the Bears*, chap. 11, for his preserving of special
seed potatoes for the Rossville growers.

78 The meeting, which began on 26 July 1872 in Winnipeg, was the first Methodist
church conference held in Manitoba. W. Morley Punshon, conference president, and
Enoch Wood, then superintendent of missions for the Wesleyan Methodist Church,
both attended to meet with and receive reports from all the Wesleyan missionaries in
the region (Young, "First Conference in Manitoba," ucca, Young fonds, box 2, file 3,
Notebook, Berens River [187?], 168–75). For Young's account of his illness and recovery,
see Part iii, sec. 8. The deaths of Elizabeth's father and brother from typhoid five years
earlier meant that she recognized the disease and knew its deadliness.

79 Young, in *By Canoe and Dog-Train*, wrote of Memotas's "knowledge of the roots and
herbs of his native forests." Familiar with "some of the simpler medicines of the whites,
he was often styled our 'village doctor'" (180–81).

thankful for. Wm Memotas was one of our most trusted Christian Indians, living what he professed & professed what he lived.[80]

The Birth of Nellie and the Pitfalls of Hospitality

In 1873 [September 1872], our dear little Nellie was born. Another dear little Girl, bright, healthy, and beautiful.[81]

While we were at Norway House Dr George Young visited us; also Dr Lachlan Taylor, [and] a Rev Mr Armstrong visited the mission.[82] And as Egerton was invited by the Church to visit Ontario and with Mr Crosby give the missionary meeting a helping hand by increasing their funds,[83] & as his Brother was on his way to Ontario, we talked it over about my coming with him, when, if I waited to come with Egerton it would be very cold for the children. So we thought it best to get ready & come with Mr Armstrong.

---

80 To this, Elizabeth added, in a note at top of the page: "The conference sent Rev Mr Semmens out to relieve Egerton." Indeed, in September 1872, hearing of Young's illness, the Reverend Morley Punshon arranged for John Semmens to go to Rossville to assist him. Semmens was specially ordained in October and reached Rossville on New Year's Day 1873 to find Young "in the best of health and spirits." Young left on his winter travels later that month, leaving the mission in Semmens's care. Semmens, "Notes on Personal History," typescript, 12–16, UCA, Conference of Manitoba and Northwestern Ontario, Winnipeg.

81 Norway House baptismal register, no. 1494, Eleanor Elizabeth, baptized November 1872, aged two months. In *Stories from Indian Wigwams and Northern Camp-fires,* Young wrote that because she was born in the fall, she received a Cree name meaning "the rustling of the falling leaf" (36), but he did not record the Cree. Keith Goulet suggests it might have been *kitoweyastun neepee,* 'the leaf makes a sound as it flies or floats in the air' (e-mail, 11 March 2013).

82 Elizabeth misremembered here: George Young did not visit the Youngs at Rossville, but rather at Berens River, in December 1874. In June 1873, however, Lachlan Taylor, the general secretary of the Methodist Missionary Society, and Armstrong came from Toronto to Norway House on a tour of the missions in the region, and Egerton escorted them from Rossville to Oxford House and back (George Young, *Manitoba Memories,* 253–59).

83 The Reverend Thomas Crosby became a mission school teacher and then an itinerant preacher in British Columbia in the 1860s; he was ordained in 1871. His enthusiasm and success brought him to the attention of church leaders, and he was sent on furlough to Ontario to travel with Egerton R. Young raising support for missions. Clarence Bolt, *Thomas Crosby and the Tsimshian: Small Shoes for Feet Too Large* (Vancouver: University of British Columbia Press, 1992), 36. According to Young, together they spoke at eighty-nine missionary meetings from Sarnia to Québec (*By Canoe and Dog-Train,* 256).

On 2 January 1873, George Young had written privately to Egerton Young: "In regard to Dr. Taylor's contemplated visit. . . . *Confidentially* — do not fail to let him see some of the "*Shades*" of a missionaries life — let him *rough* it. Do not buy and bring out delicacies — if you do he will think it is a specimen of your living & go back & say "the Bro[ther] lives *like a Prince*" — I want him to see & *feel* things as you have to see & feel them. I fear you will be *generous to a fault* in his case. Be wise *O Egerton*." Elizabeth's wish to be generous prevailed, however, as her son recalled in his 1962 memoir:

> There came to the Mission field a distinguished minister and lecturer who visited the mission stations at the request of the mission secretary. When mother heard of the coming of such a distinguished man she thought they ought to have something special to give him to eat. So when father was in Winnipeg he bought a few tins of canned peaches. The Rev. Dr. Lachlan Taylor came to Norway House; he not only visited at the mission house but was entertained at the Trading Post by the officers of the H.B.C. They spread before him as a Scotchman, glasses and liquor; he drank all that was set before him. When he came to our house he seemed to enjoy the entertainment that mother had provided, especially the peaches, for he said, "Mrs Young, may I have a second helping of peaches," and she obliged him. But when he returned to Ontario, he told all and sundry that the Missionaries were living in luxury, that he was served canned peaches.

Taylor's acceptance of HBC hospitality also drew a reaction from the Rossville people: "After that visit the Indians told father, 'Your boss can go to the Trading Post and drink liquor with the officers of the company out of glasses, and you won't let them serve us liquor in tin cups.'"[84]

---

84 Traveller and HBC man Henry Halpin noted that Taylor also partook of rum found in an old unopened keg at Oxford House "and pronounced it 'good' on several occasions" (Elliott, ed., *Adventures in the West*, 88).

Two Farewells

There was much to be done to get ready, & leave everything in good condition as we were not coming to Norway House again. House to clean, our clothing to pack & leave ready to move to Berens River. We are to leave dear Egerton with Sandy boy [Sandy Harte] to look after things, ere Egerton leaves for good. There is very much to be done. The house to be cleaned, our things for Berens River to be cleaned and packed ready to be moved, Egerton's things to be left ready for his leaving. We must not forget Sandy boy, for we may never see him again. He will go back to Nelson River to his own people, so he will have much to fix and make ready.[85] Then the children's things, for a long journey. Three, Egerton, Lillian, & Nellie, not saying anything about myself. Clothing ready & packed, food to be prepared and the last thing to be done was to scald milk & put into jars & bottles seald tight and placed in a cool place, and that is under the stern sheets of the boat. Now [end of July 1873] we are ready & long to be away. Father & Sandy come with us for the first night, and then we say goodbye. Father saying to Nellie, "It will be a long time ere I see you again." He did not think then that he would never see his darling again.

We were terribly delayed on our journey, head winds and storms, food diminishing, Nellie's milk getting less and less, each day. The sun pouring down on us, as we had no canopy, or shelter of any kind, from the weather. Nellie began to be poorly & now we were nearing the first part of our journey. Egerton & Lilly were breaking out in spots, from the strong pemmican they were eating. You may imagine my anxiety when this occurred.

Now that we were landed at the Old Fort [Lower Fort Garry], baby Nellie sick. We at once called a Dr, he had to [come] ten

85 This is Elizabeth's only reference in these memoirs to Sandy Harte, the Nelson River Cree boy whom the Youngs virtually adopted in 1870 and to whom they and Eddie were strongly attached. See Part III, sec. 7, for detailed accounts of him from her other writings and other sources. See also Part II, esp. chap. 2, and Egerton R. Young, *Indian Life in the Great North-West*, 9–50.

miles with the mudd up to the hub of the wheels so he could not come in a hurry and this was imperative as the darling was very ill, and when he did arrive nothing could possibly be done. This did not add to our happiness. So the dear passed away from us leaving us depressed, unhappy.[86] All alone amongst strangers, much kindness was shown us by strangers. The Indian men that brought us this far, made the dear loved one's coffin, & here we left our precious darling's body to be buried in the great North West, here we said goodbye to all that was left of our darling. At the same time thankful that the other two were spared, although they too were quite poorly. We left the Lower Fort sad & sorrowful, but thankful for friends although strangers, who were kind helpful & sympathetic. Arch Deacon *Cowley,* who was sincerely sympathetic and called in a most Brotherly way to help & comfort & give assistance, in any way possible.[87]

Now we got on our way as quickly as we possibly could, as my darling children Eddie & Lillian needed immediate attention as they were poorly. Now we had left poor food, poor attention, poor traveling, for all that was good & helpful which was a happy & welcome change, for we were all tired and exhausted from our long open boat journey, & poor accommodation & poor food, and the loss of our eleven month old little *Nellie.* A kind overruling Providence raised up kind friends all the way along.

86 Egerton Young used the empty pages of an 1867 diary to make later notes about the family, and there, under April 7, he wrote, "Nellie Elizabeth at Stone Fort died of spinal meningitis" (UCCA, Young fonds, series 2, box 1, file 13). The Red River doctor must have made the diagnosis when he came.

87 Archdeacon Abraham Cowley of the Church Missionary Society (Anglican), who served at St. Peter's Church and mission on the lower Red River, quickly wrote to Egerton, assuring him that Nellie could be buried in the graveyard there. Cowley to Young, 15 September 1873, letter preserved in Young's scrapbook in the UCCA, Toronto. When Young came to Red River in late September, Cowley conducted a burial service for Nellie in the St. Peter's graveyard (*By Canoe and Dog-Train,* 255).

Back in Ontario, 1873–74

The children were very different to the civilized children, for many questions were asked about them as their English was very limited. Even when we reached our own dear ones, how they amazed & surprised them in so many very strange ways, in their speaking, in their expressions, especially Eddie. When eating an apple, he said, "I do not like this apple, it has too many fish scales in it."[88] However, they were very quickly learnt to like many civilized things, fruits, of all kinds and also vegetables, were all strange to them.

We were not in the civilized land [long] ere our little ones had some of the ills of the young children. And as we were home amongst our own people, and knew that it was only for a short time, so we had to make the most of it. Our loved ones were scattered, we had to be busy & make the most of the time allotted to us. Dear Egerton had to leave us and with Mr Crosby visit the different Towns & cities giving missionary lectures, rousing up the churches to greater zeal for the missionary work. So we were left to visit and see our dear ones as best we could *alone.*[89]

We left Eddie with his grandma Bingham in Bradford, but we had not gone very far, while at an Aunt Laura Bowels [Bowles] (Brighton, Ont.),[90] Lillian had contracted measles, where & how, was utterly impossible for us to conceive, but the fact was there before us, & there we had to stay. We were most kindly cared for. As they had pigeons, I remember Uncle Bowles very sweetly & kindly killing one for Auntie B. to make some dainty broth for the sick girl. This was at Brighton not far from Trenton where Grandfather Wm Young lived, Egerton's Father. Our visit home thus was [a] series of enjoyment mingled with all sorts of variations

---

88 Eddie described this incident in chapter 7 of his memoir (Part II). His version was, "I do not like this potato"; he had no experience with apples.

89 See Part III, sec. 12, for Elizabeth's second account of her sojourn in Ontario, with some further details.

90 Laura Waldron Bowles (1811–83) was a sister of Egerton's mother, Amanda Waldron Young (d. 1842) and married to William C. Bowles (Waldron-Young genealogical records, in Wilson Brown, family history files). "Grandma Bingham" was, of course, Elizabeth's mother, Clarissa.

sometimes glad, sometimes pleasant & agreeable. Whatever
happened we tried to feel it was amongst all things make the best
of everything, as it had begun so sadly. We tried to make the best
of everything as we went along. Our friends were not of the wealthy
kind that could give us much luxury, or even attention, so our visit
was indeed a work of labour, and a good deal of endurance. At that
time there were no homes for returned missionaries on furlow, so
we were forced to trott around and visit our loved ones here and
there, Trenton, Brighton, Bradford, Bond head.

Mother dear lived in Bradford, sister Lottie, & Brother Joseph,
with her. This I made my home, going out from there & coming as
the case might be. While there Eddie had the measles. So it was
nursing & caring, anxious and trying to recuperate. As for myself,
I had had quite a strain traveling alone all the way from the mission,
Norway House.

As Egerton went up & down ocean to ocean [actually, not west
of Ontario] with Mr Crosby, sometimes they would be on some of
our old circuits & then the friends would invite me to join them.
This would mean leaving the children or taking them with me. Of
course it would be joy to meet Daddy & have a visit with him as well
as with the friends. I remember one visit at Mrs W. E. Sandford's
[Sanford's] in Hamilton. While there the Church presented us with
a silver tea & coffee set, it was beautiful. Mr & Mrs Sandford were
very kind & helpful to us in many ways, and we fully appreciated
all their attention for Mr Sandford [had] sent to Norway House
mission our Jack & Cuffy, of which the address on Jack's collar was
inscribed, "A *Poor Missionaries Dog. Don't steal him.*"[91]

This was certainly a splendid, thoughtful, and most useful
present to the missionary, who fully appreciated the grand pair
of dogs, for the mission work, as the journeys were long, cold, &
dreary, but were absolutely necessary to be taken to cope with the
work. The winters were long, & these two dogs were strong, and

91 Senator William E. Sanford was a leading Methodist businessman in Hamilton.
He had given Jack, a St. Bernard, and Cuffy, a Newfoundland, to Egerton, arranging
for them to be sent to Norway House. See Young, *My Dogs in the Northland*, 66, 125.

with other native dogs, were just what was needed to accomplish the many miles of travel over Lakes of Ice & snow, to reach many of the outposts of Indians who were keeping up the Macitonian [Macedonian] cry for a missionary of their own.

From Ontario to Berens River

The time has now arrived for our dear one to return to his mission work as the winter is closing in, and the last boats are soon leaving for Berens River & Norway House means haste as there is much to be attended to, supplies for building the mission House & church at Berens River.[92] That means my being left alone to travel again later on. If ever a woman needed wisdom and a guiding hand, I was that woman while it was joy to see loved ones. It was also sorrow to leave them but duty before pleasure so with a dear boy & girl I started on my way back to work.

I had company: two dogs, two missionarys one old & one young, & a young lady going out as a Teacher, Miss Batty.[93] Sometimes I thought she was Batty, often on leaving the boat for [railway] cars, I was left alone with children, luggage, dogs, and my lady would take pencil & notebook, march and take

92 Elizabeth misremembered the season: Egerton left Hamilton, Ontario, on 4 March 1874 (see Part III, sec. 13) "and reached Beren's River after twenty-three days of continuous travelling" (*By Canoe and Dog-Train*, 257). He had with him two St. Bernard dogs given to him by a Mrs. Andrew Allan of Montréal; she also gave him two other dogs, which Elizabeth brought with her that summer (*My Dogs in the Northland*, 195).

93 The ministers were Lewis Warner and a man whose surname was Morrison; Warner was bound for Edmonton to chair the missions in that district. See John Maclean, *McDougall of Alberta* (Toronto: Ryerson Press, 1927), 85. George McDougall reported that by October 1875 Warner was "infirm and desiring to return to Ontario," although he stayed for that winter (quoted in J. E. Sanderson, *The First Century of Methodism in Canada*, vol. 2 (Toronto: William Briggs, 1910), 321). According to Sanderson (301–2), the party went by rail and ship, sailing from Sarnia on 11 July 1874. Two Miss Battys came west to teach at Methodist mission schools. The one travelling with Elizabeth was Elisabeth Sarah Batty. Clementina Batty arrived in Winnipeg in June 1875; Egerton Young met her there, and she visited Berens River on her way to teach at Rossville (Sanderson, *First Century of Methodism in Canada*, vol. 2, 319–20). She married the Reverend Orrin German, missionary at Oxford House, in 1877 (Paul Gibson, descendant, letter to Harcourt Brown, 24 August 1975). On her Rossville teaching, see Part III, sec. 9.

notes by the way. Of course who needed someone to look after her. However as long as strength & health was given, all went well. How we longed for the end of the journey.

At last we reached Mr Young & Winnipeg, & glad we were to meet and greet our loved one, and proceed on our journey. As the weather was getting very uncomfortably cold, as our mission house & church had to be made liveable for the winter, as also our church to worship in. So haste was the order. And while this was going on, our home was a log and mud hut, when it rained the mud ossed [oozed] through between the logs. One night it rained so hard and so long that a great lump of mud dropped down on our little girl, if it had fallen on her head it would have killed her, fortunately we were spared that dreadful catastrophe.

Our Carpenter pushed on quickly as he had to leave us by the last boats of the season. Although the mission was not be any means finished yet — we worked hard & made it very comfortable, did some painting, did some unpacking and gradually made our Berens mission quite homelike & habitable. The mission school was passable. The bell tower in good order, so that the Service could be announced on Sunday morning, & our friends Mr & Mrs Ferrier of Montreal were our very kind friends, making the bell, carpenters tools, & many other things a donation to Berens River mission.[94] Many came to church, & S[unday] School, and also day school. Some of [the] Indians from Norway House were with us, but not as many as expected. Our mission house was one storey and a half high. Three rooms downstairs, the minister's study, the living room, the kitchen & pantry & cupboard, the bedrooms upstairs, quite a palace to the mud hut.

94 Senator James Ferrier, a prominent Montréal businessman, was active in the Methodist Church. Gerald J. J. Tulchinsky, "Ferrier, James," *Dictionary of Canadian Biography* online. Figure 14 illustrates another Ferrier gift — to Elizabeth.

"Where Are My Quilts?"

Elizabeth and Egerton Young appeared to agree on almost everything, but E. Ryerson Young, in his 1962 memoir, recalled a poignant scene that left his mother feeling hurt and sad. It probably took place after she joined Egerton at Berens River in the summer of 1874 and unpacked the belongings that she had left at Norway House for transport to their new station:

> When mother opened her goods that were brought down from the mission home at Norway House, her heart began to tremble, and she turned to her husband and said, "Where are my quilts?" Father said, "What do you mean, those white blankets?[95] I gave them to the Indians with all the others. We can get a new outfit when we get to Toronto." Mother's dismay was almost heart breaking. "You can't get quilts like that again. Think of my mother trying to take care of her children and keeping boarders so as to have something with which to feed them, and then when all were in bed and still to have her get out her quilting frames and spread out her sheets and sew away with those skilled fingers of hers, and her eyes filled with tears and her heart praying alone for Libby up in the mission field. Those quilts were saturated with her prayers and tears and now you have given them away, those sacred quilts as though they were a bundle of rags."
>
> It is hard to picture either mother or my father, for he had not the slightest idea of the delicacy and love that women have for the nice things they have made. He never knew in his boyhood what nice bed clothes were, and in his long journey to the mission field he knew nothing of the clothes that love and skill had made. Around the campfire in zero weather all he saw was clothes that kept him warm. It would take a loving and tender heart to try to sympathize with my mother to come through that terrible journey down Lake Winnipeg, the loss and burial of her babe and now to lose the things that she considered almost holy, to be thrust aside by an unthinking and un-understanding heart.

95 Egerton's term, "white blankets," indicates that these were "whole cloth quilts," as opposed to quilts made of different-coloured pieces of fabric pieced together. Their decorative patterns were executed as the maker sewed the two sides of the quilt together — more subtle than crazy-quilt designs — and the "whole cloth" chosen had to be of high quality. Thanks to Anne Lindsay (e-mail, 28 March 2013) for interpreting this description and providing insight.

A Mother's Crisis
In the early winter of 1874, not long after Elizabeth's arrival at Berens River, a local Ojibwe mother came to her, desperate for help. Elizabeth vividly recalled the incident in an article she wrote two decades later for *The Indian's Friend:*

> One day there came to me at our little poplar-log hut, our first home among the Saulteaux, a poor Indian mother. Her tale was most pitiable. Although she had a babe only a few months old, her pagan, tyrannical husband had come into the wigwam with the word that he had shot a deer, and at once ordered her to leave her child and take a couple of carrying straps and go for it. There was nothing for her to do but obey, and so away she hurried, following the back trail of his snowshoes until she found the deer, lying just where he had shot it. It proved to be a very large one, and so she had not only to put one of the straps across her forehead but the other one across her breast in order to be able to carry the heavy animal. After a great effort, she managed to carry the deer home, a distance of two or three miles. When she reached her wigwam her baby was crying bitterly for attention, but her tyrant husband would not allow her to nurse her child until she had skinned the deer and cooked him some of the meat. When she went to nurse her babe, she found that the heavy pressure of the straps had so bruised and injured her breast as to make this impossible.
>
> Terrified, she came to me, the missionary's wife, for help and sympathy. Fortunately Mr. Young had brought out with a great deal of trouble, the previous summer, a good cow from the Red River settlement and so I had quite a number of large cakes of frozen milk. I dressed her wounded breast and then gave her a tin cup that had a spout at one side over which I drew a soft cloth, telling her how to break off some of the frozen milk with her hatchet and melt and heat it in the cup. I sent her home with this to feed her crying child. Strange as it may appear, she succeeded in raising the child, but she made large demands upon our pile of frozen milk; and happy were we that we had it to give her.[96]

96 This story appeared in Elizabeth's "The Transformed Indian Woman," published in *The Indian's Friend*, vol. 10, no. 6 (February 1898), 9–10, and no. 7 (March 1898), 9–10.

Christmas Anxiety, 1875

Christmas & New years as usual with the Indians. It was up to us with the help of the H.B.C. to make it as pleasant as possible for the natives. But an unexpected thing happened to us. Mr Young had to leave on business accompanied by an H.B. official, and fully expected to return before Christmas.[97] Unfortunately the man went mad with drink & Mr Young hoping against hope he would become sober that they might hasten on their journey, but alas the journey could not be undertaken alone so the good had to wait for the bad, and the poor lone ones had to *look*, to *long, to despair*, to *wonder* what was the trouble. No word, no Telegraphing, day after day, and no word, no sound of the Sleigh bells. Of course the holidays had no merriment for us. It was all too, too, utterly sad, discomforting, and disconcerting. So this was the way we spent our first [actually, second] Christmas at Berens River. We were an unhappy household, the missionarys wife sad not knowing whether Mr Young was alive, or if on the way something had happened. Yet hope predominated & kept us from being too utterly prostrated under such severe circumstances. At last Captain McDonald came to himself and became normal, so that after the holidays were all over they made their appearance. We were glad to know that our loved one was quite all right, at good temperance, talk, in favour for prohibition. We were too much agitated to make any comments. Thankfulness was written all over us and everything, and we soon got into the swim of our regular work again, building up the mission & visiting.

97 The man was in fact a free trader, according to HBCA B.16/a/8, Berens River post journal, 16 December 1875: "Mr Young started for White Mudd River and the free-trader McDonald went along with him he goes to Red River." Young described the trip to Sandy Bar and back in chapter 14 of *By Canoe and Dog-Train*, though misdating it to 1877.

The Birth of Florence and Other Memories

May came & with it a wee Babie girlie to cheer us, by the name of Florence.[98] Harriet Papanakis was my nurse, Martin her husband was our Interpreter & man of all work.[99] The Ice was so strong that it was quite safe to travel on it, so you can see that in May how cold the weather is, & how careful you have to be in dressing for such severe weather. How we long for food for the inner man, and clothing for the outer man, but the all-Wise and all good God provided for us, in many ways we never dreamt of. My little girlie was now my anxious care to see her properly fed. Fish liquor, Rabbit soup, milk, much of her food without very much sweetening, however the little dear got on beautifully.

In late July 1875, Clementina Batty, a new teacher bound for Norway House, visited the Youngs at Berens River. Having met Egerton in Winnipeg, she travelled north with him in a fleet of five HBC sailboats. At the Youngs' "neat and comfortable parsonage," "two dear little children were wild with excitement, 'cause Papa's come home." But their mother was not having an easy time: "We found her and her sweet babes subsisting chiefly on sturgeon, with a very limited supply of the poorest flour."[100]

Witnessing Treaty 5 (and Two Mysterious Deaths)

One morning to my wonder and astonishment, an old Indian by the name of Berens was looking very eagerly at a lamp, the bowl of which was resting on the shoulder of a boy. He was interested, & thought the boy would get tired if kept there too long.

98 The Young family Bible gives her name as Florence Mary Ferrier, born 9 May 1875 and baptized by her father on 15 August 1878 (? last digit not clear). Elizabeth's memoirs say nothing about the Ojibwe naming ceremony initiated by the local chief, "Souwanas," which Eddie described in detail. See Jennifer S. H. Brown, "Growing Up Algonquian: A Missionary's Son in Cree-Ojibwe Country, 1869–1876," in *Papers of the Thirty-Ninth Algonquian Conference*, ed. Karl S. Hele and Regna Darnell (London: University of Western Ontario, 2008), 72–93. This section is out of sequence, as the Sandy Bar trip was in December 1875.

99 Martin Papanekis and his wife were Rossville Crees who, along with Tom Mamanowatum, came to help with the Berens River mission. See Young, *By Canoe and Dog-Train*, 259.

100 Sanderson, *First Century of Methodism in Canada*, vol. 2, 319–20.

Morning after morning he came and seemed to be wonderfully pleased, interested, and amused.

This "old Indian" (actually not so old) must have been Jacob Berens, born in the early 1830s, who was the first member of his family to become known by the surname Berens. He and his family were Methodists, and at the signing of Treaty 5, on 20 September 1875, the Youngs saw him become the treaty chief for several bands in the area. Elizabeth Young's memoirs do not mention Treaty 5 or the fact that she and Egerton Young signed it as witnesses.[101] However, a paragraph about the event survives in the papers of E. Ryerson Young (JSHB collection) who evidently typed up his mother's recollections of it:

Treaty-making. Gala day with the Governor (Morris) from Manitoba! While at Berens River [the] Gov. visited the "Fort" the H.B.C. trading-post and passed the Mission house. Great excitement was caused among the natives and Mission people at the moment. The Missionary was at the Fort. The Indians [were] anxious to fire a salute and wished to use Mr. Young's gun. Timothy Bear, our Interpreter, tried to fire it as the Governor passed but not being able to work it, appealed to me for help and so where ignorance is bliss it is folly to be wise, I immediately took the gun in my hands feeling sure of doing justice to it and the firing. As I had seen Mr. Young often using it, I succeeded admirably in saluting and welcoming the great man.

In her 1927 memoir, Elizabeth continued her recollections of Berens River:

It was here the old Indian women asked me to leave our tea leaves in a bowl for them when they came, so that they could have a drink of tea. I have known them sometimes, when in the kitchen to actually lift the lids of the Kettles to see what the missionarys wife was cooking.

101 Alexander Morris, *The Treaties of Canada with the Indians* (Toronto: Belfords, Clarke, 1880), 348).

It was here where our successors had Twins and the thought came to the Indians was, that they would need two nurses. So two appeared & made the request to be made nurses for the two babies. Unfortunately the missionaries wife was not accustomed to Indians, or to luxury. If she had been to the Indians, she might have averted the sad catastrophe that occurred by employing one as nurse & engaging the other to do some work to assist in the care of the babies. But unfortunately she engaged one, and the unhappy one went out saying she won't need her very long. The Sunday morning while the missionary was preaching he was called into the mission, baby was dying, and in the afternoon the other baby passed away. This was cruel, had they understood the Indian nature this might have been averted. Thus wisdom, common sense, were necessary to avert this uncalled for trouble. We are more than thankful to our Heavenly father for His unspeakable goodness to us.[102]

Berens River Mission being established — by the Rev E. R. Young, meant much care & anxiety, however with push, pluck, & perseverance much was being accomplished and encouragement was being established & thus work went on. Gradually the House was being made very comfortable with what things we had given to us when we were in Civilization, paints, tools, & everything for our comfort. We needed much of that sort. We worked away for about three years [Elizabeth was there for just under two], & then we returned to civilization & into the regular work.

Comment: Elizabeth Young's Berens River Experience in Retrospect

A typed page in the papers of E. Ryerson Young records some of Elizabeth's further memories: "The demands upon us were a little too much to bear. Health gave way. Symptoms were explained and the home physicians ordered us to return for special treatment. It was a heartbreak to give up the work that had meant so much to us; but it was surrendered. Our fine

102 The Youngs evidently heard about this incident some time after they had returned to Ontario. The missionary who lost the twins has not been identified; John Semmens was not married when he served at Berens River in 1876–78. Ojibwe people themselves had concerns and fears about "bad medicine" being used by persons who might take offence at some action and cause harm, even when no offence was intended.

dogs [except for Jack] were taken over by the Rev. John Semmens" (JSHB collection). Unmentioned is the fact that Elizabeth from February 1876 onward was also pregnant with her next daughter, Grace Amanda, born late that October in Port Perry, Ontario. Including her pregnancy with Florence, born in May 1875, Elizabeth was carrying a child for fifteen of her approximately twenty-two months at Berens River. She also had the care of Eddie, aged five going on seven, who as his own memoirs indicate was a lively child whose supervision must have caused some anxiety, and his younger sister, Lillian. Elizabeth's health issues were not specified but they, with her pregnancies and family responsibilities, doubtless diminished her stamina.

Other difficulties, as Elizabeth recounted, were the initial housing problems when she, Eddie, and Lillian first arrived, and the fact that the Youngs were founding a new mission. At Rossville, six missionaries and their wives had already worked there for twenty-eight years by the time the Youngs arrived; the Methodist village and its church were in place, with established routines and shared understandings. To assist in the Berens River work, the Youngs brought a few of their Rossville associates (Timothy Bear, Martin Papanekis and family, Little Mary, and Alex Kennedy), but they were all relative strangers to the Berens River people. Egerton did have some prior connections with the Berens family (see Part II, introduction), but he was often travelling, as when his unexpected absence at Christmastime in 1875 left Elizabeth in such great anxiety. Eddie also recounted an episode in which he and his mother were bullied by a HBC trader who thought that the few ermines Eddie had trapped among his rabbits represented the Youngs dealing in furs with the Indians. Eddie, however, generally had a happier time at Berens than his mother; of all the family, he seemed to form the closest ties with the local Ojibwe, assisted by his facility with the language — though that, too, could cause family tensions, as when he participated in an Ojibwe dance, to his father's distress (see Part II, "An Ojibwe Invitation"). Elizabeth kept on with the activities she performed at Rossville, organizing Christmas and New Year's feasts, and tending the sick (particularly during the measles epidemic that struck in the winter of 1874–75), along with her daily responsibilities. But the comfort that she developed in interacting with the Rossville people seemed not to develop at Berens River.

Leaving Berens River, 1876

Early in the summer of 1876, we left our Berens River mission
for home. Our journey was one of real hardship in the H.B.C. sail
boat, head winds, Storm, Rain.[103] So we had to go ashore drenched
to the skin, and not much to eat, after being out for [a] day, and
here we were near the mouth of Red River, but could not reach it,
and we were obliged to go ashore and make a fire & try to make
ourselves as comfortable as we could in wet blankets. Indians
put up the tent for us, and we put our children in the middle and
one at the back and the other at the front. But all too anxious to
sleep. Ere long we heard the stentorian calls of the Indian Guide,
calling How, How, the wind is fair, be quick up & we may reach
the mouth of the river ere it changes. So without any breakfast
of any kind we got into the boat and fortunately just reached the
mouth of the river as the wind changed & glad we were to even
have a breakfast on (Catfish); and as we got farther on and closed
in we were nearing the home of Mr Sifton, between the upper and
lower Fort Garry.[104]

Where they sent the servants down the bank to bring us up
to their luxurious home, the trite expression was from Earth to
Heaven, really it was a good comparison, for we were wet, cold, &
hungry. While there the *bath* was at our disposal. We were thankful
and made good use of it, giving all a good wholesome sponge & put
them to bed, how we did bless and thank our Host & Hostess for
their great kindness to us and ours while in that terrible condition.

After this it was steam boat, cars [railway], no more sail boats,
for which we were more than thankful. The next trouble was our
precious baby took disentry [dysentery], from boat to [railway] cars

---

103 The *Manitoba Free Press* reported on 12 August 1876 that Young reached Winnipeg
"last Tuesday on his way to his new station in Ontario. He and companions were some
ten days on the lake between the Mission and the Lower Fort and encountered very
heavy weather." Thanks to Anne Lindsay for this reference.

104 John Wright Sifton was a devout Methodist businessman who, in 1874, received
contracts to build a telegraph line and sections of railway in Manitoba. His better-
known son was Clifford Sifton, minister of the interior who aggressively fostered
immigration to western Canada. See David J. Hall, "Sifton, Sir Clifford," *Dictionary of
Canadian Biography* online.

it was a constant care, and every place we stopped or changed cars, we tried to get a Dr as the disease was getting worse. It continued until we reached my mother's home in Bradford, Ontario, and there the Dr mastered it and the dear gradually improved.

While on the steamer I caught my foot in a rope ring it throwing me, giving me a sprained ankle. This was exceedingly painful so much so that I was forced to stay on my back for nearly a week and with my boot laced up tight at the end of which I unlaced my boot & found my ankle almost black, but fortunately I was able to walk. However I was thankful and happy at that, for with sick Florence & very much to look after. Anyone travelling will know how [much] there is to look after, with three children and one expected. Poor Florence was not expected to live for some time & not until we reached my home or my mother's home, & called in the Dr, could we check the disease. To say I was nearly worn out is only speaking mildly, very mildly. What with three children & one coming, it was a trying position, but it was coming to civilization & home, and where we could be cared for.

Life in Ontario Parsonages: Port Perry, Colborne, and Bowmanville
Our new home was to be Port Perry. Here we found kind friends, and we were happy, glad, and contented, feeling we were where we would be taken care of. And not depending on ourselves if anything occurred.

Here is where Egerton & Lillian began school work & I was very much annoyed with the boys teasing and calling him Indian names.[105]

One man simply & emphatically said we do not want a returned missionary, and yet that man was one of our warmest friends. He was just a wee bit of a wagg, so it passed off as fun.

It was here our dear Grace was born bless her, & where dear Granpa Wm Young christened her, but she very strenuosly objected to it for she cried & howelled all through the ceremony.[106]

---

105 See Part II of this volume, especially the opening sections of E. Ryerson's 1962 memoir, and Brown, "Growing Up Algonquian," for detailed accounts.

106 Grace Amanda Young was born in Port Perry on 29 October 1876 (Young family Bible). She is pictured in figures 4 and 15.

We enjoyed a musical choir. Father, Mother, & children all belonged to the choir. The father was leader, the mother soprano. The daughter Miss Herrington [not further identified] was organist & soloist — It was delightful to hear her singing. It was a great pleasure joy & delight — such an addition to the church services, and here we had the pleasure of seeing our dear sister Clara married to Mr Aaron Ross's son, Wm Ross. It is just fifty years ago, now, Clara & Willie have just had their Golden Wedding.[107] We have had the pleasure of being there, & sharing with them the festivities of the occasion.

Mr & Mrs [Aaron] Ross, Sr. were very kind and thoughtful. Mr Brown's family; Mr Bruce's family one member of the family who visited the Parsonage very often, who always gave me great pleasure & delight. He since then has become a great and prominent man or I should say Dr.[108]

This is where our son & Daughter first went to school & what a trial it was for him as the school children called him an Indian, & bothered him intensely on that account. Here is where our *famous* dog Jack caused much excitement at one place near bye, Mr Young was calling & of course [Jack] was along, & was a privileged dog, he stretched himself out in the Hall. The Lady of the house passing through the hall tripped over him several times. At last she said, "*how much dog is there?*" Jack [fig. 5] was a big St Bernard. This same dog caused much merriment and a good deal of excitement.

In those days there were Gipsys going around, & at that time there were a number living in Port Perry. They had a dog & they said he could whip Jack. Jack was tried, tested, & but for a bite on his shoulder, where he could not touch it, if he could have touched it, he would have healed it, and if he had been with the other dogs, he would have been cured but alas poor Jack was doomed, everything was done for him that love for the grand dog could

---

107 Clara and William were married on 18 September 1877 in Port Perry. This statement thus helps to document the time at which Elizabeth was writing this memoir.

108 This is probably a reference to Herbert A. Bruce (b. 1868), who was attending school in Port Perry. He became a medical doctor, had a distinguished career, and was appointed lieutenant governor of Ontario in 1932. See www.scugogheritage.com/misc/pioneers.htm.

think of.[109] So the Gipsies were satisfied, that their dog had whipt good old Jack.

I remember very vividly one night when dear Dr George Young was visiting us & in the night, we were disturbed by Jack's growling & as [the] Dr was sleeping quite near to the noise, Mr Young, E. R., got up & sternly spoke to Jack.[110] Then Jack was quite [quiet]. But in the morning when we got up and found the Babies carriage gone and also all the clothes that were on the line, so now we were sorry we did not listen to Jacks cry for help, and as the little boy [Eddie] said we never had anything stolen from us when we were in the Indian country, quite a black eye for civilization. Our poor little baby Grace now had to do without her little carriage.

We had much to remember Port Perry by. This is where my sister Clara was married from the Parsonage to M. W. Ross, son of Mr & Mrs Aaron Ross. This is where through Egerton's instrumentality many were brought into the church who became true devoted members of the church, & great helps by being faithful workers therein.

Colborne was the next place we went to. We followed Dr & Mrs Joseph Locke. The Parsonage was very small. So we requested the officials to provide another one if possible for us. And they very kindly did so, much to our great pleasure and delight. Hear we had a beautiful ring-dove, dear Egerton was so fond of them [it]. We let it fly through the house. We had a dear old lady visiting us who wore caps and when we were at prayers, this beautiful dove would come and nestle in our friend's cap, and be quite at home there. It was most provocable of laughter and most disconcerting, and quite upset our equalebriam. We came to ourselves soon.

---

109 Young, describing Jack's death in *My Dogs in the Northland*, 123–24, recalled how one of his northern dogs, Rover, had been a "dog doctor," licking the other dogs' injuries and making them better. Jack had no Rover here.

110 George Young had left Winnipeg in the summer of 1876 to take charge of the Richmond St. Church in Toronto and became conference president of the Methodist Church in 1877 (*Manitoba Memories*, 320, 324).

We moved to our new home, we had more room outside as well as inside, much to our delight. We had fruit trees, we had to keep a cow, so we made butter had plenty of milk & cream. Mr Young was told to keep the barn door & gates well locked up, and even the Sacremental Wine secularly fastened up or she would get it. Sure enough one night she did get out of the barn and out through the gate and away she went. It was several days before we got our cow again. One very funny thing occurred & happened. Our son [Eddie] who was at a mischief age, put the wonderful cow to the sled & told his sisters to jump on. They had not gone very far when they were all upset in the snow, and glad were they to get off so easily.

Our Last Two Children and Another Loss

Here is where our baby girl was born on the fourth of February 1880.[111] Laura Winnifred Young, bless her, a sweet little miss. My Dr's name was Gold, he was gold to me. He watched me carefully as there was something in my looks he did not like, for a few days he was most assiduous & very attentive. I had much to be thankful in having such a good Dr.

It was very unfortunate to have to move out before Conference time as the people who owned the place wanted to come in.

While there I had my mother & Sister there some of the time. I had a dear little friend while there, called Mrs Dewey. She was such a comfort & help. She had two nice sons & one daughter, her husband a nice man, but [two lines crossed out] so many ways.

Soon we left Colborne & went to Bowmanville, to a nice church & Parsonage, & nice people. While there I sang in the Choir, & enjoyed it very much. We had a very busy time, we had many Entertainments & many nice young people who were interested & very happy. Mr Young had a young men's class, & many of the young men went out as missionaries, & ministers, much to our delight.

---

111 The date is given as 1881 in the Young family Bible, which also records the earlier death of an infant: "Eva at Port Perry 1878. A wee flower too frail for earth's cold blasts." Copies of pages in the JSHB collection.

Thus we put our trust in the Lord, & He shall bring it to pass, &
today dear Father's [name] is revered & honored by those who were
there when we were.

While there we had a little son given to us, soon after he came
the children had the measles & the dear latest arrival took them so
we had quite a Hospital for a time. We soon got around & thankful
to say all well & happy, but our dear little William Joseph was not
to be with us very long. A few short months & we had to part with
him & lay him away, dear little man, & that was while dear Father
was away again.[112] It did seem so cruel that I should be alone each
time we had to part with our dear little ones, & yet I was not alone,
O how much have I to be thankful for. For the One who said,
"Lo I am with you unto the End," was with me, throughout — [not]
seen, yet felt, Who's comfort sustained and comforted in sorrow.
This was in Bowmanville & while there we enjoyed our sojourn
there. Of course we had some rough places to pass over, yet on the
whole we had many friends there & were happy, good meetings,
good choir, [I] being happily one of their number.

112 William Joseph was born on 22 March 1883 and died in October: Young family
Bible. He appears in the family portrait reproduced in figure 4.

Postscripts

Elizabeth Bingham Young: Method in Her Methodism

Elizabeth Bingham was brought up a firm Methodist, and, as noted in the introduction, her father held an important position as a Methodist class leader in Bradford. Although lacking the higher education received by Emma Crosby and a good many other Methodist women of the rising generations,[1] she was well schooled in how Methodism worked at a local, small-town level and in what was expected of its adherents, as the opening lines of her memoir indicate. She recalled a happy girlhood, finding satisfaction and pleasure both in many social amusements and in helping people in need, likely assisting her father in his pastoral rounds. Her memories correspond with Neil Semple's observation that "Methodism was not a joyless, puritanical retreat from the world. Rather, it was profoundly sociable and convivial, providing a warm, outgoing sense of fellowship."[2]

There is no sign that Elizabeth taught school before her marriage as Egerton did for a while, although her church activities likely involved Sunday-school teaching, as they did at Rossville. As a girl she probably took

---

1 Emma Douse obtained a Mistress of Liberal Arts degree at Hamilton Female College and, in 1870, began teaching there in the "academic" stream. Her first meeting with missionary Thomas Crosby, in January 1874, led rapidly to courtship, marriage, and their departure for British Columbia in May of 1874. See Jan Hare and Jean Barman, *Good Intentions Gone Awry: Emma Crosby and the Methodist Mission on the Northwest Coast* (Vancouver: University of British Columbia Press, 2006), 5, 11–19. See also Johanna M. Selles, *Methodists and Women's Education in Ontario, 1836–1925* (Montréal and Kingston: McGill-Queen's University Press, 1996), for broader context.

2 Neil Semple, *The Lord's Dominion: The History of Canadian Methodism* (Montréal and Kingston: McGill-Queen's University Press, 1996), 56.

music lessons, in the same way that her younger sister Sarah was doing in 1868–69 (see Clarissa Bingham's letters in Part III, sec. 4). Before her marriage, she may also have taught music and singing, for which she evidently had a talent. The Youngs brought a melodeon to Rossville, and her singing was a feature of the church services there.[3] On 11 August 1873, after she had left Rossville, Egerton wrote to her, "When I scolded some of the [HBC] Scotchmen for not coming to church, their answer was that the church seemed so sad and drear without Mrs. Young's sweet strong voice that they felt better at home. So you see even those poor fellows miss you" (see Part III, sec. 11, for the complete letter). Her singing of Cree hymns within and outside church surely assisted her language learning. It was also a means of reaching people, as in the instance of Sandy Harte, the Nelson River boy whom the Youngs took into their home at Rossville. Once settled in and happy, he sometimes would "burst into song," singing hymns in Cree. (A full account of Sandy is provided in Part III, sec. 7.) Music was her own sphere of activity; records make no mention of Egerton taking initiatives in singing or music. Also, it was Elizabeth who showed interest in Indian dances. In chapter 14 of his memoir, Eddie recalled his mother asking to see an Ojibwe dance at Berens River, and in her own account of Sandy Harte (in Part III, sec. 7) she mentioned asking an old Rossville Cree woman to show her some dance steps.

Elizabeth had other skills that were central to her success at Rossville. The making of clothing was critical and, as she recalled, also involved scrounging for supplies of flannel and sometimes cutting up some of her own garments to recycle the cloth. Egerton's accounts of expenditures in 1868 referred to the purchase of a sewing machine and needles to take to the Northwest.[4] Although Elizabeth must have used the sewing machine at Rossville, her memoir makes no explicit mention of it, and the items made by Little Mary (and perhaps by other Rossville women) that survive in the Royal Ontario Museum's Young collection are all hand sewn.

---

3 Melodeons were small table-sized reed organs with foot pedals. The Youngs' melodeon resided in their home (see *By Canoe and Dog-Train Among the Cree and Salteaux Indians* [London: Charles H. Kelly, 1890], 60); it would have been too small for church use.

4 Notes taken by Harcourt Brown, from Egerton's account records now in the Young fonds, UCCA, Toronto.

Elizabeth also made no reference to teaching the Rossville women to sew; they already had skills in that area, particularly in working with leather garments. But she did encourage their sewing, providing them with materials and a warm place to work in her home — and, as she also noted, flour, tea, and soap on request. She may have hoped to encourage their making of craft items that could be sold for their benefit, but such an enterprise proved to demand more outlays of resources (and probably time) than she could afford. In the end, the main producer of sewn goods was Little Mary, making items for the family's own use. Part III, sec. 6, presents some brief texts by Elizabeth and Egerton on the sewing activities of the Rossville Cree women and the things they made, and several items preserved in the Egerton Ryerson Young collection (ROM 999.133) are illustrated in figs. 1, 2, and 7–13.

Elizabeth's most demanding responsibilities at Rossville were concerned with food management. Cooking was not new to her, but the need to make do with foods of limited variety and to cope at times with genuine scarcity both among the local Crees and in the Youngs' own larder posed immense challenges. The Youngs took seriously the Methodist egalitarian ethos of sharing and helping the poor. All who joined Methodist communities were expected to give themselves "wholly to Christ and to one another." United by "strong spiritual and emotional bonds, they were "substantially brothers and sisters, fathers, mothers, and children, in Christ," overriding "such temporal divisions as class, race, or nationality."[5]

Food and food practices were powerful means of enacting this ethos, as well as forms of communication around which mutual understandings had to be built — and rebuilt. Methodists faced considerable cultural dissonance when their closest neighbours were Hudson's Bay Company personnel, who organized their social relations among themselves and with Aboriginal people on quite different principles (even though the Youngs at Rossville came to be on good terms with some HBC officers). Elizabeth and Egerton were bemused by HBC ranking and gender distinctions when they arrived at Lower Fort Garry on the Red River in July 1868. The "law of precedents" prevailed: at dinner, "no clerk of fourteen years' standing would think of entering before one who had been fifteen years in the service, or of sitting

5 Semple, *The Lord's Dominion*, 58.

above him at the table." Another custom that stirred their comment "was the fact that there were two dining-rooms . . . one for the ladies, and the other for the gentlemen of the service." The Youngs found this "so contrary to all our ideas and education on the subject" that "we presumed to question it," but they were told it was an old custom that worked well and that if business were discussed in the women's presence, "all our schemes and plans would soon be known to all."[6]

Elizabeth Vibert has looked more broadly at how HBC food practices embodied British colonial outlooks, providing "a ready means to shore up social boundaries." In the 1820s, the company laid down rules to limit social and racial mixing at meals. Gentlemen officers tended to get the best foods — fresh meat and vegetables; the lower ranks got fish, flour, or whatever country produce was at hand, and Aboriginal people were not at table at all — except insofar as some employees were of Aboriginal descent. As Vibert observes, "The daily rituals of the table provided a key venue for the performance and reproduction of class and racial status. . . . It was all part of the constant theatre of the fur trade, a set of self-conscious performances that extended beyond food to dress, personal conduct, and cross-cultural ceremony" — all manifest in "the allocation of food, the tradition of high table, the arrangement of chairs around tables, the exclusion of women." In short, "the rituals of everyday life both symbolized and enabled the hierarchical class, race, and gender relations that structured fur trade society."[7]

At Rossville, the Youngs enacted their own Methodist set of performances around food, blending their values with those of the Crees as they began to understand them. Having already experienced HBC practices, they faced a new learning curve as their Cree hosts sounded out their values and responses. Their first visitor, whom they both wrote about, was the woman who gladly ate what Elizabeth set before her and then carried off the entire loaf of bread, corned beef, and dish of vegetables sitting on the table. Egerton later came to understand the etiquette behind her taking everything that she

6 Young, *By Canoe and Dog-Train*, 44.

7 Elizabeth Vibert, "The Contours of Everyday Life: Food and Identity in the Plateau Fur Trade," in *Gathering Places: Aboriginal and Fur Trade Histories,* ed. Carolyn Podruchny and Laura Peers (Vancouver: University of British Columbia Press, 2010), 130, 134–35.

believed was being given. But the woman also doubtless perceived the new-comers as well endowed with both goods and status, and hence as obliged to be generous; Mary Black-Rogers's classic article, "Varieties of 'Starving,'" is of help in interpreting the episode.[8] Elizabeth learned to set out in future only what she could afford to give.

Their second lesson came from the man who presented two ducks as a "present" to the missionary. After he lingered much of the day, he finally made the Youngs understand that he was awaiting the "present" they were to give him in exchange. Evidently, he conceptualized their acceptance of the ducks as initiating an exchange of the sort he might have expected over at the HBC post and, in Cree terms, a reciprocal relationship. To avoid such situations in the future, the Youngs took an economic approach, deciding to be very careful about "gifts" and to pay (based on HBC trade standards) "a reasonable price for everything we needed which they had to sell."[9] In the absence of a cash economy, this entailed calculating what they really needed and what they could spare from the supplies they received only a couple of times a year.

As the Youngs settled in, Elizabeth's food practices and offerings were central to the building and maintaining of relationships. Her collaborative organizing of the New Year's feasts and the invitations to all, from HBC traders to "pagans" coming from some distance, were striking examples. The Rossville spirit of inclusiveness extended to the sending of food from the feast to all those who could not attend because of age or sickness, and afterwards all the remaining food was divided among those in need.[10] From a Cree perspective, the event would have evoked parallels with the custom

8 Young, *By Canoe and Dog-Train*, 58–59; Black-Rogers, "Varieties of 'Starving': Semantics and Survival in the Subarctic Fur Trade, 1750–1850," *Ethnohistory* 33 (1986): 353–83.

9 Young, *By Canoe and Dog-Train*, 60. Timothy Bear early began to assist as interpreter, but it is unclear whether he was on hand in this episode.

10 Young, *By Canoe and Dog-Train*, 68–70; see also Elizabeth's account in her memoir ("The New Year's Feast"), above. Methodist organizing of such feasts was not new. On 1 January 1856, for example, the Reverend Robert Brooking described a New Year's feast to which the Indians contributed beavers, rabbits, and venison (*Wesleyan Missionary Notices*, no. 12 [15 May 1857], 180). But the scale and inclusiveness of the Rossville event described by Elizabeth were remarkable.

of the eat-all feast or "*wihkotowin*, a feast of game at which a large surplus is prepared and entirely consumed."[11] In anthropological terms, the feast was a grand example of commensality, the act of eating at the same table, as an expression of social solidarity or bonding. The Methodists saw the feast in that light, as a positive expression of their values, but their writers also portrayed it to Christian audiences as a replacement for the "dog feast" — their simplified rendition of Cree-Ojibwe ceremonies that epitomized the paganism that the missionaries sought to wipe out as they brought everyone together in new observances (which the Cree could relate to as offering some parallels to the old).[12]

Elizabeth's memoirs reveal many examples of the role of food as symbol and vehicle for setting relationships in motion, but Egerton in his writings described some of her food "performances" and hospitality in more detail than she did. On the first Sunday after the Youngs' arrival, for example, a venerable old man, "one of the first converts of the early Missionaries," said to have been a hunter for the HBC for eighty years, arrived from some distance for the morning service. The Youngs invited him home to dine and to rest so that he could stay for the afternoon service, and his visits became a pattern each Sunday. William Papanekis became a close friend and a class leader, and his three sons were important in the Youngs' Rossville life: Samuel as the leader of the smallpox relief expedition in 1870, Martin as Egerton's trusted guide in summer and winter and later as aide to the Berens River mission, and Edward, converted by Egerton and ordained in Winnipeg in 1889.[13]

Then one June, perhaps in 1869, a visiting stranger told Egerton about meeting the Reverend James Evans as a boy back in the 1840s. As he was

11 See Robert Brightman, *Grateful Prey: Rock Cree Human-Animal Relationships* (Berkeley: University of California Press, 1993), 214–30, for a fine discussion of the social and spiritual aspects of the feast.

12 Young's *By Canoe and Dog-Train*, 66, and illustration, 212, joined other published mission works in dramatizing the contrasts between old pagan rites and new observances.

13 Young, *By Canoe and Dog-Train*, 130–32. The first Methodist missionary to conduct baptisms at Norway House, Robert Rundle, baptized five children of William and Ann Papanekis in July 1840: Norway House baptismal register, nos. 49 and 55–58, including Samuel, aged twelve, and Martin, aged six.

an orphan, Evans had taken him into his home and was very kind to him, explaining to him about the Christian faith. However, a Cree family trading at Norway House from a great distance persuaded him to come live with them, with unhappy results. He grew up far away and had a family. Years later, after a terrible winter hunt, a voice spoke to him urging him to remember the missionary's message, and then game animals became plentiful again. Now he had arrived with his wife and children, "to ask you to help us to become Christians." Egerton recorded that when Elizabeth heard the story, she rose to the occasion: "Out of our scant supplies we gave the whole family a good hearty meal, and we both did what we could by words and actions to make them feel that they were our friends." Some older residents remembered the orphan and his parents and pitched in to give the family a home.[14]

Another initiative, organized mainly by Elizabeth, was a striking kind of Methodist (midday) dinner theatre. As Egerton wrote in *By Canoe and Dog-Train*, this "novel plan" involved the Youngs visiting individual families for a prearranged meal to encourage wives to keep their homes "decently and in good order." Egerton would announce at the Sunday service that, on following days, he and Elizabeth would come to certain homes for a meal and that they would see to the accoutrements and bring provisions as needed, if the family would prepare their home for the visit. In mid-morning, Elizabeth would get her dog-train harnessed and her cariole loaded with dishes, knives and forks, tablecloth and provisions, and have her young dog-driver, Alex Kennedy, drive her to the home. (Egerton recalled elsewhere that, "My wife was also the owner of a capital [dog] train, that was generally kept well employed, under the charge of an efficient driver, in taking her around, as, on her missions of comfort and helpfulness, she visited the wigwams and other lowly homes of the Indians, where sickness prevailed.")[15]

14 Young, *By Canoe and Dog-Train*, 151–57.

15 Young, *My Dogs in the Northland* (New York: Fleming H. Revell, 1902), 68. I. O. the *Indian Trail and Other Stories of Missionary Work Among the Cree and Saulteaux Indians* (London: Religious Tract Society, [1897]), 49–50, Young identified Kennedy as Elizabeth's dog driver, adding that "[we] each had our favourite dog-trains." Cuffy, the Newfoundland, was the lead dog in Elizabeth's train. For more on Alex Kennedy, see Part III, sec. 15.

Elizabeth and the woman of the house would then prepare the meal and spread the dishes and cutlery on the tablecloth, usually arranged on the floor, as tables were few. Egerton would arrive about noon, and all would enjoy a plain feast, commonly fish and potatoes, and "cheery conversation" with the family, followed by prayer and hymn singing. Egerton would then leave on his various duties while Elizabeth helped in cleaning up and in any other matters, such as clothing, with which assistance was wanted. The aim was to set an example, to provide a model for good Methodist house-keeping, while also fostering sociability and commensality — the notion of fellow worshippers sharing meals as equals. Egerton sometimes extrapolated from these dinners in his preaching: "Better far is it when Jesus comes. He spreads out the feast, and he invites us to sit down and feast with Him. O let Him in!"[16]

Food sociability and sharing, cultivated by Elizabeth and often by Egerton as well, brought more families to Rossville and into the congregation. The difficulty with their mission success was the fact that the larger economic landscape was being reconfigured as Hudson's Bay Company business practices shifted. The resources of the area were also under severe strain. Big game was getting scarce, and rabbits were a limited substitute. Fish was the mainstay for both people and dogs; the Youngs wrote several times about eating fish twenty-one times a week. Their son in his memoirs (see Part II, chapters 2 and 6) recalled his parents' concern about food shortages and the depletion of fish, and agriculture was scarcely viable in the Norway House environment, even as Egerton's new variety of potatoes proved highly successful and as plowing with dogs aided in their planting. Food concerns were major factors in Egerton's urging the church to establish a mission at Berens River as a new home for at least a portion of the Rossville

16 Young, *By Canoe and Dog-Train*, 229–32. This evokes Jesus's words in Revelation 3:20: "If any man hear my voice and open the door I will come in to him and will sup with him and he with me." On a more mundane scale, tea served the purpose of commensality well enough; in *Stories from Indian Wigwams and Northern Camp-fires* (New York: Eaton and Mains, 1892), 38, Egerton wrote that "even old Tapastanum, the conjurer, became friendly and frequently called to have a talk over a cup of tea." In *By Canoe and Dog-Train*, 234–38, Egerton told another story of sharing and its results. He and seven Cree associates ran out of food on a trip from Oxford House. One man caught a pike, and, when cooked, a third of it was given to the "praying master." Egerton insisted that it be evenly divided among them all, a gesture that later influenced some of them, so they said, to be "fully decided for Christ."

people; he was to be disappointed that so few of them followed him there after his own relocation in 1874. Governmental authorities directed them instead to Sandy Bar and White Mud River, whereupon they were relocated to a reserve on the Fisher River to make way for incoming Icelandic settlers.[17]

One story that Egerton told in a letter evidently addressed to the *Christian Guardian* and written on 31 March 1873, a few months before the Youngs left Rossville, expressed the strain on everyone's food resources and the compulsion felt to share whatever one could:

> One morning . . . after making a few visits among the people, as
> I was putting up a little flour for a poor, sick woman, my good wife
> said, "My dear, that is the last bag of flour, and there are several
> months yet before boats can arrive with more." My answer was,
> "Wrap yourself up and go and see her sufferings for yourself."
> She did so, and returned home about dinner time. When the table
> was set, and grace said, after Mrs. Young had received her portion,
> she put it all in a little pail, and sent it to the poor, sick woman,
> and while our little ones and I were trying to eat our dinner,
> there came to our ears the wailing, importunate prayer, "Oh Lord,
> pity the poor." The little three-year-old boy looks up and says,
> "Papa, is God cross with us, that mamma cries so when she prays?"
> It is not the first time that food has gone from our table, and we
> have combined fasting with our prayers for our poor Indians.[18]

Egerton in this letter did not mention another factor pressing on the family's resources: the Youngs' taking of Little Mary and Sandy Harte into their household on a lasting basis. Mary and Sandy were not simply charity cases; they made real contributions to the household and became warmly attached to the Youngs. But their previous injuries had also left them with physical disabilities such that the Youngs' support was important to their well-being.

17 Frank Tough, *"As Their Natural Resources Fail": Native Peoples and the Economic History of Northern Manitoba, 1870–1930* (Vancouver: University of British Columbia Press, 1996), 146, 148–49.

18 Copy of printed letter preserved in Egerton R. Young's scrapbook, UCCA, Young fonds, Toronto. The letter lacks documentation, but it opens with a reference to receiving the latest issue of the *Christian Guardian*.

As of 1873, when Young wrote, he and Elizabeth could only partially grasp the scope of the HBC-related changes beginning to affect the Cree around Norway House. For decades, Norway House had been the key axis of transport and communication from England to York Factory to Lake Winnipeg and beyond, but as rail and steamship transport began to reach areas to the south, York Factory was losing importance, with implications for both Norway and Oxford houses. The need for York boats and boat-men was declining, and the Hudson's Bay Company shifted its investments and interest away from the old labour-intensive modes of travel.[19] By 28 September 1875, the Reverend John Ruttan was writing from Rossville of the pressing needs "of our people who are now thrown out of employment without any means whereby to procure the necessary things for themselves and families."[20] Given that the missionaries were generally on short rations themselves, Methodist generosity and sharing could not resolve the larger problems that were arising. The Youngs, as they later realized, were living through the end of an era.

Mission Wives at Rossville: Some Comparisons

How do we situate Elizabeth Young among missionary wives of her time, and, indeed, can we generalize about them? Rosemary Gagan was able to gather considerable data about the single women who worked for the Women's Missionary Society of the Methodist Church of Canada in the years from 1881 to 1925 because these women had some visibility and left biographical and career records, even if their careers were short.[21] In con-trast, the lives and identities of mission wives were largely submerged in those of their husbands; it takes some detective work even to find out their

19 See Tough, "*As Their Natural Resources Fail*," figures 2.4 and 2.5, comparing the HBC transport system of York boat brigades in 1868 with the rise of rail lines and of steam transport on Lake Winnipeg, in 1875–85.

20 Ruttan, 28 September 1875, to *Wesleyan Missionary Notices*, 1875, 87.

21 See Rosemary R. Gagan, *A Sensitive Independence: Canadian Methodist Women Missionaries in Canada and the Orient, 1881–1925* (Montréal and Kingston: McGill-Queen's University Press, 1992).

first names. It is unusual to come across such extensive memoirs such as Elizabeth left or to have available such a large family correspondence as Emma Crosby's from British Columbia.[22] Most wives left few or no personal writings that have found their way into archives or into print.

Various sources, however, offer glimpses of the mission wives who lived and served at Rossville before and after Elizabeth, which provide the basis for some comparisons. In the late summer of 1840, James and Mary Evans (who had married in 1822) and their daughter, Eugenia Clarissa, aged about seventeen, settled at Norway House. Their relations with the company and Donald Ross, the HBC officer in charge, began well but soon deteriorated. By summer 1843, the Methodists could not remain comfortably in the post and began building mission accommodations beside a small Cree village about two miles distant. Ross wrote to his colleague, James Hargrave at York Factory, on 2 December 1843, "our *pious* neighbours removed down to their new Establishment at the village in the latter end of November the old Lady is quite savage, about what she calls being 'turned out of the Fort' — never mind, let her grumble . . . I only wish they were 'on their own hook'" (referring to HBC outlays for transport and other services contributed to the mission).[23]

Egerton Young, in his biography of James Evans, naturally viewed Mary Evans very differently. Perhaps recalling some qualities that he saw in his own wife, he cited Mary as one of "the many noble brave women" whose "coolness and bravery in trying hours quite equals that of the men. Their tact and skill, their patience and endurance, their faith and belief in the ultimate triumph of the gospel, easily place them in the front." His hagiography, however, had some basis in concrete knowledge of the Evanses gained through oral history. After James Evans's death in England in 1846, Mary returned to Canada, and Egerton recalled a time "when, as a little boy in my father's parsonage," he sat at her feet and "listened with intensest interest" as she talked of the Rossville mission and of its people such as John Oig and other

---

22 See Hare and Barman, *Good Intentions Gone Awry.*

23 G. P. de T. Glazebrook, ed., *The Hargrave Correspondence, 1821–1843* (Toronto: Champlain Society, 1938), 460. Hargrave's wife, Letitia, wrote in the same period of growing friction between Mary and Mrs. Ross. Yet Donald Ross was recognized in the naming of the new mission village as "Rossville."

Evans associates whom he was later to meet and who also shared their memories with him. Mary Evans initiated prayer meetings and Bible readings for the mission women; she also encouraged the women's "wonderful cleverness . . . in their bead work, and silk and porcupine quill work," and the Evanses sent for "quantities of flax and wool and spinning wheels, as well as yarn and thread" to foster their industry. (Elizabeth was to carry on some of the same activities twenty-five years later, although she never mentioned spinning.) The women, he said, also gathered and selected the white birch bark used in printing Evans's first syllabic texts and then stitched the pages together with deerskin covers. Another task of the women, surely organized by Mary Evans (although this is not explicitly mentioned), was the making of duffle dog shoes; James Evans used many of them on his long trips, as did Egerton in later times.[24] Indications are that Mary established a round of activities that later mission wives at Rossville would replicate to varying degrees. The details of her practical work are not well recorded, however, and the Evanses' Rossville legacy was darkened by their difficulties with the Company and by the turmoil surrounding accusations of Evans's improper behaviour with young girls and his falling out with his younger associate, the Reverend William Mason.[25]

The next missionary wife, Sophia Mason, lived at Rossville almost twice as long as any other. She had a signal advantage over the others: she was fluent in Cree and at home in the region. Born in 1822 in Red River, she was the youngest daughter of HBC governor Thomas Thomas and his Cree wife, Sarah. After her father's death in 1828, she resided in two successive Red River Anglican clergymen's homes and completed her studies at the Red River Academy. In 1843, she married the Reverend William Mason, and later that year the couple arrived at Norway House to assist with the mission. They stayed on when Evans left in 1846, and Sophia took up scriptural translating, building on and refining the work being done by Henry Bird Steinhauer and John Sinclair. The Bible translations that resulted bore William Mason's name, but Mason recognized that her "perfect command and knowledge

24 Egerton R. Young, *The Apostle of the North: Rev. James Evans* (New York: Fleming H. Revell, 1899), 113, 253, 154, 191–92, 166.

25 For a succinct overview of the issues, see Gerald M. Hutchinson, "James Evans' Last Year," *Journal of the Canadian Church Historical Society* 18 (1977): 42–57.

of the Indian language" was central to "the most correct rendering" of any passage in Cree. He credited also her labours at the mission day school and her "visits to the Indian tents" while also tending to a large family despite "her feeble and delicate constitution." Sophia had four children baptized at Rossville in 1844, 1846, 1848, and 1850. The last two, although listed in the Norway House Wesleyan baptismal register, were baptized by Anglican clergy, a clue to Mason's coming move to a new connection.[26]

In 1854, William Mason left Rossville and engaged to serve the Church of England, spending the next four years at York Factory. The Masons then sailed to England to see the Cree translations printed while Sophia worked on completing revisions to the Cree Old Testament. She died in London in October 1861, shortly before her fortieth birthday and three months after the birth of her ninth child.[27] Her Cree language skills and translation work set her apart from any other wife. She exceeded most of the others in another respect: she was pregnant during much of her mission service, bearing nine children in a marriage that lasted only eighteen years. Unfortunately, Egerton Young's writings say nothing about Sophia, given the deep rifts that developed between Evans and Mason and between Mason and the Methodists. In his biography of Evans, Young wrote, "We do not put his [Mason's] name here on our pages."[28]

In the summer of 1854, the Reverend Thomas Hurlburt and his wife, Betsy, arrived to take charge of Rossville. Hurlburt, in his mid-forties, was appointed to chair the Hudson's Bay District missions. He had married Betsy Almira Adams in 1832, and the two had served at numbers of eastern missions and for seven years in the Mississippi-Missouri region. He was known for his mastery of several Native languages and for his Cree and Ojibwe translations. Betsy had one child baptized at Rossville, on

26 Norway House baptismal register, no. 423, Sarah Jane, born 21 August 1844; no. 581, Mary Ross, born June 1846; no. 658, Charles Edwin, born June 1848 and baptized by the Reverend John Smithurst of Red River; and no. 715, Frederick William, born March 1850 and baptized by the Bishop of Rupert's Land. Possibly another child or two were born at Rossville after 1850 but recorded in Anglican registers.

27 Bruce Peel, "Thomas, Sophia (Mason)." *Dictionary of Canadian Biography* online.

28 Young, *Apostle of the North*, 195–96. The fact that Mason's name appeared alone on the Cree translations published in England also much irritated all who knew how hard the native Cree-speakers had worked on them.

23 September 1855.[29] Hurlburt cited her contributions in visiting the sick and holding "female prayer meetings."[30] But her poor health caused her to leave for Canada; in May of 1856, Hurlburt took her as far as St. Paul and returned to spend one more year at Rossville. The mission had an important female helper, however. Miss Charlotte Adams, a cousin of Betsy, had come west with the Hurlburts to serve as a "devoted school teacher," who "spent her evenings in the training of the mothers and daughters in household duties, and in visiting the sick and needy in their homes," while also studying the Cree language and gathering girls to stitch and bind three thousand copies of one of the gospels and four epistles, all written in Cree syllabics, for circulation in the region.[31] Hurlburt described her other contributions: "With the girls and women, Miss Adams is very acceptable; and they now crochet a variety of fancy and useful articles for themselves, and also some to sell. . . . Hoods, caps and bonnets are taking the place of shawls and blankets, as articles of headdress among the women: these Miss Adams is very busy just now in preparing for them." One skill was lacking, though: "Some one to teach singing is very important. Our people are very urgent about it."[32] Miss Adams and Hurlburt left Rossville in June 1857, and she does not seem to have been replaced.[33]

The next Rossville missionary, the English-born Robert Brooking, arrived at Rossville in August 1857 with his wife, Elizabeth, and they stayed for three years. Brooking had served on the Gold Coast in Africa for six years, before coming to Canada and working in missions there until his appointment to Oxford House in 1854. Brooking had started out as a manual labourer and his forte was building things — houses, schools, fences, boats, and so on. After Hurlburt left Rossville, Brooking and "his equally committed wife"

29 Norway House baptismal register, no. 969, aged one month fourteen days.

30 Thomas Hurlburt, journal extract dated 29 December 1854, published in *Wesleyan Missionary Notices*, no. 5 (November 1855), 69.

31 John Maclean, *Vanguards of Canada* (Toronto: The Missionary Society of the Methodist Church, 1918), 78–79. Trained as a teacher at the Toronto Normal School, Charlotte Adams taught at Rossville until she and Hurlburt left in 1857. Thanks to Anne Lindsay for identifying Adams.

32 Thomas Hurlburt, letter of 15 December 1856, to *Wesleyan Missionary Notices*, no. 12 (15 May 1857), 179. Elizabeth Young with her love of and talent for singing would have been greatly appreciated that year.

33 Arthur G. Reynolds, "Hurlburt, Thomas." *Dictionary of Canadian Biography* online. Hurlburt's last baptisms listed in the Norway House baptismal register were in mid-June 1857.

replaced him, staying until late summer 1860, when they went back to mission work in Canada. Elizabeth died in 1862.[34] Brooking's writings made a few references to her at Oxford House. On 3 December 1856, he noted of the Oxford Crees, "Christianity is improving their general appearance. . . . I cannot tell you how many ladies' dresses, and white shirts, Mrs. Brooking has got to cut out and make by Christmas." (Unlike Elizabeth Young, neither Miss Adams nor Mrs. Brooking seemed to place emphasis on Cree crafts such as quillwork or beadwork.) Records do not speak of her mission work at Rossville; she may have been in poor health. She had no children baptized at Rossville.

The Reverend George McDougall, experienced in eastern Canadian missions, began work at Rossville late in 1860 and remained till early summer 1863 — except for his travels to the west in 1862, which confirmed his wish to pursue mission work on the western plains. He and his wife, Elizabeth, had eight children, and she, of all the wives in this group, had the longest career running the domestic side of a mission and raising a family in that context. But her Rossville service was relatively brief and less well known than her later years. She had one child born at Rossville: George William, baptized by Charles Stringfellow on 18 June 1862.[35]

The McDougalls were followed by Charles and Ann Stringfellow, who, in 1857, soon after their marriage in Upper Canada, had been dispatched to serve at Oxford House when the Brookings moved to Rossville in Hurlburt's place. The Stringfellows began their Rossville service in summer 1863. They had one child baptized there, Sarah Elizabeth, born 18 February 1866, and, as noted earlier, lost a small child in a scalding accident.[36] When Egerton and Elizabeth Young took their place in August 1868, Ann Stringfellow was in poor health; she probably lacked the stamina to engage with mission work as Elizabeth was to do.

The story of the Youngs' successors, the Reverend and Mrs. John Ruttan and the Reverend Orrin German, whom Egerton Young met briefly before he left Rossville in early September 1873, offers a few more glimpses of mission wives. John Ruttan, aged about twenty-three, arrived newly ordained and newly married to Ellen Beddome, aged about nineteen; writing to Elizabeth

---

34 Anthony J. Hall, "Brooking, Robert." *Dictionary of Canadian Biography* online.

35 Norway House baptismal register, no. 1148, aged 8½ months.

36 Norway House baptismal register, no. 1262, 27 May 1866. As Sarah Elizabeth turns up in later censuses, she was not the scalding victim.

in September 1873 (see Part III, sec. 11), Young remarked that "Mrs. Ruttan is very young and will have much to learn. The Lord help her." The Ruttans were musically inclined: in the same letter, Young wrote, "They have a beautiful organ, so our dear little melodion has its song put out." The Reverend George Young, reporting on his visit to the Rossville mission in January in 1875, praised them both, writing that Ruttan's "excellent young wife, right from the Wesleyan Ladies' College, Hamilton, only a few weeks elapsing from the day she left her studies till she entered upon her duties in this far-off mission, has been 'a helper indeed' to her husband." On 3 January 1875, he baptized their first child, Eva, born 26 April 1874.[37] The extent of Ellen's involvement in mission work is not clear; certainly she and John arrived without prior experience or knowledge of the people and language. Her family responsibilities grew apace; the Norway House Wesleyan baptismal register recorded two more children born in 1875 and 1876, just over a year apart.[38]

When John Ruttan began serving at Rossville, the schoolteacher was Peter Badger, a Cree of mixed descent from Red River who had been teaching there since the 1860s. He was bilingual; according to David Pentland, "he must have been an excellent interpreter, able to switch easily from English to the most colloquial Cree."[39] In June 1875, however, Badger left Norway House with twenty families who were departing to settle at White Mud River, the first landing place of the Rossville people who were soon to be relocated to Fisher River.[40] In early August 1875, Miss Clementina Batty arrived from Ontario to teach the school, and by 28 September Ruttan was writing to his church superiors that Miss Batty "cannot be too highly spoken of"

---

37 George Young, *Manitoba Memories: Leaves from My Life in the Prairie Province, 1868-1884* (Toronto: William Briggs, 1897), 295, and Norway House baptismal register, no. 1560.

38 Norway House baptismal register, no. 1619, Sarah Ann, born 20 July 1875, and no. 1696, William Arthur, born 25 August 1876.

39 David H. Pentland, "The Rossville Mission Dialect of Cree: Egerton Ryerson Young's 1872 Vocabulary," in *Essays in Algonquian Bibliography in Honour of V.M. Dechene*, ed. H.C. Wolfart (Winnipeg: University of Manitoba, 1984), 37, analyzing Badger's contributions to the word lists in Young's document.

40 Badger's original arrival date at Rossville is not clear, but the Norway House baptismal register, no. 1307, records the baptism, in November 1866, of Rachel Harriet, daughter of Peter and Harriet Badger, born 11 October 1866. On Badger's move to become the teacher at White Mud, see Ruttan's report dated 18 June 1875 in *Missionary Notices of the Methodist Church of Canada*, 3rd ser., no. 4 (October 1875), 62.

for her diligence, piety, and emphasis on teaching English. Included in Part III (sec. 9) is Egerton's description of some aspects of Rossville schooling under the Youngs, followed by Miss Batty's account of some changes that she began to make; her story of the shawls is reminiscent of Miss Adams's tireless production of "caps and bonnets" to replace traditional female head coverings. Both Miss Batty and Ruttan were more insistent in their efforts to promote European dress, and also the use of English, than the Youngs or Peter Badger had been, and the role of Cree in the students' schooling was surely diminished.[41]

Then, in 1877, Miss Batty and the Reverend Orrin German were married, and she joined him at his Oxford mission; her sister, Sarah Elizabeth, evidently stepped in for a while as the Rossville schoolteacher. When the Ruttans left Rossville in June 1879, the Germans moved there from Oxford House, remaining until summer 1883. Orrin German was learning Cree, and by late 1876 he thought he could do without an interpreter: "I am far from being thoroughly master of the language, but I think I shall be able to make myself understood." Available sources do not comment on the closeness of the Germans' involvement with their parishioners. Clementina German, like Ellen Ruttan, had three children baptized at Rossville; both had heavy family duties, and no record indicates that they had an equivalent of Little Mary to help out.[42]

In sum, from 1840 to 1883, a total of nine Methodist missionary wives served with their husbands at Rossville. The only one whom we can know reasonably well, through her own writings and those of others, is Elizabeth Young. Further details about the other wives and their work may be gleaned from closer archival study. But unless new sources surface, it appears that knowledge of them must come mainly from the writings of others. The information

41 In a column titled "Rossville Mission, Norway House," Miss Batty wrote rather disparagingly about Badger: "Unhappily, the school for the last fifteen or sixteen years has been taught by a native teacher, and though the children read the English with tolerable fluency, they neither speak nor understand it." (A copy of the column, probably written in 1876 for *Missionary Notices* or the *Christian Guardian*, is in the Egerton R. Young scrapbook.)

42 *Missionary Notices of the Methodist Church of Canada*, 3rd ser., no. 11 (January 1877), 187; Norway House baptismal register, no. 1896, Williamina Batty, born 18 September 1878; no. 1997, Orrin Charles Clement, born 7 June 1880; and no. 2108, Jacob, born 18 December 1881 and baptized 28 March 1882, noted also as the date of his death.

at hand, however, conveys some sense of the range of variation among them, as well as their similarities. In age, they ranged from the nineteen-year-old Ellen Ruttan to women in their forties. The younger ones were of course more prone to pregnancies; Sophia Mason had at least four children while at Rossville, and Elizabeth Young, Ellen Ruttan, and Clementina German each had three. The Hurlburts, McDougalls, and Stringfellows each had a child born there, too; only the Evanses and Brookings had none. The wives' formal education, so far as known, ranged from small-town schools (Elizabeth Young) to courses of study at ladies' colleges (Ellen Ruttan). Some were daughters of ministers or class leaders (Betsy Hurlburt, Elizabeth Young); Sophia Mason grew up in the Church of England and came to Methodism through marriage.

Elizabeth's work at Rossville paralleled much of what other wives did there — sewing, making garments, visiting the sick — and all bore major responsibilities, even if unspoken, for food and housekeeping. Like Mary Evans, Elizabeth encouraged Cree women's crafting of traditional items. With Little Mary's residency in the household, she had a resource at hand that no other wife likely had, as well as an appreciation for such skills (compare the image of Mrs. Brooking sewing white shirts and dresses to "improve" the appearance of the local Native population). Sophia Mason was unique in her Cree proficiency. Elizabeth, however, worked hard at learning the language, and her practice in singing Cree hymns surely helped. Sources do not mention whether the other wives had their own dog trains, but Elizabeth's team (and driver) certainly extended the scope and independence of her work in the community. She was also on her own more often than most of the other wives. Egerton took seriously the extension of his circuit duties to as many communities as he could reach "by canoe and dog-train," and was often gone for weeks at a time. Evans and George McDougall also travelled widely from Rossville, but the other missionaries do not appear to have taken long trips — except to the Oxford mission and to Red River, with stops along the way.

Methodist churchmen from the mid-1800s to the early 1900s recognized, after their fashion, the critical contributions of missionary wives to their husbands' vocations. As noted in the introduction, the Reverend Morley Punshon, in his valedictory sermon to the Youngs and other missionaries who were about to leave for the northwest in May of 1868, exhorted his listeners to pray that their wives, "with frailer organizations, though perhaps

a well-knit network of nerves — for there is not so much of the robust muscular strength — may be preserved for the trial."

Fifty years later, the Reverend John Maclean devoted the last ten pages
of his *Vanguards of Canada* — brief biographies of thirteen men notable
for their importance to Canadian Methodist missions — to a chapter titled,
"Heroines of Western Canada." "Who shall give a record," he asked, " of the
heroic women of the mission house, far removed from the haunts of civilization, with dusky maids and mothers as their only neighbors, and exposed
to the hardships of the frontier . . . in primitive log houses and disjointed
frame buildings, on the shores of northern lakes and far inland rivers, and
even in the Arctic wilds, women of beauty and refinement have lived in dense
solitude, that they might win a few savages as disciples of the great Christ."
The chapter then related several anecdotes about individual wives and their
courage, faith, and suffering — among them "Mrs. E. R. Young, patient and
faithful, telling the wonderful story of love." Maclean ended with an assur-
ance that "the days of heroic endeavor have not passed away. . . . Brave
women like Mrs. S. D. Gaudin and Mrs. Fred Stevens on Lake Winnipeg,
and others in the far west, are still standing at the outposts of civilization,
guarding the frontier for Christ, and glad of opportunities to do their bit for
the Empire and the human race."[43]

If Elizabeth Young read Maclean's words in 1918 (and she probably did,
as she maintained a life-long relationship with her church and church literature), she doubtless was pleased about his recognition of mission wives
and their work. But she herself never wrote about outposts of civilization,
frontiers, or empire; her portrayals of her work are concrete and down to
earth. "Heroines" is hagiography, with a few anecdotes tucked in, to round
out Maclean's previous 250 pages of stories about heroic mission men. It is
fortunate that a few missionary women on occasion have spoken of their
work and experiences in their own words.

---

43 Maclean, *Vanguards of Canada*, 252, 259, 261–62. Maclean's generalization about
dusky maids did not allow for highly placed HBC officers' wives such as Mrs. Robert
Hamilton (mentioned earlier), whose mother was half Cree, or Mrs. Donald Ross, long-
time resident of Norway House, who, as the daughter of Red River Selkirk settlers, was
not a "dusky" neighbour.

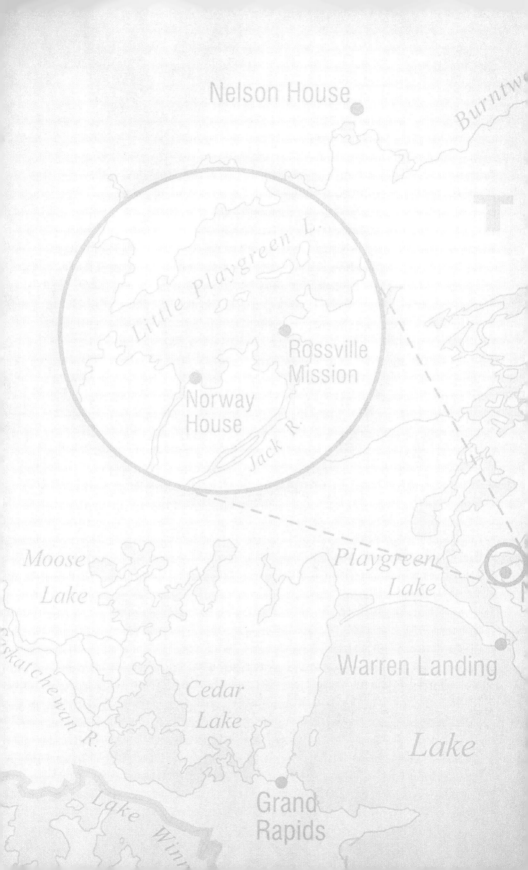

II

"A Missionary and His Son"
and Subsequent Reminiscences,
by E. Ryerson Young

Introduction

In around 1935, E. Ryerson Young, the eldest child of Egerton and Elizabeth Young, composed a memoir of his experiences at Norway House (the Rossville mission) and Berens River titled, "A Missionary and His Son." We know its approximate date because, at the end of chapter 7, "My Mission Sisters," E. Ryerson mentions Elizabeth's burial site (in Bowmanville, Ontario), and she died on 29 May 1934. The manuscript numbers eighty-one typed pages and contains a number of small inked corrections and edits. It is well written and organized, having the look of a text that was prepared with publication in view. But it offers no clue about Young's publishing plans, if any. Possibly he intended it mainly as a contribution to family history — in which he took a keen interest and about which he often wrote. The text is not a chronological narrative; rather, each of the fourteen chapters covers a particular topic or theme.

During the 1930s, Young became increasingly deaf and his eyesight was failing as well.[1] But his mind remained strong, as did his commitment to keep on with his writing as best he could. By the mid-1930s, he had published several books and numerous articles in church publications.[2] Several unpublished manuscripts survive as well, of which the most notable is his biography of Cree singer and performer Frances Nickawa (1898–1928), completed in 1931–32. Nickawa was schooled at Norway House and adopted by a teacher there who brought her to Vancouver, where training in elocution and music

---

1 Young's obituary in the Toronto *Globe and Mail*, 6 March 1962, stated that he lost his sight a year after his retirement and learned to read Braille at the age of sixty-five.

2 The books were novels and short stories set in northern Ontario and on the plains, with a Christian theme; they included *Duck Lake*, *The Camp Doctor*, *Three Arrows*, and *When the Blackfeet Went South*.

launched her on a career that echoed that of Mohawk performer Pauline Johnson (d. 1913) in some respects, yet differed from it in that Nickawa devoted her life to performing on behalf of the Methodist Church and missions, travelling across North America and also to England and Australia. Young met her in Toronto and saw her perform. He could identify with her childhood at Norway House, where he was born, and was much moved by her untimely death in December 1928.[3] His writing of her life doubtless encouraged him to think, soon thereafter, of writing up his own youthful experiences there and at Berens River and to set down his memories of what he later went through in Ontario, branded as "Indian" by schoolmates and others who found him different from themselves.

On 16 January 1962, at the age of ninety-two, he undertook a new effort to record by dictation to his housekeeper not only his memories of his childhood years at his parents' missions but also a record of his later life and his own family. He was not able to complete this task; the last date on which he recorded telling his story was 10 February 1962. ("This is February 10/62," the typescript reads. "I am 92 years old and the only living Minister of my class.") He died on 5 March 1962. But the memoir he managed to compose in that brief period amounted to seventy-five typed pages, ending with an outline of and anecdotes from his service as a Methodist minister in Ontario.[4] At times, it reflects some confusion of memory and chronology. Still, it adds valuable details to his mission memoir of the 1930s.

It also provides a unique account of the family's experiences after leaving the mission field, in the various small-town parishes where Egerton Young served until 1888, when he became a travelling lecturer and author. "Eddie" recounted in lively detail the challenges of being plunged into the foreign setting of Ontario rural life and the vicissitudes of his formal and informal education in his teenage years as the family was moved from one parsonage to another. The Canadian Methodist church still followed the old pattern of itineracy whereby ministers were reassigned every three years to

---

3 For a study based largely on Young's biography, see Jennifer S. H. Brown, "Frances Nickawa: 'A Gifted Interpreter of the Poetry of Her Race,'" in *Recollecting: Lives of Aboriginal Women of the Canadian Northwest and Borderlands*, ed. Sarah Carter and Patricia A. McCormack (Edmonton: Athabasca University Press, 2011), 263–86.

4 The memoir, which was left untitled, in now in the UCCA, Young fonds, series 6, box 11, file 6.

a different posting, a practice that, as Neil Semple observes, "was considered essential for the vitality of Methodism." It also served as "a significant check on clerical independence in conduct or doctrine. . . . Ministers had little time to secure a substantial personal following in the local community." The problem for families was that they could not build long-term community connections, while their children had to change schools every three years, facing new teachers and finding new friends.[5] Eddie's memoir well portrays how that itinerant life affected him and his siblings. He managed to adapt to such an existence both then and later, when he himself joined the Methodist ministry. At the end of his narrative he listed his own itinerancy. From the early 1880s to 1932, he served thirteen different church communities across central and southern Ontario, typically for three-year terms, travelling on horseback much of the time (see fig. 6), as his father and grandfather had done before him.

The first memoir, "A Missionary and His Son," which ends with the the Youngs' departure from Berens River in 1876, is published here in full. It is followed by the latter portion of the 1962 memoir, with its vivid portrait of the Youngs' lives as returned missionaries in Ontario, picking up the story at the point where the earlier memoir closes. In addition, the later memoir sometimes supplies useful details or observations about the mission years that are not found in the 1935 account. On such occasions, passages from the earlier sections of the 1962 memoir have been inserted within square brackets into the text (or, if brief, simply provided in footnotes). The 1935 manuscript shows some over-typing and inked corrections, but punctuation, capitalization, and paragraph breaks are in short supply: E. Ryerson was unable to read and edit the text as he would have desired. I have silently corrected punctuation, spellings of proper names, and other small errors and have added paragraphing to mark new topics as they appear.

Both memoirs say more about the Youngs' years at Berens River than at Norway House. Eddie's time at Norway House ended when he was a little over four years old. He retained some strong memories of life there —

---

5 Neil Semple, *The Lord's Dominion: The History of Canadian Methodism* (Montréal and Kingston: McGill-Queen's University Press, 1996), 232–34. In 1894, the church ruled that, with due permission, "itinerants" could remain with the same congregation for five years, but by then Egerton Young had changed his career path.

notably, the bond he formed with Sandy Harte, the Nelson River boy who lived with the Youngs from mid-1870 until their departure from Norway House in the summer of 1873. However, he engaged much more actively with life at Berens River in 1874–76. There, he evidently enjoyed remarkable freedom for a child aged five to seven, setting traps for rabbits (and the occasional ermine) as Sandy had taught him, driving a small dogsled on his own, and spending time with Ojibwe people who took a particular interest in him, for some good reasons of their own.

At Berens River, Eddie was befriended by a traditional Ojibwe leader, Zhaawanaash, whom he and his father both later wrote about. Egerton Young featured him as "Souwanas" or "Sowanas," a great storyteller and companion to Eddie and his sister Lillian (see the frontispiece), in the informal prose of his book *Algonquin Indian Tales*. This friendship had deeper roots, however, going back to September 1868 and Egerton Young's first visit to Oxford House. There, Young met an old man who "came a long distance to ask me to go and instruct his people. . . . I told him I would send word to Toronto for help. 'Ah!' said he, 'I have asked other Missionaries before, and they have said the same thing, and our hearts have melted within us from long watching.'"[6] The man, as will emerge below, was Bear, or Makwa, traditional chief at Berens River and the older brother of Zhaawanaash, who became chief after Bear died in the winter of 1873–74.

From 1869 to 1873 Young visited Berens River about twice a year, winter and summer, and increasingly urged the Canadian Methodists to consider establishing a mission there. His campaign was reinforced when, in July 1871, a number of men from Berens River visited Rossville itself. The old man acting as their spokesman addressed the missionary: "Do you remember your words of three summers ago?" Young asked, "What were my words to you?" He replied, "Your words were, that you would send to the great kecheayumeawekeemouk — English: Great Praying Masters — for a Missionary for us." In response, Young looked up his letter containing his message to Toronto of October 1868, in which he requested a missionary for Berens River, and translated it for his visitors. "We thank you for that word," the old man replied, *"but where is the missionary?"* As Young wrote,

6 Young, letter dated Rossville, 5 October 1868, *Wesleyan Missionary Notices*, n.s., no. 2 (February 1869), 31.

"I was lost for an answer. . . . I went down before it [the question] like a reed before the storm." He tried to explain that large portions of the world were unconverted and "many years would pass away before all the world was supplied with missionaries." The old man asked, "How many winters will pass away before that time comes? . . . These white hairs, and the presence of my grandchildren in the wigwams, tell me I am getting old." Red River and Norway House had missionaries and schools, he added, and, "I do not wish to die until we too have a church and school." Young, writing to *Wesleyan Missionary Notices* about this conversation, then (successfully) begged the "friends of missions in Canada" to come up with "$200 from you to enable us to commence this mission immediately."[7] In 1873, Young deputed his Cree interpreter and assistant, Timothy Bear, to begin to lay a basis for mission work at Berens River. (But, of course, $200 did not go very far, as the Toronto Wesleyans observed, and Timothy suffered from growing health problems after settling at Berens River.)

Two of Young's books describe other encounters with the old man and help to identify him. In *Indian Wigwams and Northern Camp-fires*, Young wrote that on one of his summer trips to Berens River, he heard a story about a zealous missionary (quite likely the Methodist John Ryerson) who had visited there some years before.[8] Preaching on a Sunday, the visitor declared that, among other things, the Great Spirit had appointed every seventh day as a day of rest, and those who did not keep the Sabbath holy would be punished. An old chief sprang up, rejecting the preacher's words; "I am not afraid to hunt or fish on this day," he declared. Then he jumped into his canoe with his gun and paddled off. Some time later, a shot was heard, and

7 Young, letter dated Norway House, 29 July 1871, *Wesleyan Missionary Notices*, 1 February 1872, 211–12. In response, the next issue of the *Missionary Notices* contained a letter dated Hamilton, 2 March 1872, from Sanford, Vail, and Bickley, strong corporate church supporters, commending Young's "noble work" and instructing "Mr. John Macdonald and the Rev. Dr. [Lachlan] Taylor, Treasurers Wesleyan Missionary Society, Toronto" to "draw upon us for the two hundred dollars necessary to start a mission at Berens River" (copy in Egerton R. Young scrapbook, p. 68).

8 When the Reverend John Ryerson visited Berens River in the summer of 1854, he wrote of two "medicine men" who opposed his speaking to the local Ojibwe people. Jennifer S. H. Brown, "As for Me and My House: Zhaawanaash and Methodism at Berens River, 1874–1883." *Papers of the Fortieth Algonquian Conference*, ed. Karl S. Hele and J. Randolph Valentine (Albany: State University of New York Press, 2012), 81.

shortly afterwards the man appeared, paddling slowly with one hand. The other was nearly shot off, and he had twisted his sash belt around his arm to stop the bleeding. The storyteller, who was present at the time, stated that the chief then said that he should have stayed and listened: "Now I believe there is a God who is angry with and can punish those who do not keep his day." Young found that, on his visits to Berens River, "no Indian more cordially welcomed me than the old man with only one hand."[9]

In *By Canoe and Dog-Train*, Young expanded on how warmly "this venerable old man" received him. At his morning and evening prayers, the old man came and asked him, "Missionary, please pray in Indian, and pray out loud, so that I may hear what you say." Young wrote that he "became very much attached to my old friend with the snow-white hair, who was so hungering and thirsting for the teachings of the Word."

In April 1874, when Young finally arrived at Berens River as resident missionary, he learned with sadness that the old man had died in the winter, always hoping that the missionary would come again to talk and pray with him. At the last, "he raised himself up and said to his son Jacob [Berens], "O, I wish the missionary were here!'"[10] Invited into a wigwam among the old man's relatives, Young learned more about his last days from a grandson. Not long after Young's visit the previous September (1873), the grandson said, "Mismis [*nimishoomis*, my grandfather] got very sick, and after some weeks he seemed to know that he was going to leave us." He called his family together and told them that they should listen to and remember all the good things the missionary said and follow his guidance. As for himself, he said,

9 Young, *Stories from Indian Wigwams and Northern Camp-fires* (New York: Eaton and Mains, 1892), 40–42. Young did not name the man, perhaps echoing Ojibwe etiquette, which avoids using personal names when people already know who is being referred to. A well-known elder might simply be known as *akiwenzii*, the old man; all would know his identity. Young probably last saw Bear on 11–19 September 1873 when he visited Berens River briefly before continuing on to Ontario (Berens River post journal, HBCA B.16/a/7, fos. 22d–23).

10 Young, *By Canoe and Dog-Train Among the Cree and Salteaux Indians* (London: Charles H. Kelly, 1890), 218; *Stories from Indian Wigwams and Northern Camp-fires*, 42. Jacob Berens also fostered his family's acquaintance with missionaries; he was baptized at Rossville by the Reverend George McDougall in 1861. For more on the family, see William Berens, as told to A. Irving Hallowell, *Memories, Myths and Dreams of an Ojibwe Leader*, ed. Jennifer S. H. Brown and Susan Elaine Gray (Montréal and Kingston: McGill-Queen's University Press, 2009), 11–13.

his memory was failing. "Get me my old drum and medicine bag," he told them, "and let me die as did my fathers." The family brought the drum and bag and, "as he drummed he fell, and as he fell he died." Young was "deeply affected" and asked to be shown where the old man was buried — under the place where his wigwam fire had burned, as the ground was otherwise too frozen. Young lingered after the others left, kneeling alone in the snow to "weep out my sorrow as I thought of this old man's precious soul passing into eternity under such strange circumstances."[11]

In 1930, nearly fifty years later, an American anthropologist, A. Irving Hallowell, came to Berens River to do fieldwork. Chief William Berens, who made his work possible, told him his memories of his grandfather, Bear, the eldest son of the great "conjuror" Yellow Legs. Bear, he said, "practiced the old Indian religion," the Midewiwin, and the shaking tent, too, even though he "had lost all the fingers of his left hand except the thumb." "How," he wondered, "could he have shaken the tent himself?" The shaking of the tent proved his grandfather's special powers.[12]

In sum, a gathering of sources shows that Egerton Young's "old man" was Bear, Berens River chief and older brother of the Youngs' friend Zhaawanaash ("Souwanas"), who became chief after Bear died. His relatives, numbers of whom took the surname Berens in the next generation, made it clear that Bear had not converted. But Young seemed to earn the respect and confidence of Bear, as of the other "conjurors" with whom he carried on extensive conversations (Tapastanum at Rossville and later Zhaawanaash). Bear's relatives were surely impressed by Young's expression of grief at his death. Zhaawanaash moved quickly to affirm a relationship with Young, discussing spiritual matters while also enlisting his aid regarding treaty and supply issues, and he and his grown son, Jake or Jacob, took Eddie on expeditions and told him old stories that the boy long remembered.

11 Young, *By Canoe and Dog-Train*, 220–21.

12 Berens, *Memories, Myths and Dreams of an Ojibwe Leader*, 42. See pp. 198–99, n. 15, for Berens River post journal references to Bear, the last dating to mid-October, and probably to his burial, 13 February 1874 ("Buried an old Indian today that died here": HBCA B.16/a/7, fo. 26d). For a detailed discussion of the shaking tent, in which spirit beings offered information about the future or about people or events at a distance, see Jennifer S. H. Brown and Robert Brightman, *"The Orders of the Dreamed": George Nelson on Cree and Northern Ojibwa Religion and Myth, 1823* (Winnipeg: University of Manitoba Press, 1988), 146–57.

The Youngs came to know Jake as Jakoos, probably because his father referred to him by that personal diminutive.[13] Bear also had a son named Jacob — Jacob Berens, who became the treaty chief in 1875 and whose son William was around eight or ten years old at the time the Youngs were at Berens River. The Youngs never mentioned either Jacob Berens or his son William by name in their writings, although the latter, in telling his life story to Hallowell, recalled knowing the missionary, and the Berens family was closely associated with the Methodists. The Youngs' personal tie was with Zhaawanaash — later baptized by the Reverend John Semmens, who had no idea of his importance.[14]

In a letter to me of April 1985, the Reverend H. Egerton Young, E. Ryerson's son, pointed out that his father "was both blind and deaf when he dictated his memoirs" early in 1962, shortly before his death, and indicated that the text "was typed by his housekeeper." The 1935 memoir, he suggested, "may have been typed by Mr. Harry Smith," who assisted his father in Toronto, "after Dad lost his sight." E. Ryerson may still have had some use of his eyes at the time, however, as the 1935 memoir bears signs of his corrections (even though his assistant may have typed it). His hearing loss began much earlier, as his 1962 memoir relates, and brought his pastoral work to an end in 1932.

In the face of his failing eyesight, E. Ryerson still possessed a strong visual memory, which surely helped to hold in place the many details that filled his texts. In "A Missionary and His Son," he commented on his visual recall as he remembered the book of Bible pictures whose stories he told to

13 Jakoos was evidently the "Jake Sowanas, or South-wind," mentioned by Egerton R. Young as the runner leading his dog train on his December 1874 trip with the Reverend George Young from Winnipeg to Berens River (*Stories from Indian Wigwams and Northern Camp-fires*, 283). Young identified Jake as the son of Souwanas in John McDougall's *"Indian Wigwams and Northern Camp-fires": A Criticism* (Toronto: William Briggs, 1895), 16. Another demonstration of the special relationship that existed between Zhaawanaash and the Youngs was Eddie's sister's naming ceremony, held by Zhaawanaash in May 1875 (Brown, "As for Me and My House"). In *Algonquin Indian Tales* (London: Charles H. Kelly, 1903), 17, Young described how "Souwanas and Jakoos" would sometimes arrive together to carry Eddie and Lillian off for stories and a feast (as Eddie recalled in chapter 4 of his memoir).

14 On Zhaawanaash, who retired as chief when his nephew, Jacob Berens, was installed as treaty chief in 1875, see Jennifer S. H. Brown, "As for Me and My House."

the Berens River Indians while his father was waiting for them to come into the church: "I have always loved pictures, and in fact I think my memory is 'pictorial,' for when I could get anything into the shape of a picture it seemed to stay for a long time 'on memory's walls.'" His verbal skills were strong too, as evinced by his ability to master the Cree language and, later, to function in Ojibwe as well. One of his granddaughters, Dale Young, recounted a story he told of walking in the woods with his father. They were identifying a certain plant, and Eddie said, "In our language, Daddy, we call it "————," and he gave the Cree name.[15]

15 Thanks for this story to Dale Young, who spent a lot of time with her grandfather, walking with him and reading to him. She heard about Little Mary and a good many other things that he also recorded in his memoirs.

A Missionary and His Son

1 Born at Norway House

When Louis Riel and his *Metis* were disturbing the peace of Canada's newly-formed province, Manitoba, at the southern end of Lake Winnipeg, in 1869, I came to disrupt the peace of the household of a young missionary and his wife at Rossville Mission, Norway House, at the northern end of that great Western lake. It may be said at once that both the province and the mission house survived these disturbances, and peace, at least intermittent peace, was established after the period of childhood was passed.

The rise of the province of Manitoba, with its rail connections with the older parts of the Dominion of Canada, meant the passing of the glory of Norway House. For many years it was the most important and the strategic centre of the far-flung operations of the Honourable Hudson's Bay Company in the northwestern section of North America. In its Council Hall the directors and factors of "The John Company,"[1] as it was familiarly called by Indians, and its other servants, annually assembled. In the "Compound," hundreds of tripmen — voyageurs *par excellence* — who manned the "great brigades" used to meet as they moved to and fro, carrying the furs to Hudson's Bay and the trade goods to the various outposts of the traders. These were days when Norway House "Fort" was full of life, with its complete quota of Officers of the Company and workshops running at full time, winter, and summer, to keep the brigades supplied with

1 The John Company was a nickname commonly applied to the British East India Company, although not usually to the Hudson's Bay Company. One suggested origin of its use for the East India Company is that it derived from the often written abbreviation, the Hon. Company, which was also a rubric used for the Hudson's Bay Company.

"York" double-pointed, flat-bottomed boats and high-prowed canoes to conquer the rapids on the rivers and the storms on the lake in the summer tripping, and dogs' sleds and harness, etc., etc., for winter travelling. Near the Fort an Indian village of considerable proportions grew up, many of the inhabitants being regular tripmen or servants of the Company, and from among the choice young women of the village, workmen, and even Officers, found their wives.

Thus in the heyday of its glory Norway House had representatives from almost every section of the British Isles — Englishmen, Scotsmen, Irishmen, Orkneymen — as well as the lively "Couriers [coureurs] de Bois" of Quebec. I have been given to understand that I was cordially welcomed by them all, as it was whispered around that I was the first "thoroughbred" white boy born at that place.

So I had my "adoring Magi" and their acts were treasured in my mother's heart. The giant Orkneymen, with their great beards, would hug me to their breasts, and often tears would trickle down their beards as my white face made them think of little ones they had left far away across the wild northern seas. The lively voyageurs would toss me up and catch me with laughter and joy, to the annoyance of my father's great sleigh dogs, which had quickly established themselves as my sworn protectors and did not like this dangerous tossing of their master's son. In fact they became so warlike that some of those men dare[d] not reappear on the mission property, and that demonstration had to be performed when the dogs were *in absentia*. Of all the demonstrations of the white men of the Fort the Indians seemed to be jealous. "He belongs to us," they would say. "He was born here." So they held a big pow-wow and gave me the name of "Sagastaookemou," which, according to their interpretation, meant "The Gentleman from the Sunrise Land." One of the gentlemen of the Fort wrote on a pane of glass in the church with his diamond ring an account of this proceeding. I was told that when the old log church was taken down and replaced by another, the Indians were more concerned about the careful transfer of that pane of glass and its placing in the new church than about anything else. However, that glass has gone now, for the second church was, unfortunately, burned one winter.

But apparently all the Indians who came to do me honour were not so successful in achieving the heights of a white babe's Court etiquette.

In those days, when Indian hunters from outlying districts came in to trade their furs at the Fort they were "treated" by the traders with rum. After they had been so treated and were feeling the effects of the "spree" they determined to visit the mission house. At that time my mother had for a helper a bright-faced Indian girl. At the sight of her in the kitchen, mischief at once took possession of these visitors, "for beauty provoketh thieves sooner than gold," Shakespeare says, or, we may add, the adoration of a babe.[2] So they started to chase the girl, who screamed and beat them off. Mother, who was in the inner room, hearing the disturbance, quickly rolled me in my blankets, shoved me into a little "cubby-hole" under the stairs, and pushed the dining table against the door of my hiding place. Then she ran out of the front door to get help. She found some Christian Indians from the village, who came and sent the drunken visitors about their business.

But what a wreck they had made of that little dining room! Not meeting with any success with the girl, except terrifying her, they had pushed on to the inner room. They tore the pictures from the walls and smashed the chairs. Fortunately for me, upon that occasion I did not attempt to acknowledge the adoration of these visitors and made no outcry. So when the Indians took their departure my mother almost forgave the visitors for their demonstrations as she found her babe untouched, and so unharmed.

When my father returned home and realized what had been done he was not so easily satisfied. He laid his complaint before the officers of the Company, and as there was a "Grand Council" of the managers shortly afterwards he took the matter up with them, with the result that an order was adopted that henceforth no more "treats" were to be given to the Indians.[3]

2 The reference is to *As You Like It*, act I, scene 3.

3 Young's complaint appeared to coincide with a shift in company policy. On 18 August 1870, Chief Factor Robert Hamilton told the Reverend Henry Budd at The Pas that at a council at Norway House, the company "had abandoned the use of Rum, with all kinds of spirituous Liquors, as an article of Trade throughout the whole of the Territory" (*The Diary of the Reverend Henry Budd, 1870–1875*, ed. Katherine Pettipas [Winnipeg: Manitoba Record Society, 1974], 36). Enforcement, of course, was another issue.

Little Mary

Thus, early, a "Temperance battle" was fought over my little head. But if strong drink caused some of my "worshippers" to misbehave and to be driven away, in a very strange manner it brought to me one of the best and most comforting friends of my childhood. We called her "Little Mary," and this is her story:

She was the daughter of a chief, tall, athletic, straight as a young pine, and skilled in dealing with furs, deerskins and all manner of needlework.[4] Her father was a pagan, and according to the custom of the Indians that had been untouched by Christianity he sold his daughter to the man who had brought him his price. Mary went away submissively with "her man." Being ambitious, she inspired him to work hard at his hunting, while she dressed the beautiful furs he brought in. She made him a fine deerskin coat and adorned it with all her skill. So when they visited the trading post the next spring they had a valuable pack of furs. Mary had discussed with her husband what they were to receive for these furs. He was to get a suit of clothes and she was to have cloth for a dress. Each was to have a new gun and he some more traps, so that they might do better in the next winter's hunt. Blankets and supplies were considered, and like two happy young white people, they looked forward to a prosperous married life.

Indian custom in those days left the trading entirely to the men. So Mary's husband went to the post with the furs, while Mary was left to build the wigwam. One day passed and the husband did not return. "Oh, well," thought Mary, "He is cautious and is buying slowly and carefully."

Two days passed. Three days passed, and no sign of the man, Mary then became anxious, and even suspicious.

On the fourth afternoon, as she was looking through the woods toward the trading-post, she saw an Indian, coatless, come staggering through the trees. As he came nearer, the truth, and the whole truth, dawned upon her. Before he had started to bargain over those fine furs he had been "treated" to white man's rum. Then he wanted more and more, until not only were the furs all sold for rum, but also the beautiful coat that she had made for him.

---

4 This was Mary Robinson, whose sewing skills Elizabeth Young remarked on: see Part III, sec. 6. Egerton R. Young, in *Algonquin Indian Tales* (London: Charles H. Kelly, 1903), 32, recorded her husband's surname.

Mary had a sharp tongue and was as eloquent as any of her forebears in any war council, and all her fury blazed into fire that day, as she tongue-lashed that man. Then, with a feeling of disgust and frustration she turned from the man and would hide herself in her tent. The drunken sot, not able to say a word in reply to her angry outburst, looked around to see what revenge he could have. Unfortunately, an axe lay handily by. He seized it and ran at her in his fury and struck her across her back. The blade was buried in her vertebrae. With a scream she fell to the ground. That scream roused the man to what he had done. He ran into the woods and was never seen or heard of again.

Poor Mary's scream was heard by some Indians and they came to her. But they knew not what to do for her. Her own relatives, as pagans, called in their "medicine men." They were of no help, and the sufferer lay for months in agony and neglect. Her own people had grown weary of looking after her, when she was discovered by some of the Norway House hunters who were members of our church. They did what they could for her and told her they were sure that if she would let them take her to Norway House the missionary could help her.

At first Mary did not like to think of this, for she had been proud of her father and her Indian ancestry and had said many times: "The religion that is good enough for my father is good enough for me." But now her father's people had deserted her and left her in the hands of these strangers upon whom she had no claim. They had been kind and gentle and had done all they could for her, as they said, "for the love that was in their hearts." At last they won her consent to come back with them to Norway House. They brought her down in a large canoe that they had made for the purpose and took her into their own home. Here the missionary had met her and he did what he could for the woman whose back had been so cruelly wounded.[5]

5 Both this and the 1962 account suggest that Mary's people were "Wood Indians" (mentioned also by Elizabeth) of the Cross Lake area — living at some distance from the mission. The 1962 memoir adds that some of her Norway House relatives took her in and that "Mother was soon at her side . . . arranging for her comfort. For some time, mother's visits were almost daily, but it was a long, long time before she was able to walk." When she finally visited the mission house, "she looked around to see if there was anything she could do to express her thanks. She saw a little black haired boy in his cradle and she exclaimed, 'Oh, I'll take care of him,' and she constituted herself as my nurse."

After many more weeks of nursing and care Mary was at last able to rise from her bed. But it was not the tall, athletic young woman who had gone so bravely into the forest with "her man." Her back was bent and she looked like a hunchback. Little Mary soon found her way to the mission house. She said she wanted to do something for the missionary and for the people who had been so kind to her. When she saw the baby boy she made a quick decision. She installed herself as my nurse. The Indians were pleased with this and neither of the parents had any cause to regret it. But to the boy she was "an Angel of love."[6]

2 So Little to Do With

While Norway House as a centre of fur-trading has declined, and the buildings of the Fort suffer from disrepair and the Indian village has all but vanished, the place now boasts of several Residential Schools under the management of religious denominations, an Experimental Farm, an Airways Station, and an outpost of the Royal Canadian Mounted Police. Above all, it has a hospital with resident physician and his staff. How different it was in the early seventies of the last century! The storehouses of the traders were full of furs for export, or with imported goods for trading — all the buildings spick and span, and the workshops humming with hardworking and clever mechanics, Indians and white, working side by side, and the "Compound" often crowded with voyageurs in summer or with dog-teams in winter, with one day school and one lone missionary, whose amateur medical skill and his mission house were all the doctor and hospitalization the place afforded!

My mother's one complaint, as she looked with retrospect upon those days of pioneer service, was, "we had so little to do with." Still, that brave little woman and her husband, with that "little" at their command — little log house, little food and less clothing, little communication with the outside world, three or four hundred miles from the nearest "regular doctor" or "registered nurse" — did not hesitate to use their "little" in the fullest possible way for the advantage of their parishioners.

6 For a more detailed account of Little Mary, see Jennifer S. H. Brown, "A Cree Nurse in a Cradle of Methodism: Little Mary and the Egerton R. Young Family at Norway House and Berens River," in *First Days, Fighting Days: Women in Manitoba History*, ed. Mary Kinnear (Regina: Canadian Plains Research Center, 1987), 19–40.

Sandy Harte

A sample case of their work along this line brought to me one of the most interesting of my childhood friends. On one of his extended trips [to the Nelson River, in September 1869], in his apostolic eagerness, to Indian bands "in regions beyond," my father came upon a bright-faced Indian boy who was lying under a rabbit-skin "blanket" in a wigwam on a summer day.

"Why are you not out running about with the other boys on a lovely day like this?" the missionary asked.

For his answer the boy threw back the covering, and the missionary was saddened to see one of the boy's hips badly mangled by a gunshot wound that had rendered him helpless.

After speaking a few words of sympathy to the boy, the missionary sought the father and asked him what were his plans for the lad's treatment. He was shocked to learn that the Indians had come to the conclusion that as the boy would never again have the use of his limbs and be a good hunter the best thing was to destroy him so that he would not be a burden to the tribe.[7] My father remonstrated with them and said that they should send the boy to some place where his wound might be treated and he educated. He might later return and be their school teacher. Then after doing what he could for the wounded boy, the missionary pressed on with his evangelistic tour.

Not long after he had returned to Norway House a large canoe came to the mission "dock," and when the missionary hastened down to see who had arrived in such a canoe he found the wounded boy surrounded by his father and his friends.[8]

"We have brought the boy as you said," declared the Indians. "We would like to have him healed and educated so that he might come back to us and teach our children."

My father had not offered to undertake such a task when he impulsively made the suggestion. The "little to do with" was, at that time, even more straitened by disturbances in Manitoba, and communications with the

7 This varies from Egerton Young's account in his *Indian Life in the Great North-West* (Toronto: Musson Book Company, [1899?]), 14, in which he stated that Sandy, as the chief's son, was being cared for. Young also reported to the *Christian Guardian*, in a letter of 29 September 1869, that the "principal Chief" spoke warmly after the services: "I see every day that which convinces me there must be such a god as has been described to us."

8 He would have arrived in early summer 1870, once canoe travel became possible.

outside world were almost entirely cut off. It was a severe test of faith, but the missionary and his wife opened their hearts and home and took the boy in.

He was in a grievous state from neglect — not only with a neglected wound, but neglect of body, and clothing alive with vermin. But the missionary and his wife labored over him with all their love and skill. He was really only a "wild boy" from the woods, and he must have been frightened when he saw his clothing thrust into the fire, had his hair shaved off, and other "heroic" measures taken with his wounded leg.[9] But the work of the missionaries with the body seemed to be the least of their troubles. He was far from being an amiable or an eager pupil of the white man's ways of thinking. He was, however, wonderfully skilled in Indian arts. He could make the best of snowshoes and was an expert hunter when taken out on a dogsled along a trail. So the missionaries prized him for the good work he did, patiently labored for his mental improvement, and prayed for the enlightenment of his mind and soul. They had their reward, and perhaps, I played a little part, for from the first I liked him and he saw how readily I accepted him as a friend. Whatever he did for me pleased me. He made many little things, such as bows and arrows and snowshoes. When I was able to run about he showed me how to set rabbit snares, and in this way we made some contribution to the dinner table. When the dogs were not all needed for tripping we were allowed to take two old trusties and a sled and go a little farther afield and there set our snares.

The boy was named Sandy Harte, and in time was able to hobble around with the aid of a crutch. Then he went back to his own band and served them for years as their schoolmaster.[10] The lessons he taught me as a hunter I did not forget.

9 This varies from his parents' first-hand accounts, in which the clothes were not burned but washed and returned and no mention was made of the cutting or shaving of hair; instead, Elizabeth lent or supplied combs. Eddie, who was very young when Sandy arrived, may have generalized from what he later heard of the practices in residential schools.

10 It is difficult to trace Sandy Harte's career, as the Nelson River mission was irregularly staffed and funded. The Reverend Orrin German, in a letter dated 17 August 1881 and reprinted in the *Missionary Outlook*, no. 2 (1882): 15, reported that on a June trip to Nelson River he found about sixty children of school age and that "Sandy Horte [*sic*] has undertaken to teach them the syllabic characters during the summer. Sandy is a very earnest and faithful leader. I hope he may get a small allowance for teaching during the summer." For further details on Sandy's interest in Cree syllabics, see Part III, sec. 7.

Trapping at Berens River and Troubles with Ermine

After serving at Norway House Mission for five years father was sent to
Berens River to organize a mission there. That point was considered a most
desirable place for the Indians to establish a village as an overflow from
Norway House.[11] The advantage to me of this place was that it enabled me
to do a little more and better hunting close to the mission house. The last
winter I was there I had two score or more snares and would visit them
regularly. I was so successful as a hunter that it got my family into trouble.

The Hudson's Bay Company claimed a monopoly over all furs caught
in the country. Along with rabbits, ermine would get into my snares. The
appearance of these in the mission kitchen pleased both mother and Little
Mary. A little fair-faced chubby sister [Lillian] had come, who was a grand
playmate. Mary took these ermine skins and dressed them beautifully, and
skillfully made a lovely ermine coat for my sister.[12] Spying Indians had seen
these ermine skins being dressed by Mary, and they had reported their
discoveries to the trader at the Hudson's Bay Company's post. He came hot-
footed to the mission house and demanded what the missionaries meant by
buying furs from the Indians, adding that they had better "change their business." As father happened to be away, my mother had to suffer the brunt of
the attack. She resented the charge and said they had bought no furs from
the Indians, that her own little boy had caught the ermine that had come
into the house. The trader had seen me, a little boy, over at the post, playing with his children, and he could not believe her words. When my father
learned of the visit he immediately went to the post and told the trader that
if he had any complaints to make he was to deal with him, and not with his
wife, and also intimated that he had been longer in the country than had
the trader, and that he had friends among the managers of the Company.[13]

11 Egerton Young hoped that many Rossville people would indeed choose Berens River,
but instead a good many were directed towards Sandy Bar (White Mud River) where
resources were few (*By Canoe and Dog-Train Among the Cree and Salteaux Indians*
[London: Charles H. Kelly, 1890], 168–69).

12 The 1962 memoir added that "when I visited my sister [Lillian, in 1937] in England,
she said some of that jacket is in existence today."

13 The complaining trader was not named. The HBC clerk most often mentioned by the
Youngs was James Flett, from Birsay, Orkney, who was serving at Nelson River in 1869
when Young first visited there and was then at Norway House and Rossville. It seems
unlikely, however, that he was the one who took so hostile a view of the matter — and
he had been in the HBC service since 1846. HBCA biographical sheets: Flett, James (B).

One day, when the skins were laid out and ready for sewing into the coat, some more "spies" reported that they had seen "many, many skins," and again the trader hastened over in high wrath. It was a snowy day, but with my two dogs and sled I had made my rounds and came into the mission kitchen all covered with snow, and with my "catch" in my hands.[14] I found the Trader there and my mother in tears.

"There he is," said my mother. "He has caught every skin that we have here."

The man turned, seized my shoulder in his strong grip and shook me. "Where's the Indian that caught these furs?" he demanded loudly.

"I had no Indian," I replied. "I caught these all by myself."

He stormed at me and asked again and again, who was the Indian that set my snares and took out the ermine? I shook myself free of his grip and said: "I don't need any Indian now to help me. Sandy taught me and he never came to this place."

In the "contest" over me my father weakened and said that for the sake of peace and "the good they wished to do," I had better give up my hunting.

My mother did not see it that way. "This is none of their business," she declared. "It is our boy's own work and pleasure. The trader has no monopoly rights and this is a free country now." Neither the trader nor my father shook her assertion of "free rights" for her boy and I continued my hunting.[15]

14 Egerton Young, in his lightly fictionalized *Hector, My Dog: His Autobiography* (Boston: W. A. Wilde, 1905), chap. 8, described how Eddie (Sagastao) learned to drive a dog sled and work with dogs.

15 Both the HBC and the churches were on the alert for signs of missionaries trading in furs. On 31 March 1873, Young complained in a letter to the *Christian Guardian* that after some church officials had visited their western missions the previous summer, "some busy-bodies were circulating the erroneous idea that we were becoming fur-traders." He added that others "will answer for themselves," but, as for himself: "The best fur cap I have in the world is a second-hand one sent out in charity by Mr. Sanford, of Hamilton; and my wife's best, is one made out of the one I wore all last winter." (This may be the hat worn by Young in figure 11.) The Reverend John McDougall was to have some conflicts and trouble over his dealing in furs: see James Ernest Nix, "McDougall, John Chantler," *Dictionary of Canadian Biography* online.

3 Going to Church

Of course I was taken early to church services. How early I do not remember. But Indians did not stay home because of their babes. An Indian mother has had a babe on Monday and been at church the following Sunday. Going to church was too much of a luxury for them to let even babies keep them home.

It is not recorded either how early I asserted my protest against the complete indifference of mission churches towards the comfort of children and to the discomfort of benches and high seats. As I had a mind of my own, and also the courage to make its viewpoint known, "church behaviour" was not mastered too quickly. Anyway, there were many things happening in a mission church that were not conducive to perfect reverence on the part of a lively boy. The church had a single aisle up the middle. On one side sat the men and boys, and on the other the women and girls. A row of pegs was also on the wall on each side. The men hung their caps, some of which were beautifully beaded [see fig. 10], or their black "slouch" hats, if they were wealthy enough to buy such from the traders. The women, on their side, hung their babies on the pegs. These babes were laced up in "moss-bags" fastened to boards with a wooden band like a basket handle over the front of the board. Only the faces of the babes were to be seen. And what an array they were! Black-eyed, bronze-cheeked and fat, generally with doleful looks upon their countenances, unless they undertook to protest and raise a cry. This would sometimes start a chorus that would rival the Indian choir, which occupied the left-hand corner of the platform, while the "official" pew of the Hudson's Bay Company Officers was on the raised platform to the right of the minister.

Indians have been declared "imperturbable" by many writers, and their general conduct in Divine worship exceptionally reverent. Small boys, however, notice small things, such as petty attempts of the girls to imitate any new style that appeared in the Traders' pew that was so glaringly set before them, [as] for example, when a Trader brought home a bride "from Winnipeg" who had a veil that came part way down her face. At prayer time the girls who had hair-nets were busy with their heads under their shawls, and when the "Amen" was said and the shawls were slipped back, these girls had their nets pulled forward and hitched to the ends of their noses.

Little Mary's Defence of Her Charge

The day came, however, when I had transgressed beyond bounds and father thought that I should be punished for my misconduct in the church services. What happened has been repeated so often that I might here give it as I have heard it from my parents:[16]

"What are you going to do, Missionary?" Little Mary the Indian nurse, asked, as she hurriedly approached the missionary and his son and tried to crowd in between them and place herself in a position of protection over the boy.

"The boy has misbehaved in church, Mary, and he must be punished and made to respect the House of God," he replied, and proceeded to use a birch switch that he had cut from the woods on his way home from the log mission church. Mary, with greater energy, crowded in to protect her precious charge. Like most of the Indians of the place, she could never see anything wrong in the boy, and did not approve of whipping a boy, anyway. A boy, she thought, should be brave and courageous. Physical punishment was both humiliating and tended to break his spirit.

"Stand aside, Little Mary," the missionary said gently (for he respected this Indian nurse), yet firmly, for when he undertook a task he usually saw it through.

Little Mary did not stand aside, but held her ground, and straightened herself as well as she could. "Missionary," she said quickly, for she had been thinking very hard, "haven't you been teaching us Indians to keep holy the Sabbath day?"

"Yes, Mary, I have," he replied. "But what has that to do now? Stand aside, for I must punish this boy."

But Little Mary went on: "And haven't you been telling us that we should not do anything on the Sabbath day that we can do on other days, that it is doing unnecessary work on the Sabbath?"

"Yes, Mary," said the missionary, somewhat shortly. "But please stand aside, so that I may get on with my work."

---

16 This event probably happened at Rossville, as "Eddie" wrote that he was drawing more on his parents' retelling of it than on his own memory, and Mary made the point the next day that he was too young to understand the belated punishment.

"You could punish this boy some other day, Missionary," Little Mary asserted, pressing home her argument, "and if you do it today you will be doing unnecessary work."

The missionary, in his turn, straightened himself up and looked at the Indian nurse. Her eyes, however, were upon the boy. She knew that her words had struck home, for the threatening switch had been lowered. The missionary thought that there was something in what Little Mary had said and he must not be inconsistent.

"You can punish him some other day," Little Mary added, making sure of her victory, "and you will not be breaking the Sabbath."

"Well," said the missionary, "take the boy away, but bring him back to me tomorrow morning." Mary threw her arms about the boy's shoulders and hurried him away as though fearful that the white man might change his mind and even yet punish her darling boy. The missionary laid the birch switch on pegs on the wall, so that it would be handy for the morrow.

The next day he called for his son, and Little Mary appeared also. "What are you going to do, Missionary?" Little Mary asked blandly.

"Why, Mary, you understand," the Missionary replied. "You got the boy away yesterday, but you were to bring him back today for his well-deserved punishment."

Mary had not made any promise to bring her charge to be punished. Her head, however, hung down, for she was thinking hard. "Missionary," she said, earnestly, "does it do anyone any good if you punish them for anything they do not know anything about?"

"I don't suppose it does, Mary," he replied, and almost smiled as he saw the Indian woman twisting herself around the boy.

But Mary did not smile. Punishment may be an amusement to the punisher, but it is not to the punished, nor to those who feel for him.

"Missionary," Little Mary said as she slyly looked at him, "you know that little boys have short memories. If you punish this boy now he will not know what you are punishing him for and you will hurt him and do no good by it."

"Well, Mary," the missionary said forcefully, "but you had better see to it that the boy behaves, for if I catch him in mischief again I'll punish him right on the spot."

Little Mary and Storytelling at Rossville

There was another way that father attempted to punish me in his adherence to the commands of King Solomon not to spoil a child by soft usage. The Mission house was constructed of logs and was an affair of a story-and-a-half. A stairway without railing went from the middle or dining room to the attic. The under part of the stairway was boarded in and made a convenient "cubby-hole." One day when my conduct met with parental displeasure I was landed in this cubby-hole and the door was shut. Sometime afterwards, when my father thought I had had enough of solitary confinement to consider my ways and learn to be wise, he opened the door and said: "Well, my boy, are you ready to come out?"

"Oh, no, Daddy," came the astonishing reply, "not as long as Little Mary will stay here and tell me Indian stories." Into that little hole the loving nurse had crowded herself and had endured its cramped space to comfort and entertain her charge.

This experience gave my father much food for thought. Whatever had that Indian woman told that boy that made him so satisfied with the dark hole that he was ready to stay there and listen to her? A few days afterwards, when he thought perfectly amicable relations had again been established between himself and his son and that old things had been forgotten (though, to tell the truth, that son adored his father, and such resentment as arose from anything in the way of chastisement disappeared like the morning dew), the father said: "What stories does Little Mary tell you, that you like so much to hear?"

I told him some of the Indian legends, and he was soon as deeply interested in these Indian stories as I was. He wrote down all that he heard in the Northland and sought for more. About thirty years after the cubby-hole incident he wrote his book, "Algonquin Indian Tales" [1903] in which he told the legends that interested him most. At that time the occupant of the White House, Washington, was the distinguished President Theodore Roosevelt. Mr. Roosevelt sent my father a letter saying that it was the most interesting book that had come to the family reading table that winter.[17]

---

17 A letter from Theodore Roosevelt to Young, dated 20 June 1907, reflected their prior contact and also alluded to author Jack London's borrowing some of Young's writings on dogs: "Your letter gave me real pleasure and I look forward to receiving the copy of 'My Dogs in the Northland.' London's faults are far graver than those I touched on. . . . I know of your work, not merely as a writer but as a missionary under very hard circumstances, and I hope you will let me express to you my personal regard and good wishes." Copy in JSHB collection.

The Question of Discipline

But lest anyone might think that I escaped well-deserved punishment from my parents through Little Mary's watchful and quick-witted protection, there is another side to be told. Little Mary could never put any tricks or arguments over my mother. These two women got along well together, but whipping was one point upon which they tremendously disagreed.

"Stand aside, Mary," mother would say. "I'll not allow anyone to come between me and my child."

Then, when Little Mary saw that there was no avail to save the boy she would snatch her shawl from its peg, and, throwing it over her head, would rush out of the house. She would not stay and work for a woman who whipped her son.

And as Mary stayed away this was a serious matter for the mother, for the boy had two little sisters and household tasks were onerous in those primitive surroundings. However, without a murmur mother would rearrange her work and carry on. She knew her Indian nurse would come back to that boy, if not to her, and the little girls. And it was so. Sometimes Little Mary's anger burned for three days, but that was the limit. Then, while playing in the yard about the house the boy would hear a whistle. He would know that no bird ever made that sound and would look sharply at the bushes. At last he would see what he had suspected — Mary peeking out from the side of a bush. The boy would rush to her, throw his arms about her neck, and fairly drag her into the house. Little Mary would then hang her shawl on its accustomed peg and things would go on as though there had been no interruption in the household routine. Neither woman would make any reference to what had happened.[18]

18 "Eddie," in his 1962 memoir, related a specific dispute between his mother and Little Mary at Berens River: "Mother was sitting in her rocking chair in the corner of the living room sewing. Beside her were her little girl and boy. Lillie snatched something out of my hand and I slapped her. Mother quickly dropped her sewing, seized me by the back of my coat and put me face down across her knee, and reached for a clothes brush that had a long handle. Little Mary, coming in from the kitchen, saw what was taking place and quickly crossed the room. She put her hand on the little boy's [back] between the little boy and the brush, and caught the blow. Mother was very angry and said, 'Stand back. I'll not let anyone come between me and my child,' and struck me again with the brush. Little Mary left the room as much annoyed as mother was. She went to a peg in the kitchen, took down her shawl, and left the house. Mother did not say anything. She put the boy down on the floor and put aside her sewing. She went to the kitchen, looked over the stove to see how things were progressing, made necessary touches to what was cooking, and then went back to her sewing. Supper was served in due course but with no little Mary."

4 "Lend Me Your Little Boy"

To the annoyance of Little Mary, I found other Indians who would tell me Indian stories and legends. Perhaps what annoyed Little Mary most was that in visiting the wigwams of these story-tellers I would eat what they gave me — fish or rabbit or partridge — and would come home with face and hands, and often clothes, very dirty. The psychological reaction from the stories that I heard may also have had some effect, for these Indians rather delighted in stories that had a cruel suggestion in them, and this did not improve the native cruelty that was in me.

Here is a sample of these stories. Nanahbazhoo was a lively mischief-maker. Being a Great Windegoo,[19] he could take the form of any animal or bird in the woods. One day he took the form of the jay we call the "Whisky-jack." He visited the wigwam of two blind men. They were good fellows and worked quietly on baskets or canoes that other Indians had set before them. They seemed too good and happy to please the mischievous Nanahbazhoo. Then he went to their wigwam he watched them to see what he could do to annoy them. Occasionally he would fly down and remove a tool which one of the Indians had laid down, but if the other discovered it he quietly put it back where his friend might find it. Not doing much this way, the mischief-maker flew up into the tree and bided his time. This came when the Indians brought out their food. As soon as one picked up a piece of meat to eat it into his mouth the jay swooped down and snatched it out of his hand. The poor blind man accused the other Indian of snatching his food from him. This the other quickly denied. Then when the second took some food and was about to put it into his mouth, the jay swooped down and caught that away also. And then he in his turn accused the other Indian of snatching away his food. This was angrily denied. Then the first one tried again, but once more the food was caught away before it reached his mouth. He then snatched up a stick of wood and flung it at the other, hoping to hit him. The stick did not, however, but the other realized what had been done.

19 A "Windegoo," or windigo (Cree, *wîhtikô*), is in fact a distinct powerful, cannibalistic being associated with winter and ice; human beings can also become windigos, developing a craving for human flesh. Nanabozho or Nanabush (the more common spellings) has a Cree counterpart, Wisakedjak — the name more often used at Berens River.

Then, when he had another piece of food stolen from him, he jumped up, and, running at his companion, started to beat him. How Nanahbazhoo laughed to see these two friendly old blind Indians roused to fury over their stolen food fighting each other.

When the blind men heard the raucous laugh of the jay they knew they had been tricked by the mischievous Nanahbazhoo and quickly stopped their quarrelling and fighting. They apologized to each other and said they must be on their guard not to be tricked into fighting again. This sort of story did not make me any kinder to dogs or to Indian boys.

It used to puzzle my people to see great sleigh dogs, that immediately resented even lifting a stick against them, stand perfectly still and let me pound away on their backs. In some way they seemed to know that I was the son of their master and a sort of privileged character, even in a passion of anger. Perhaps the Indians looked upon me in a similar light.

One day my father caught me hammering an Indian boy who was a head taller than I was. The boy was standing quietly while I beat him about the legs with a stick. Whatever my father said just then I do not now remember, but he took me into the house. Little or nothing more was said until dinner time. For dessert that day we had a little cracked wheat porridge, but it was so rare and such a treat in that mission home that it was called "pudding." When my dish was placed before me my father said: "You were very naughty to hit that Indian boy the way you did. Now you must take that pudding out to him and tell him that you are sorry that you hit him, and ask him to accept this from you."

I stoutly protested. My father seemed pleased that he had found a way to punish me that made me appreciate what I had done. He had to be obeyed, however, and so in the end I had to carry out his command. I took the pudding out to the waiting boy and hurried in to hide my anger and falling tears.

The young Indian quickly disposed of the pudding and brought back the empty dish. As my father took the dish from him the Indian boy said: "If you will give me another dish of that I'll let the little boy hit me again." As I overheard this I think my parents realized that their attempt to chastise me had "backfired."

In spite of the protests of Little Mary, I was not stopped from visiting the Indians in their wigwams. In fact, if I did not go often enough to suit them they came for me. Here is a colloquy that my mother has often told me:

One day a big Indian approached her. "Lend me your little boy?" he said.

"You have plenty of children in your wigwam," mother replied. "Go and care for them."

"My papooses are all right," he said. "My wife throws a net into the water and catches plenty of fish and feeds the children and keeps them fat. Lend me your little boy."

"What do you want of my little boy?" asked my mother.

"He likes Indian stories," the Indian declared. "I'll give him a boat ride and tell him a story." So he carried me away.

The big Indian would put me in his canoe and paddle through the most picturesque surroundings to one of the beautiful islands. In the most primitive manner, often with just a string, a bent pin and a bit of red flannel cut from his shirt, he would catch a fine fish. This he would wrap in marsh grass and mud. He would make a fire on the sandy beach. When this had burned down he would pull away the embers, dig into the sand, place the fish in the hole and pull the hot sand back over the fish. Then, while the fish was cooking, he would tell me an Indian story.

Jakoos Tells of the Flood and the New Earth

Here is one that would be quite appropriate to the place, and of which I never tired hearing. In his mischief-making the Great Nanahbazhoo had gone too far. Like many naughty people, he did not know when it was time to quit his nonsense. He made many enemies and they gathered together and drove him westward, far up into the mountains, and they appealed to the god of the waters to put an end to him. So the rivers overflowed and the whole land became a great waste of waters. Up and up the mountains Nanahbazhoo climbed. Then when he saw that the god of the waters meant to drive him out of the world, he took great trees and made a raft for himself, and on it he floated out on the waters. He did not go alone, for some of the strong swimming animals, like the otter, the beaver, the mink and muskrat joined him; also the wolf, the fox, some mice and other animals.

After floating about many days Nanahbazhoo said: "If I only had a little of the old world I could make a new and a better world." So he and the animals talked over the matter, and it was conceded that the otter was the best swimmer and that he should make a try to get some of the earth of the old world.

The otter accepted the challenge, and with a great plunge, he disappeared into the wild waste of waters. All eyes watched for the first sign of his return. Sure enough, he came again to the surface. But, alas, he was limp and appeared almost lifeless!

Nanahbazhoo took him out of the water and laid him on the raft. The otter revived and said that he had gone a long way down, but had not been able to find the land.

Then the Great Windegoo said to the beaver: "You are a grand swimmer. You may not swim quite so fast as Otter, but you are stronger, and so ought to go farther than he did."

The big fat beaver accepted the challenge, as had the otter, and with a jump and a splash disappeared in the water. He was away a much longer time than Otter, and it was thought that he had surely won his way to the old world. But to their disappointment, when his body broke the surface he was upside down. His pluck and determination to win where Otter had failed nearly cost him his life. Nanahbazhoo pulled him in and laid him on the raft to regain his breath. As the two great swimmers of the woodland waters had been conquered, for a time it seemed as though there was no chance of getting Nanahbazhoo some earth so that he might make a new world.

Then Mink spoke up and volunteered to try where the others had failed. There were some that laughed at the idea of Mink succeeding where Otter and Beaver had been baffled, but when in straits there is no choice of your champions. So Mink was allowed to make a try to touch ground and bring up some of the coveted earth.

The Mink is almost as fast a swimmer as the Otter, and it could be seen going through the water like a brown arrow. Then it was out of sight. Alas, for all his bravery, Mink was seen floating on the surface! His neat, shapely little body, with its active muscles, was now limp and lifeless! In pity Nanahbazhoo drew the little fellow out of the water and scanned his body to see if there was any life left in it. Then he breathed on it and the Mink came back to life.

With Otter, Beaver and Mink conquered, all hope seemed gone, and a spirit of gloom settled over the group until someone turned to the chubby little muskrat and said: "Why, here is Muskrat! He can cut his way through beaver dams, he is so strong! And see how long he can stay under water without having to come up for air! He may succeed where the others have failed."

"That is so," said Nanahbazhoo. And he turned to see what the chubby little muskrat had to say about it.

"I can but try and do my best," he said. "I cannot do worse than fail as these fine fellows have done."

So he gathered himself for his plunge. He was not the neat, clean-cut diver that Mink was. He flopped into the water and made almost as big a splash as did Beaver. He seemed so clumsy that he made his watchers laugh at him. But he meant business, nevertheless, and was soon under the surface of the water and swimming as hard as he could for the earth. He was away as long a time as Beaver, and, in fact, some thought that he would not come back. When they were giving up hope his body was seen to break the surface of the water, but he was limp and he appeared to be as lifeless as the others. Nanahbazhoo, with a feeling of hopelessness, brought in the body of this brave little champion and handled it gently. As he was caressing the body Nanabbazhoo noticed that Muskrat clutched his claws tightly.

"Oh, joy!" he exclaimed. "Muskrat has succeeded where the others have failed. He has brought back some of the earth of the old world. It is a very little bit, to be sure, but it is enough."

So he carefully gathered all the bits of earth from the claws of Muskrat and blew upon it until it was very dry. He worked on it and it grew larger in his hands. Then he spread it like a little lily-pad and placed it on the water. Here it grew more quickly and it seemed to become quite strong. To test it Nanahbazhoo placed the mice upon it and they ran around and around and seemed to be overjoyed at their new freedom. The fox was the next to try the new earth, and it held him all right, but he did not go far, for he seemed to be afraid of falling into the water, or that the new earth would break off and leave him on an island. ("The fox is a silly fellow, anyway," put in the Indian.) By this time no one could see the ends of the new earth. Every way one looked, it had passed the horizon, and even some bushes appeared and little trees.

Nanahbazhoo then told Wolf to try and see if he could tell them how far the new world had gone and how great it was. The wolf ran away in almost a straight line and went so far that he disappeared from their sight. He never came back. Then Nanahbazhoo declared the new world was strong enough and large enough for them all, and when he gave the word they all joyfully left the raft and went to find homes for themselves in the new world.[20]

Seldom was this story told me in the same way. Some would leave out Mink or Beaver, but it was always the fat, chubby "We-chuck," the Muskrat that was the hero.

When the story was told the Indian would pull away the sand, and the wrapping around the fish would be like a mummy case. The man would crack this and off it would come, leaving the fish beautifully cooked. Its meat tasted like honey and did not lose anything in being eaten amidst such romantic surroundings, the breezes of the northern lake meanwhile filling my youthful lungs with health. After I was stuffed with fish I wanted to sleep, and to protect me from any harm the Indian took me in his arms and never moved so long as I slept. Often the shadows had begun to gather ere I awoke.

Not meeting me at the supper table, father would ask as to my whereabouts and would be told that "Jakoos was here with his 'Lend me your little boy,' and I could not refuse him." Father was no more pleased about these excursions than was Little Mary, but mother thought the Indians treated her boy properly. He told her all that happened and she saw much through his eyes of the Indian character.

Then, after supper, when the darkness descended, father would pace the floor anxiously and complain. "It is so dark outside," he would say. "I wish those Indians would leave him alone." If they did, mother knew that he would complain about that, but she did not challenge him about his inconsistency, even though she sympathized with his fatherly anxiety.

Then would come a kick at the door. Usually the Indians did not hesitate, morning, noon or night, when they came to that mission house, to put their hands on the latch and walk in. But these kicks would sound like a soft knock.

20 The "earth-diver" story is a northern Algonquian classic, oft-told with numerous variations. For an overview, see Jennifer S. H. Brown and Robert Brightman, *"The Orders of the Dreamed": George Nelson on Cree and Northern Ojibwa Religion and Myth, 1823* (Winnipeg: University of Manitoba Press, 1988), 129–33. In Young's *Algonquin Indian Tales*, 186–89, Souwanas was the teller and the story was told in greater detail. The protagonist at Berens River was surely Wisakedjak, however: see William Berens, as told to A. Irving Hallowell, *Memories, Myths, and Dreams of an Ojibwe Leader*, ed. Jennifer S. H. Brown and Susan Elaine Gray (Montréal and Kingston: McGill-Queen's University Press, 2009), part 4. The Youngs probably adopted the name Nanahbazhoo as the one more familiar to their Ontario audience.

The missionary would spring to his feet and find the big Indian holding the sleeping boy in his arms. Even though I had wakened from the after-dinner nap, I would often fall asleep again on the home trip.

Quickly and with glad heart father would seize me from the arms of the Indian. Perhaps something in father's manner might make the Indian turn as though he would go right away, but mother would hasten to his side and thank him for being so kind to her little boy. Then she would exclaim: "Wait a minute." She would then go to the pantry, and though her stock of provisions might be low, she would share her tea and sugar. Placing the packages in the man's hand, she would thank him again for being so good to her little boy.

Her words and gift always made him happy and he came again and again.

5 Scientific Evenings

To his son, and apparently to others, my father seemed to have the gift of a fascinator. Once when I thanked the Rev. Mark Guy Pearse for the wonderful way in which he had introduced father to the people of England, Mr. Pearse promptly replied, "I only opened the door and your father entered and won by his own charm." He knew how to attract attention. His personality was indeed charming, and his stories never missed their point. How much his early life and training contributed to developing his winsome powers it is difficult to say. He was the second boy in a family of seven sons and one daughter. He was always an exceptionally good student, and when he had graduated from Bond Head Grammar School he pled to be permitted to go on to the University. He was told [instead] that he now had a "Teacher's Certificate" and that his brothers were to be considered.

So, at sixteen years of age, he left his father's roof and never entered the house again except as a visitor. He taught school for a year, and then went to the Model School at Toronto and won a higher Teacher's Certificate. Then he took charge of another school and used his earnings to continue his studies at the Model School until he won the highest, the First A Certificate, and at twenty-one he was Principal of Madoc Public School. It was from this place that, in 1863, he was persuaded to enter the ministry of the Wesleyan Methodist Church.

He always thought himself fortunate in having this experience as teacher before he entered the ministry. He contended that the average preacher does not know whether his sermons find intelligent response or not. This is vital with the teacher if his work is to be a success and his pupils are to pass their examinations. The teacher-preacher, by the intelligent expression on the faces of his audience, would know that they had grasped the point of his message. Whatever there is in this, Egerton Young was a boy-teacher who had worked for his own education. He found the keenest enthusiasm in every step of his studies. He was fascinated by astronomy and geology. In his free days he studied the rocks, and at night he was following the stars in their courses. He was as fond of athletics and games as he was of God's creations and man's inventions and discoveries. It was his boast that he was on a good Toronto cricket team and at "the slip" stopped many a "hot one." He was also a good chess player.

When he was ordered to the mission field to "evangelize" the Indians there was the boy-teacher again in evidence. He thought what had thrilled him would awaken the keenest of interest in the minds of the Indians. So he took with him to the mission field the best instruments that he could secure. He had a double-barreled breech-loading shot gun and a Martini-Henry carbine, the latest inventions as weapons of the chase. Then he had a microscope, a large magnet, a pair of binoculars, a telescope, a kaleidoscope, a coal-oil "Magic" lantern, with painted slides, and globe, maps, etc.[21]

During the week the missionary would have an "open night" at the Mission House, and would exhibit and explain some of these inventions. Most of them were "beyond" the Indians, except merely to make them think "the white man is too clever for us," and instead of rising to grasp the truth they gave way to the "inferiority complex," which is the greatest of their handicaps to their progress to this day. However, the "Gentlemen" and officers of the Hudson's Bay trading posts took the keenest delight in these "scientific evenings," as they called them, and most enthusiastically encouraged the missionary in his work.

The kaleidoscope seemed to be the instrument that interested the Indians most, with its tumbling bits of coloured glass and ever changing formations. Then, next to the lantern, was the big "horse shoe" magnet.

21 Elizabeth Young described their visitor's interest in some of these items in her own memoir (see "The Visit of Tapastanum").

The way that needles would jump from the table where they were buried in earth, and adhere to the magnet, or [how] needle would cling to needle until there was a long string of them, was ever an astonishment to the Indians.

Lanterns were really "magic" lanterns in those days and were very crude affairs compared with the wonders of later invention. The light was from a broad-wick coal oil lamp and the picture was thrown on the screen from the rear. They let the picture shine through the great sheet that had to be kept wet. Housewives may imagine the condition of the floor of the "living-room" after one of these nights of scientific demonstrations. The slides, however, were wonders of artists, for they were hand painted, as photography was as limited then as was lantern optics. There were pictures of various animals of the world. But how much interest the Indians took in Australian kangaroos and South American sloths none of us ever knew. However, a double-acting slide that showed a cat trying to catch a mouse — a very simple fore-runner of the moving picture — never failed to bring forth screams of delight.

How the white man worked "behind the screen" was also a matter of interest to them, and some were "courageous" enough to get down on the floor, lift up the sheet and peek under. One Hudson's Bay officer who had the job of keeping the sheet wet by throwing dipperfuls of water on it, when he saw a big red face appear under the curtain accidentally (?) missed the curtain and let the Indian have the water full in his face.

How much scientific knowledge the Indians accepted is doubtful, as the following experience with one "doubting Thomas" will show: This Indian could not accept the fact that the earth is round and he was brave enough to come to the missionary and say so. The missionary was very ready to talk and did his best to explain the natural phenomenon.

"After your talk," the Indian said, "I went out and sat on a rock beside Lake Winnipeg, thinking that when the world turned around, as you said, the water would run out. It is there now, just as it always was, and I told the Indians you had made a mistake there."

The missionary showed him a great map of the world in two hemispheres and explained it patiently. Shortly afterwards the missionary learned that the man had told his fellows that "perhaps the missionary is right in a way, but the world has two flat sides and Lake Winnipeg is on one of the flat sides and so the water has not run out."

The man was invited back and another lesson in geography was given to him. With the help of a little "globe" that stood upon an iron tripod, the missionary explained the round earth whirling through space, etc. He pointed out how it was round every way. The Indian was invited to ask what questions he wished and the teacher-missionary answered them as fully and considerately as he could. The interview seemed to be thoroughly satisfactory as the man went away, but soon after the missionary heard that the Indian had declared, "Well, I guess the missionary is right when he says the world is round every way, but it stands on three legs."

If father was so interested and enthusiastic in doing all this for the Indians it ought not to be difficult to comprehend what he did for his son. He keenly watched my widening intellect and directed attention to the interesting things in Nature. As my ability to comprehend increased, the scientific instruments that he had were explained to me. The wing of the fly that enabled that little creature to do such wonderful flying, and the "needle" of the mosquito that had punctured the boy's skin, were shown him in the microscope, and the wonderful Northern Star that had guided his father home over snowy trails, was seen through the telescope. And that lantern! When would he grow up so that he could work those slides while his Daddy talked and told the Indians such wonderful stories of all those animals and the countries in which they lived!

So when father called me, with a peculiar thrill in his lovely voice, I would hasten to him, for I knew that he had discovered something that was worthwhile seeing. One day I was to see a little nest that a mother mouse had made of shavings on the bench in the workshop where she had brought forth her little ones. Perhaps the most remarkable sight was to see snow made. During the New Year season a great feast was held in the church. To get ready for this feast, boilers were placed on the big iron stoves of the church, and the meat contributed — venison, moose meat or bear — would be boiled. The church then would be filled with steam. On one such day, which was bitterly cold outside, the missionary noticed a pile of snow at the bottom of a window. He drew the attention of the sexton to the snow and the man quickly cleared it away. Coming around again, the missionary saw snow there again and spoke again to the Indian sexton. The man said he had cleared snow from there several times. This aroused the curiosity of the missionary and he investigated more closely. It was no place for boys to be playing tricks with snowballs. The thermometer was down in the thirties below zero, and no one was out in the bitter wind unless it was a necessity. But as the missionary stood there the pile of snow grew before his eyes! One of the window panes had a crack, and a tongue of sharp, keen, cold air came through that crack. As soon as the cold air came in contact with the warm air in the church, the water vapour was condensed and frozen so quickly that it exploded into snowflakes. After watching this for a short time the missionary thought of his son and soon had the boy at his side showing him an act of Nature that few ever see and which he has never forgotten.

6 The Food Supply

The fact that I was so appreciative of a bit of cracked wheat porridge as to have called it "pudding" may have awakened some wonderment. It is to be remembered that Western Canada had not then risen to the dignified position of being known as "The Bread Basket of the Empire." It was still in the grip of the fur traders. Though the Hudson's Bay Company had sold their monopoly and "good-will" to the Canadian government [in 1869–70], their officers on the spot did all in their power to keep out enterprising traders and settlers. They wished to hold that land for raising fur.

Then again, Norway House and its environs were of rock formation and little suitable for agricultural activities. In its early days it was a hunter's paradise, but having become a popular centre of trade, with its many servants of the Hudson's Bay Company, their families and "adherents" that always flock to such centres, the matter of food supply became a very serious one.

This situation is seen to be more acute when the improvident nature of the Indian is taken into consideration. Father trembled for the Indians when he saw seventy nets in close proximity to the mission house in Little Playgreen Lake. How long could the fishing stand that strain?[22] Then, in the winter, the rabbits provided much of the "staple" food for the Indians. But Norway House at that time boasted a thousand or more inhabitants. It is true, the traders looked well after themselves and brought in flour from

22 Hudson's Bay Company fishing also tested local resources. On 12 November 1870, for example, the Norway House post journal recorded that 21,000 whitefish had been taken as of that date (HBCA B.154/a/69).

England and pemmican from the prairies, but very little of this passed into the hands of the Indians. There was never enough flour for them to bake "raised" bread — only "beavers' tails," hard as ship's bannocks.

Then there were times when the fish seemed to leave the nearby waters and the rabbits suffered from diseases that made them so repellent that even a hungry dog or wolf would not eat them.

The missionary saw the changes that were rapidly coming, and, along with his spiritual work, tried to make the Indians realize the new day that was dawning for that Western land and prepare them to meet it. The attitude of the Indians is reflected in the following incidents:

"That is my best child," said an Indian, boastingly, one day to my mother. "She can go longest with no food without crying." This was a criterion of excellence that did not appeal to mother. She had Dutch and English blood in her and enjoyed good eating, and was not happy in the presence of underfed, poorly nurtured children.

One summer day father was at an open window, taking keen delight in the song of a robin perched on a nearby limb pouring forth his paean of praise. There was a stunning "plunk!" and the song suddenly ceased. Father hurried out in time to see an Indian boy pick up the dead robin and retrieve his murderous arrow.

"Oh!" cried the missionary. "Why did you do that? Why did you kill that lovely songster? He had just come from the south and was singing his praises to God."

The boy stood abashed. "My mother told me this morning," he said, "that if I did not shoot something I would get nothing to eat today."

"Why," said the missionary, "I would rather have given you your breakfast than that you should kill that bird!"

"I did not know that," returned the boy.[23]

During the next winter father discovered two mink and coaxed them to come to his back door for meat scraps. It was a delight to see them poke their little brown noses out of the snowbanks along the shore, and, when they saw their friend, to come cautiously towards him. But if anyone else appeared

23 This is a truncated version of a Norway House story that Egerton Young told in full in *The Battle of the Bears: Life in the North Land* (Boston: W. A. Wilde, 1907), 139–43. The boy was hungry because his father's gun had failed, as Young learned when he visited the family in an effort to learn more about the situation. He then regretted his scolding of the boy.

they would turn and almost in the flash of an eye disappear into their pearly tunnels. One morning when their friend was a little late in appearing, they had come out of the snowbank and were hunting for their breakfasts. Bang! bang! went a gun. Father, fearing some tragedy, jumped from his desk and ran out of the house. He saw an Indian with a smoking gun picking up the dead bodies of his pet mink.

"Why did you come here and shoot those mink on my property?" demanded the angry missionary. "They were my little friends and it was my pleasure to see and feed them."

The Indian stood stolidly before the missionary and when he had finished his rebuke quietly replied: "Him fun for you; him food for me."

"I would rather have given you a bag of flour than have had you kill those mink," my father declared.

"I did not know that," the Indian replied.

The Indians soon learned of his generous heart and came in a steady stream to the mission house. There was no "Government relief" in those days and whatever "charity" was exercised came from the missionary's allowance. But as long as there was anything there it was shared and the mission house cupboard was often as bare as the poorest wigwam.

"My dear," mother has [sometimes] said to father at the morning meal, "that is the last bit of meat in the house, and if you do not shoot something we shall have nothing for dinner."

With a prayer in his heart and taking his gun, canoe and best retrieving dog, "Cuffy," a Newfoundlander, he would go off to see what he could secure. Generally he was successful, but this method of supply was too precarious to suit my father.

He built a huge stockade fence and imported some sheep. But the venture was short-lived, for huskie dogs, somehow or other, got over the fence and soon made an end of those sheep. He next made a strong log pen, with a small thick spruce door. In this he put some pigs. But one night those northern dogs, with their sharp teeth, tore a corner off the door, got in and ate the pigs.[24]

24 Young, in By Canoe and Dog-Train, 93, described bringing a sheep from Red River to Rossville in the summer of 1870. Despite his keeping it inside a stockade fence twelve feet high, the dogs got in and ate the sheep. The following summer he brought two pigs and put them in a small log stable, but the dogs one night chewed through the two-inch-thick door and ate the pigs.

His appeals for advice and help to mission headquarters were met by the declaration that he was sent to preach the Gospel, and not to feed the Indians.[25] This sort of advice only roused father to greater efforts to help the Indians. He imported a cow, with which he had better success. The Indians were ready to care for her on the promise of her calf and "Bossy" could take care of herself when sneaking Indian dogs came around.

But this did not go far in solving the economic problem. Father saw white settlers coming in and pleaded with the Indians to follow their example and cultivate the land. There was little around Norway House and he told them to go where land could be found and meet the changing conditions that were coming so quickly. It is questionable if many of the Indians saw his point of view. Certain it is that they did not appreciate his advice to become agriculturists. Nevertheless, in his missionary journeys he kept his eyes open for good arable land and discovered some at the mouth of Berens River. This place was about one hundred and eighty miles south of Norway House on the east side of Lake Winnipeg. To enforce his point he offered to accompany those who would go with him to Berens River and establish a new mission there.

In 1873 he was sent by the missionary authorities to Berens River [arriving in early April 1874], but few Indians from Norway House followed him. However, there were some Indians at that point and father determined to do his best for them.[26] But it was a venture that nearly cost him his life, and also the lives of all the rest of us.

25 On 30 March 1873, Young wrote to the *Christian Guardian* that, with fur prices falling, the H B C had almost ceased aid to the aged and destitute and that fish and fur-bearing animals were also in short supply. As a result, "we are overwhelmed with calls upon our sympathies and supplies. . . . We are often perplexed and cast down in our spirits, on account of the destitution of our people. . . . Financial embarrassments have long been clouding over us deeper and heavier, and yet we cannot, we dare not refuse to assist them, at times regardless of censure. It is very easy to write from a cosy office, or from a comfortable Canadian home, 'You must stop aiding that people,' &c, &c. It is an utter impossibility for me to turn a starving Christian red man from my door, when I know he has done his best to obtain food in the water or forest."

26 Ojibwe people had been living in the area for three generations; see A. Irving Hallowell, *The Ojibwa of Berens River, Manitoba: Ethnography into History*, ed. Jennifer S. H. Brown (Fort Worth: Harcourt Brace College Publishers, 1992). Following upon Timothy Bear's efforts to begin some mission work there, Young arrived from Ontario to take up residence in the spring of 1874 (Elizabeth, Eddie, and Lillian arrived at the end of the summer). Other Rossville associates of the Youngs — Martin Papanekis, Big Tom Mamanowatum, Alex Kennedy, and Little Mary — were also important in assisting the family and the mission.

Starting at Berens River: A Sturgeon Pond

The first night at Berens River we spent in a poplar-log hut that had a sod roof. A terrific rainstorm swept over us that night and washed the mud off the sod. Father and mother slept in the one room below, and my sister and myself in the "attic" which was reached by a pole ladder. In the morning father called his children, but there was no response. He called again and still there was no answer. Then he climbed the ladder and saw nothing but a sea of mud. The rain had washed all the earth off the sod on the roof and we children were buried in the mud. Fortunately for us, though the mud was up to our chins, our faces had been spared and we had not been smothered.[27]

The mission authorities sent a carpenter from Winnipeg to build us a new mission house, but fearing that he would be frozen in at Berens River, he left at the first sign of snow when the house was only partly finished. That winter we nearly perished from the cold. [From the 1962 memoir: "What I do remember is that mother had a very difficult time to put something on the bare board walls of that shell of a house. She got strips of cotton, pasted newspapers on it, and fastened it on the wall to keep the draft out but in spite of all they could do, the family was nearly frozen that winter."]

With what help he could secure from the Indians there, father set to work to clear some of the land to see what could be done to till it. Though he did not have so many outside calls to respond to, he still had some. The food supply was short and he hired an Indian to catch fish and see that we did not starve in his absence.

When he returned he found that things had not gone well with us. The Indian was either a poor or indifferent fisherman and the tale my mother had to tell father was far from pleasing to him. He dismissed the Indian and hired a half-breed by the name of Kennedy.[28] Even so, he was determined that there should be a more sure way of providing food for his loved ones.

---

27 Eddie remembered the experience as more traumatic than his parents' reports of it and, in his 1962 memoir, noted that from that time on, "I seemed to suffer from intermittent deafness." See also Young, *By Canoe and Dog-Train*, 262.

28 Alex Kennedy had been Elizabeth Young's dog driver at Rossville, where he also attended school. See Part III, sec. 15, for his letter of 1890 recalling his association with the Youngs and noting his later adventure as a Nile voyageur.

The thought came to him: "If his brothers at home could have pig pens so that when they needed food they had only to slaughter a porker and dress it, why could he not have a fish pen or fish pond?"

He found a little bay that he thought would serve his purpose. He then got a lot of piles, sharpened one end and drove them into the mud across the mouth of the bay. He then wove marsh grass into ropes and threaded it through the piles to keep them in place. Then with "gill nets" he caught large sturgeon out in Lake Winnipeg and dumped them into the fish pond.[29] Neither "smooth-back" nor "rock-back" sturgeon are as good eating as many other kinds of fish, but they are good food and better than starvation. So when father was away mother would say to Kennedy: "We are nearly out of food, so get us a sturgeon today." He then would take a spear and go to the pond, haul in a fish and dress it for the household.

An Experiment in Farming

However, such success as this father regarded as small stuff. He eagerly looked forward to the time when he would bring in his first wheat crop. Around the stumps the first year he planted potatoes and garden seeds, and was successful in raising potatoes, carrots, turnips and a few other vegetables.

In winter, when in Winnipeg, he got an "iron-beam" plow from an Indian agent and had a blacksmith make him three dozen big iron spikes. He dragged these home on a dog sled, and with birch poles made himself a set of harrows.[30]

A plow and set of harrows, however, were not enough. He had no tractor or horse to pull them over the land. He did not even have an ox, but he had dogs. So he hitched up two teams — that is, eight lively dogs, which gave him four pairs of dogs in tandem style ahead of the plow. He fastened the

29 It is not clear how continuously the sturgeon pen kept operating, but, as of around 1887, William Berens was netting sturgeon alive to keep in the pen at Berens River for the whole summer; they served as summer rations for the boat crews arriving there (*Memories, Myths, and Dreams of an Ojibwe Leader*, 53, 210n45).

30 In *The Battle of the Bears*, 174–77, Young told of getting a plow for Rossville from Manitoba's first governor, Adams Archibald (in what must have been the summer of 1871, as Archibald resigned early the following year), and then making the harrow. But he evidently also secured a plow for Berens River later on.

collars of the two leaders together and placed his son between them, who with a hand on the collar of each was to guide them as his father ordered. The missionary felt sure that he could handle the situation. When the dogs were a bit too eager he would stick the nose of the plow a little deeper into the soil so as to slow them down. However, amidst the unseen rocks and roots the inevitable happened. There was a jolt that even the strong-handed plowman could not hold. He was thrown aside, the nose of the plow came out of the soil, and away dashed the dogs. In a few breathless seconds plow, dogs and boy were landed in a heap at the other side of the field. I had been told that if the dogs started to run I was to throw myself back on their collars. I did so, and thus escaped injury. But my father concluded that that was too risky an experiment to try again with me, for if I had slipped under that collar-band he would have lost his son, and that was too great a price to pay, even for a field of wheat.[31]

In fact, I think my mother had something to say about this experiment. She kept me under close surveillance, and I never knew how my father finished plowing that field. But he did. Then he harrowed it and sowed his grain by hand. He reaped his crop with a sickle and threshed it with a flail. My mother sewed some sheets together and on a sunny day when there was a nice breeze they tossed the grain into the air. The wind carried the chaff away. Some prepared for wheat was put aside for seed for the next year and the rest prepared for immediate use. It was but a very little, and so was greatly prized. My mother ground it in a coffee-grinder, and so we had some cracked wheat "pudding."[32]

31 Young told this story in more detail in *The Battle of the Bears*, 177–79, recounting how Eddie in fact tumbled a few times and "two or three pairs of dogs would run over him before they were stopped." The first field was plowed for sowing potatoes. In July 1972 at Norway House, Maxwell Paupanekis, a descendant of the Papanekis family who had assisted the Youngs at the Rossville mission, told Harcourt Brown, Young's grandson, of stories he had heard about Egerton Young plowing with dogs.

32 See Young, *The Battle of the Bears*, 180, who said it also "made capital bread and biscuits." In *By Canoe and Dog-Train*, 186, he wrote that he got thirty bushels of wheat from two and a half bushels of seed.

7 My Mission Sisters

The second year after I arrived at Norway House my sister Lillian was born. She was as fair as I was dark — fair hair, pink cheeks and blue eyes. Little Mary was called in to see her. She took the babe in her hands, examined her very carefully, and, laying it gently beside my mother, she said "Girl very nice, but I like the boy better." She wanted to give all her attention to me, and it was with difficulty that my father made her understand that he was a poor missionary and had not the means to find a nurse for each of his children. So it was with a good deal of reluctance that Mary had to minister to the babe and thus make me share her attentions with my sister.

A second sister also arrived at the mission house — Eleanor, who was lovingly called Nellie. My mother often said that Nellie was her prettiest babe. But she did not stay long with us.

The Call Home: Ontario, 1873-74
In 1873, after five years of service at Norway House, my father was called "home" to do "deputation work." In the previous year Dr. Morley Punshon had aroused a great deal of interest in the churches, and the funds of the Missionary Society had been largely increased. It was feared that this advance could not be held unless something special were done to maintain it. So my father was called from Norway House and Rev. Thomas Crosby was brought from the Pacific coast, where he had done a great work amongst the Indians of Northern British Columbia. These two men were sent from Windsor to Halifax, preaching and lecturing in the interests of missions. As a result of their work the increased income of the previous year was not only maintained, but further increased by some thirty thousand dollars. (And that was a large sum in those days.)

[From the 1962 memoir: "When we were preparing to come back to civilization one of the family problems was how should the missionary's son be clothed? His Indian nurse had made him a beautiful deer-skin coat but that was not considered suitable. There still remained in mother's trousseau a velvet gown, so she cut this up and made for her boy a full length jacket, but his father promised him when they got to Toronto he would get his boy a real store suit of clothes. The dressing of my sister did not seem to trouble my mother.

"When we reached Toronto, father according to his promise took me to the Thompsons Clothing Emporium on King Street and had me arrayed in a real store suit of clothes. As we were coming out of the store, we met the Rev. Dr. Egerton Ryerson, now full of years and honours. Father introduced me to him and he seemed very much pleased to know that his name was continued down to another generation. Dr. Ryerson as a young minister in 1838 had been secretary of conference when my grandfather the Rev. William Young was ordained. On Christmas day 1867 my father and mother were married in the Richmond Street Church, Toronto, and Dr. Ryerson had performed the ceremony. Now he met a third generation in our family, and putting his hands on my little head he blessed me."]

While on this tour my father met Lord Dufferin, then the Governor-General of Canada, in Ottawa. After showing His Excellency a Cree Indian Bible, my father explained the Evans "Syllabic" characters in which the Bible was printed, and taught Lord Dufferin to read the Lord's Prayer in the Cree. "Why, Mr. Young," said the Governor, "this is wonderful! How is it that we have never heard of Mr. Evans and his work before? We have given many a man a title and a pension, and when he was dead buried him in Westminster Abbey, who has never done as much as this man for the good of humanity."

"I suppose," my father replied, "it was because he was a humble Wesleyan missionary and thought only of his work."

The Trials of the Homecoming

But the price our family paid for this visit home was heavy, for when father responded to this call of the church he brought his family with him, thinking that it would be, especially for my mother, one grand holiday. My mother was well treated in many places, especially in Hamilton, where she went as a bride when father was the pastor of the First Methodist Church. The good people of that city gave her and my father in appreciation of their work a beautiful silver service. But in spite of this and other kindly and generous gifts and hospitable entertainment, I have often heard mother say "I am sorry we came home."[33]

---

33 Elizabeth Young's memoir sheds light on her sentiments. As noted, she and the children had to leave Norway House two months before Egerton and experienced the loss of Nellie, their youngest, on the way.

Perhaps my mother's real trouble was that after the first flush of "welcome home" was over, and visits paid to relatives, this loving heart and efficient housekeeper found herself and her children without a home. She was taken from place to place and entertained always by strangers — sometimes with, sometimes without, her children. As far as we children were concerned, we soon learned the cat-like trick of "lighting on our feet" wherever we were dropped.

The mistress of a lovely home in Toronto, who entertained me for a while on this trip, gave me in after years her account of the following incident. To understand what happened we must get the background at Norway House. Many good friends thought it a terrible deprivation that I should grow up without having apples to eat. Many efforts were made to get them safely to me, but the distance was too far and the means of transportation so slow that they were always rotten when they reached their destination. However, my father grew potatoes, and a raw one fresh out of the ground is good eating and I had often had one. Then, I knew fish and all their peculiarities. As soon as I came under the care of this good lady in Toronto she made haste to make up to me this "terrible deprivation" of a missionary's boy by giving me a beautiful rosy Ontario apple. She said that I ate into one side of the apple until I got a bit of the core between my teeth. Then, in the greatest indignation, I threw that apple, or what was left of it, on her floor, declaring, "I do not like this potato. It has too many fish-scales in it."[34]

Once when my mother and I were being entertained by the wife of one of Canada's merchant princes and Senators, her son and I were playing in a room upstairs while our mothers were visiting in the parlor. Suddenly the ladies heard a "bump, bump, bump," on the stairs, and then through the door I appeared, dragging the other boy by the heels. I dragged him quickly right to his mother and dropped his feet there. My mother was instantly on her feet to get hold of me.

"Sit down, Mrs. Young," our hostess said, calmly, "and we'll see what this is about." Then she turned to me and said, "What is the matter?"

34 The "good lady in Toronto" was Annie Elizabeth Macdonald, the wife of John Macdonald, a prosperous dry goods dealer and dedicated supporter of the Methodist church. Elizabeth Young quoted Eddie's "fish scales" comment in her own memoir, but with "apple" in place of "potato," and she also referred briefly to the Youngs' visit with the Macdonalds in another short memoir: see Part III, sec. 12.

"Let him tell," I replied, with shoulders straight and my voice full of indignation.

"What is it, Alfred?" the lady asked, as she looked at her son on the floor.

"I — I called him Indian and he knocked me down," he blubbered.

"You did!" said his mother, reproachfully. "You called your guest names! That was very wrong of you and it is no wonder he resented it. Now, you boys run back to your play, and, Alfred, you see that you do not mistreat your guest again."[35]

My! How pleased I was with that lady's firm and judicial mind. I knew that after she had spoken that way my mother would not punish me. But that nick-name seemed to spring up in all sorts of places, and always filled me with resentment.

In my mother's home town [Bradford, Ontario] my grandmother and aunts had a party in my honour and several cousins were there. Perhaps these young relatives did not like to see so many amenities and favours showered upon me and sought means to have revenge. Discovering in some way that I disliked being called "Indian," they seemed to think that they would be safe from punishment if they called this out in public. They made a mistake, for then and there, defying all the rules of grace and etiquette, I fought one after another until my aunts laid forceful hand upon me. Then the question was, "What shall we do with him? Where shall we put him?"

In those days there was a sort of "holy of holies" in the "big houses." It was the parlor and it was usually kept closed and dark, from week-end to week-end. What wonderful haircloth furniture those parlors had, and heavy drapes hanging down in front of the great windows, and the wool or fuzzy ropes that tied those curtains and drapes back! It seemed to my aunts the only place for my incarceration, and so I was put in the parlor. All was quiet there for a while. Then there was a loud "whack! whack! whack!" and the aunts hastened in to see what was happening. I had dragged the sofa from its moorings and placed the chairs in front of it.

35 This episode probably happened at the Hamilton home of William E. Sanford, a prosperous Methodist businessman who (like John Macdonald) was appointed to the Senate in 1887; he supported the Youngs' mission work in various ways. Census data show that that the Sanfords had a son, Edward, born in 1868, whom Eddie likely remembered as "Alfred" from that one meeting. Eddie well knew that in these contexts "Indian" was being used pejoratively.

The sofa was my cariole and the chairs were my dogs. I had somehow got those curtain ropes off and had them around the chairs as dog harness and was using the curtain pole as a whip on the "dogs." My aunts quickly decided that it was better for me to pound my young cousins if they persisted in calling me names than to bruise their precious furniture. So I was permitted to rejoin my party.[36]

Whatever my ambitions have been in later years, in my youth I was determined to climb to "high places." When in Montreal my mother and I were being entertained by the occupants of one of the fashionable "brown stone fronts." While the two ladies were away shopping I discovered an open window in an upper room. I climbed out on to the [eaves]troughing, and then up to the roof, and had induced the little son of our hostess to follow me. While [we were] up there the ladies returned, and as they approached the house I called down to them, waving my hands and standing on the edge of the roof. The lady of the house promptly fainted and fell to the sidewalk. My mother did not meet "emergencies" that way and seemed to know the right point to attack. Taking an orange out of her bag, she held it up so that I could see it. "Come carefully down the way you went up," she said to me, "and I'll give you this orange. You come first and help the little fellow to follow you."

Mother was not trained in the "protective means" developed in a modern complex city, or she would have called in the men of the fire department to rescue us urchins from our perilous perch. She was still mission-minded and depended upon self-aid. However, I navigated the return passage all right and also brought the other fellow safely down. It is said that my first query on reaching my mother was not the slightest concern about my adventure, but, "What made the lady fall to the sidewalk?"[37]

---

36 E. Ryerson Young told this story again in his 1962 memoir but placed it in late summer 1876: "I was home [from Berens River] in time for my grandmother Bingham and Aunt Clara and Aunt Lottie and Uncle Joe to give me my seventh birthday party" (which would have been belated as he was born on 11 June). The 1876 date is more convincing on one count: Eddie would have been more able to move such heavy furniture at age seven than between the ages of four and five.

37 The mother who fainted was Mary Ferrier, the wife of James Ferrier. In her 1927 memoir, Elizabeth referred to the Ferriers as "our very kind friends," but she did not mention her son's antics here or at the Sanford home in Hamilton (nor, in quoting his comment about the apple, did she indicate the circumstances under which it was made). Surely, his behaviour in these elegant homes must have caused her some distress.

The Death of Nellie, August 1873

The real tragedy, however, of that homecoming was during the trip down
Lake Winnipeg. The only way for my mother and her children to reach
Winnipeg was by the Hudson's Bay Company's "open boat." It was decided
that mother should take us three children and go down in the boat, while
father would close up the mission house and follow by canoe.

The weather proved very hot, there were delays, and we had no awning
or any other covering from the sun. As a result, we children were soon very
sick, and mother as well. She battled hard to save her children, but in spite
of all her efforts, little Nellie died. The Indian boatmen put to shore, made
a little coffin under my mother's directions, and buried her on the bank of
the Red River.

There was not much of a place that was called Winnipeg then. Fort
Garry was the headquarters of the Hudson's Bay Company there. There was
also Selkirk colony. My mother and her surviving children were taken in
by a Mr. and Mrs. Sifton and treated with great kindness and sympathy.[38]
When father arrived later and learned of his loss he was greatly distressed.
In the neighbourhood the Church of England had a mission and a graveyard.
My father appealed to the missionary, Archdeacon Cowley, for permission
to inter his little Nellie there. In a very hearty and brotherly way he said,
"Come, brother, and in the choicest of our graveyards bury thy dead."[39] With
his Indian canoe men my father went up Red River and brought down the
little body. The Archdeacon himself met my father at the gate of the cemetery and led the way to the open grave, where he read with tenderness the
burial service of his church.

38 In her own account, Elizabeth made no reference to aid from John Sifton and his
wife in the context of this journey; rather, she indicated that it was in the summer of
1876, when the family left Berens River for good. Reaching the Red River after a bout
of stormy weather on Lake Winnipeg, they received much needed hospitality from the
Siftons as they began their return journey to Ontario.

39 Egerton had learned of Nellie's death before he reached Winnipeg. On 15 September
1873, the Anglican clergyman at St. Peter's mission on the Red River wrote to him: "As
I said before, our grave yards are open to you, and we shall be only too glad if we can
be of any service to you in the matter of permanent interment. . . . 'In the choice of our
sepulchers bury thy dead'" (Genesis 23:6).

The last thing that I remember of that Western land (for I left it as a little boy) was a visit to Nellie's grave. We were on our homeward journey in 1876. Mother was not able to come with us, and so father and I were alone except for the sexton, who pointed out the unmarked grave to us. It was a solemn walk for me, as my father's loving heart was deep in thought and grief and I could only look on and wonder. He was not only leaving his dead, but his work, "cut off in the midst of years," behind him.[40]

Back to the North and Berens River

In his earnest appeals to the people of the Home Churches [my father] not only called upon them to expand the work and establish new missions, but also to do something for the economic improvement of the Indians. He was challenged to lead the way, and did so by going to Berens River and organizing a mission there.

The trip back to the North country was a veritable nightmare to my mother. The mission party took boat at Collingwood, on the Georgian Bay, for Port Arthur [then Prince Arthur's Landing], Lake Superior. Mother was given charge over a couple of "green" missionaries, two sleigh dogs that had been given to father, her two children, and had also to "shepherd" a young woman who was going out to serve the church as a mission school teacher. She considered herself a literary person and had her notebook constantly in hand writing her impressions, but she never knew where her stockings were and had to be watched lest she should leave much of her personal belongings "by the way."[41]

But I was her chief trouble. I contracted a dose of whooping cough, and as the accommodations of that boat were of the most primitive nature it was only by the constant care and persistent attention of my mother that I reached port alive. I do not know where father was on this trip. He may have been fulfilling some last-hour deputation engagements, or receiving

---

40 Young visited the grave again in July 1892, on a return visit to Winnipeg and points north. Among his papers is an envelope labeled, "Flowers from Nellie's Grave, Mapleton near Selkirk Gathered July 31/92." JSHB collection.

41 Elizabeth's memoir tells of the party: the ministers [Lewis] Warner and Morrison, "Miss [Sarah Elizabeth] Batty," and two St. Bernard dogs. Like most travellers at that time, the party probably went on to Duluth by ship, then by rail to Moorhead, Minnesota. It being summertime, they could then go by steamer down the Red River to Winnipeg.

some last-minute instructions from the mission house, or giving orders to merchants for material for the new mission he was to establish, or he may have rushed on ahead to prepare a home for us at Berens River.[42] Anyway, he had sublime faith in my mother's abilities as a traveller and "manager of a tourist party." I wonder if Paul, when speaking so commendingly of the "women who laboured with me in the Gospel" [Epistle to the Philippians 4:3] in his missionary journeyings (such as Phoebe and Priscilla), had not the help and support of such efficient women as "Elizabeth Young," and so would at least pay some slight tribute to their faith, love, fine service and heroism!

The Birth and Naming of Florence

Berens River has at least this happy memory: it is the birthplace of another lovely sister. How well I remember the ninth of May 1875! The sun was shining brightly, but all the waters and landscape were covered with ice and snow. Winter in that land holds its iron grip often far later than that date. My sister Lillie and I were sent on a visit to the trading post, and we were having a good time with the trader's children, for Mrs. Flett was an excellent hand at entertaining children.[43] Suddenly, in the midst of a game, my father's dog driver [Alex Kennedy] burst into the house and shouted as he saw me, "You have a new sister: come home and see her!"

The play immediately ceased, and Mrs. Flett bundled my sister and me into our winter wraps and saw us well packed in the big cariole — dogsled with deerskin sides. Then the driver shouted "Marche!" and the dogs sped away at top speed, for they were going back home. It was a great ride, mostly over the frozen lake and river. It did not take those dogs long to cover the four miles. In fact, if the promised entertainment at the end had not been so exciting my sister and I would have thought the ride far too short.

But to see that wonder of wonders — a new sister! She was a beauty, with fair hair and blue eyes. My parents called her Florence Mary Ferrier, after the two daughters of Senator Ferrier of Montreal, who had done so much to help my father establish the new mission. But that did not satisfy the

---

42 Young had left Hamilton, Ontario, for Berens River on 4 March 1874 (Enoch Wood to William Young, 31 July 1874) and arrived there at the end of March.

43 Mrs. Flett was the wife of the HBC clerk James Flett, who served at Berens River from 1873 to 1885 and was at Norway House and Rossville from 1869 to 1871. HBCA, biographical sheets: Flett, James (B).

Indian chief, *Sou-a-nas* (South Wind). The pretty babe must have an Indian name and his own must be in it. So there was a great deal of discussion until someone noticed that a flock of song birds had arrived from the sunny south. That suggested the name, *Souanaquapeek*, Sou-wa-nah-qua-peek (the voice of the Southwind birds).[44] She was well named, for when she grew up she had a very fine contralto voice and sang in some of Toronto's best choirs.

Father's spirit of fun had to have its play over such an event. After having a good look at the babe our little tongues were loosened and we demanded to know where she came from. Of course neither Chief *Souanas* nor any other Indian brought her. Neither did the cold Frost King bring her from the North Pole. Hence and accordingly, she must have come from the cellar (for the new mission house had good deep cellars). So father, my sister and I went down into the cellar. The potato bin had the most vegetables in it, and though they had "eyes," we decided that they were too dirty and ugly to have anything to do with a babe like that. There were a few turnips in another bin. Their insides were white enough, but there was no outward attraction to them. The carrot bin was nearly empty, but the few that were left showed up well. The colour of their skin was most like the babe's skin and hair. So it was solemnly declared, and apparently by all accepted, that this fair little lady had popped up out of the carrot bin!

When we returned to "Old Ontario" two other sisters and a brother joined the family. The boy was a fine little fellow, but when he was a few months old he was cut off, oh so suddenly, by a summer complaint.[45] Father had left him laughing in mother's arms as he went away to attend his annual Conference. This was on a Monday morning. The Friday of that week the babe died and I was instructed to send father a telegram. Boy-like I wasted no words. "Come home, baby is dead," the telegram read, and my father said it hit him "like a sledge hammer." He came home on the next train. A couple of days later the darling was laid away in the beautiful cemetery on its high bank in Bowmanville.

---

44 For details on her Ojibwe name and naming ceremony, see Jennifer S. H. Brown, "Growing Up Algonquian: A Missionary's Son in Cree-Ojibwe Country, 1869–1876." *Papers of the Thirty-Ninth Algonquian Conference*, ed. Karl S. Hele and Regna Darnell (London: University of Western Ontario, 2008), 82–84.

45 This was William Joseph, who was born on 22 March 1883 and died that October (Young family Bible). Eddie was fourteen years old at the time of William's death.

Both my father and my mother took this blow very keenly. "We'll buy a three-grave plot, dear," father said to mother, "and when our time comes we shall lie down beside our little boy."

Father was then a poor preacher with seven mouths to fill, and he had no money for gravestones. This fact was soon noticed by some of the good church people to whom he had ministered with his usual zeal and fidelity, and they proceeded to do something about it.

One day there came a letter into the new home, and it said that the friends wished him to write for them what he would like to have engraved upon a small tombstone that they had purchased and wanted to erect over the little grave. Only people who have had like tender and considerate deeds done to them can begin to appreciate what my father and mother thought of this act. The little stone stands in the grave plot beside one a little larger that marks the resting place of my father and my mother.

8 Talking

My mother has often said that my sister Lillian had come along to teach me to talk. She might have added "in English," for Little Mary had taught me Cree. So with the work of my sister I became a bi-linguist, and as the years came and I mingled more and more with the different people in and around the trading post, I was able to converse in several different tongues. In fact, my father has said that at five years of age I was the best interpreter he had. I can well remember being called from playing some game with Indian boys when some Indians visited our place whose language my father could not understand. He would say to me, "Find out what these people want or what they are trying to tell me."

"This is what they want," or "This is what they say," I would tell him. "Tell them this back," he would answer, and I would turn his words into the dialect of the Indians, for there were other bands besides the Cree speaking Indians who called on us. And on visiting their tents on my own initiative I soon found out how to talk to them.

I do not remember that my father ever used me in a public way, though I think he must have been tempted to do so, as the adult Indians were very unreliable, their education limited, and their viewpoint biased. They have been called "interrupters" rather than interpreters, and even worse than that, for they have often delivered ideas of their own, rather than those of the man they were apparently speaking for. In translating, the child has no predilections and will at least be an honest go-between.

Then the Indians seemed to be pleased to hear me speak their tongues as one of themselves and would eagerly listen to me when I would attempt to retell some of the stories that my parents had told me in English. For my parents did not leave me to the Indians for all the stories I was to hear. They quickly introduced me to the wonderful fount of children's stories that are in the English language, and my sister and I have often wept over the tale of "The Babes in the Woods," and laughed at "Silver Locks and the Bears," and other such stories.[46] But attractive as these stories were, and often as they were called for, a greater treasure came to us one day. "A Child's Bible" was sent to us all the way from Scotland. It was a large book with full-page pictures. I have always loved pictures, and in fact I think my memory is "pictorial," for when I could get anything into the shape of a picture it seemed to stay for a long time "on memory's walls."

In this book we had those wonderful pictures of little Moses amongst the bulrushes on the Nile being faithfully watched over by his sister Miriam; Samuel at prayer, saying "Speak, Lord, for Thy servant heareth"; those pictures of Christ and his mother, etc., all made by the world's greatest artists. I wanted to know the meaning of each picture and every character that appeared in them.

The book was so constantly in use that, to preserve it, my mother put a deerskin cover on it. Then, in my enthusiasm, I would take this book out and place it on a rock or some elevation, and displaying one of my favorite pictures, would proceed to tell the story of it in Cree. I have been told that I have done this on a Sunday morning when the Indians were gathering for church service, and that my father has had to tell Little Mary to "take

46 "Babes in the Woods" was an old English tale and ballad about two small orphan children cheated of their inheritance and left to die in the forest. The Three Bears story evolved from one featuring an old-woman intruder to the Goldilocks version that became dominant early in the twentieth century.

that boy and his book into the house so that the Indians may come into the church." It seemed that these grown Indians were more ready to hear me tell in Cree these Bible stories than to listen to my father address them through an interpreter.

[From the 1962 memoir: "One bright spring day, I took my Bible on Sunday morning out on a rock near the steps to the church. I opened the Bible and Isaiah's picture, and to the Indians that came around me, I started in to tell them the story. Then as other Indians came down the Berens River and beached their canoes they joined in my audience. My mother told me that at least forty Indians had gathered around me. The church bell was rung and father came down to the church. He went past us, up the steps and into the church. This was generally the sign for all the Indians to follow him into the church. After waiting a little while and no Indians came in, he went out again. He told me to quit talking, and they called little Mary and told her to take the boy and his book into the mission house and let the Indians come into the church. I was told by my mother the Indians protested and said they would rather hear me talking in straight ahead Cree than to hear him stumbling over interpreters. Little Mary hurried me away and the Indians went into the church."][47]

But at best the business of interpreting has its troubles. It is difficult enough to turn words, and far more so to successfully pass ideas "over the language border," but many new inventions crop up and then there is real trouble. Here is a simple case. A book is "mussanhagan," the Bible is "Keche Mussanhagan" or "The Great Book." A pamphlet or letter is "mussanhaga-niss," or "little book." But what were the Indians to call an envelope? The native Indian had never known such things, and so nothing to describe it or to stand for it was in their vocabulary. Whatever it was called in other places I know not, but at Norway House in our time the observing Indians had thus "diagnosed" it: "Mussanhaganiss-miskitezenhaganiss," or "the little book's

47 The language at Berens River, where Eddie's storytelling took place, was Ojibwe. Evidently, though, the people at Berens River — who had Cree connections and were reading hymns and scriptures in Cree syllabics at the time — understood that language well enough to follow Eddie's tales. The two languages, while distinct, both belong to the Algonquian family. In addition, as is clear from the 1962 memoir (see the excerpt quoted in chapter 14, below), Eddie was quick to pick up some of the local "Sateau" dialect.

shirt." As the lucky Indian was enveloped in a white shirt, so was the letter slipped into its white garment.[48]

Having got the idea that I could help my father at home, in my ambition I thought I could help him abroad. One of the most dangerous places in that north country is the "muskeg." Some of these are very deep, and men or animals getting into them have been lost as though swallowed by the wide sea, "unknelled, uncoffined and unknown."[49] There was one near our mission which one day father tried to fathom. He fastened together two long poles over ten feet each and lowered them. But they did not reach the bottom of that morass. In the winter time these muskegs would usually freeze solid and become good roadways. Even in summer moss or grass would grow on them and the wary and sure-footed would make their way precariously over them.

One day an urgent call of distress came to father from a sick Indian who dwelt on the far side of one of these muskegs. Father, in his eagerness to render help, took the short cut over the muskeg rather than waste time going the safer way around it. When he was well started over the bog he heard a sound behind him that made his heart leap as though to his mouth. He turned and saw me in the middle of that muskeg doing my best to keep up to him. With a prayer in his heart he came quickly back, and grabbing me up in his arms, said, "Oh, my boy, what are you doing here? You might have slipped and been swallowed up in the mud and we would never have known what happened to you."

"It was all right, Daddy," I replied nonchalantly. "I just put my feet where you put your big ones and it was all right."

I have heard this little experience of mine used as a parable by teachers and preachers as they would encourage parents to render their children the best of services — that of giving their young people a good example. For happy are the children who can say to their parents when in the dangerous places of this world, "It is all right for I am putting my little feet where you put your big ones."

48 Keith Goulet (e-mail, 23 March 2013) notes that the first part, properly *musin-uhigunis*, means "little book." The second is perhaps a combining of terms for cloak or coat and for a container or dish. The term is not used in modern Cree, which has adopted the English word (pronounced *enpaloop* or *enfaloop*, as Cree lacks the *v* sound).

49 Lord Byron, "Childe Harold's Pilgrimage, canto IV, stanza 179: "He sinks into thy depths with bubbling groan, / Without a grave, unknell'd, uncoffin'd, and unknown."

9 Operations

"Poor little woman," I have heard a good-hearted soul say in talking of my mother. "Up there amongst those Indians and no neighbour near to invite her in for a cup of tea!"

"Weren't you lonely up there?" some people have asked mother.

"Lonely!" she has replied. "I didn't have time to be lonely, and when night came I just sank into unconsciousness." And I understand that I had my full share in that matter, for I was a very lively little boy.

Our kitchen stove was a big cast-iron affair, with edges almost as sharp as a knife and no pretty nickel appendages. The big wood box was around behind the stove. To get something that was hanging on the pegs above that box I climbed upon it. Losing my balance, I fell on the stove and cut my scalp badly. There was no one around but mother and Little Mary and they set to work and patched me up. The scar of that wound I have to this day.

The coming of that carpenter and his shining tools got me into further trouble, especially his adze.[50] I evidently took it for a short toboggan slide, but started too far up, and, as a consequence, nearly cut off a good bit of my "sit-down." Father was home at the time and helped mother to sew up the wound, but they kept me a day and a night upon my face so that the wound would heal properly.

The Indians at Berens River, like those at Norway House, soon realized their source of help and they made a trail to the Mission house I have often heard mother say that when they got up in the morning they would find from twenty to thirty Indians in the kitchen. Some wished only to sit, huddled in shawl or blanket, to just get warm, and perhaps see how the little white woman did things, for that place was the only "movie show" they had up there. But most of the others confessed that they were hungry, and some asked for medicine. To the best of her ability mother would minister to one and all.

She humorously tells of one Indian woman who brought in a little girl that was in distress. "What has she been eating?" mother asked. "Green gooseberries," was the answer. "Then I think she needs some castor oil,"

50 This carpenter was probably the one whom Eddie mentioned as building the mission house at Berens River in fall 1874.

mother declared, and gave the woman a supply, with careful instructions how to serve it. A few days afterwards she met the woman, who was all smiles. "How is the sick girlie?" mother asked. "Better," came the reply. "They are all better. I fried their fish in that oil."

But there were other cases that were far from being so simple, and had nothing amusing about them. One Monday morning, when mother was busy at her washtubs, the kitchen door burst open and a big Indian fell on the floor and swooned away in a dead faint. He had been chopping wood too near the limb of a tree. The axe had caught the branch and turned in the swing, lighting on his head and cutting a large part of the scalp, which now laid over his right ear.[51]

"Didn't you faint?" mother was asked by a white woman, to whom she told the story. "I would have."

"I don't know about that," mother replied. "When you realize that you are the only one on the spot to do anything you sometimes find strength to do surprising things."

"Whatever did you do for that Indian?" the woman asked.

"I promptly seized a towel out of the tub, wrung out the water, laid the scalp back in place, and bound the towel tightly about his head. Then I secured my husband's razor, an antiseptic, some sticking plaster, silk thread and a needle which I used to sew leather and went at the man."

Carefully shaving around the cut, mother laid the loose piece back and thoroughly cleansed the wound. The edges were then drawn together, tightly sewed, and the head bandaged. After that mother bathed the Indian's face with cold water. When he opened his eyes and gasped for a full breath he seemed glad to know that he was still alive. He was sure the missionary would help him, so he had run as hard as he could to the mission house after he had hurt himself.

As a boy I told mother how brave she was to do all this. She has turned on me with a look so strangely full of courage, love and tenderness. "Oh, it was nothing to patch up that Indian's head. I just sewed away as long as there was anything to sew, but it hurt me terribly to push the needle into the pinky white skin of *your* head."

51 In Elizabeth's 1927 memoir she recalled that the axe had gotten caught in a clothesline.

10 Pemmican

"Pemmican is the sweetest meat that has crossed my lips." How often I have said that I do not know, but it was the conviction of my boyhood days. My father, however, and other missionaries to the Indians of our Canadian West slandered pemmican.[52] His humorous description of it was along this fashion: If you took the meat of a dead horse, cut it into strips and hung it in the sun until it was as dry as a bone, pounded it to bits until it was like sawdust, and then poured over this dried-out meat your grandmother's melted soap grease, you would have pemmican. This is, of course, rhetorical extravagance, and is a part of the general dispute between missionaries, diplomats, agents, etc., who are called to live in a strange land, and the children who are born to them in those lands. The children fall in love with the "native food," while adults find it difficult to acquire the taste for such. There is also a qualifying condition; and that is that the native food to be acceptable even to the children must be well made and well served. This is equally true with food in "home" lands. How often have I seen an uncle of mine who had a country store work over the butter brought in by people whom he "could not refuse," and try to make it palatable so that he might sell it and save it from being thrown into the tub for soap grease, where it meant almost complete monetary loss to him![53] So it has been with pemmican. But the pemmican that the traders bought by the ton was well made.

Pemmican needs no defence from me, however. Centuries of use by the tripmen and traders of the Northwest, as well as by the Indians, and the uniform health of the users, often without any other food, has placed it high in the dietetics of the world. When other voyageurs on land, river or sea, have been forced to live on some single form of food they have soon

52 In a letter of 9 January 1870 from the Victoria mission in the Saskatchewan district, for example, the Reverend George McDougall wrote that for years pemmican "has been the staple dish on our table, yet I must confess I have very little relish for tallow and pounded meat" (*Wesleyan Missionary Notices*, n.s., no. 7 [May 1870], 99).

53 This was doubtless Samuel Squires Young, youngest son of the Reverend William Young and Maria Farley, who "for some time conducted a large and successful wholesale grocery business in Trenton [Ontario]" ("Young, Samuel Squires," obituary notice, available at www.treesbydan.com; he died on 20 March 1925).

found themselves in trouble. But this has never been the case with those who have lived on pemmican. It has been one of Nature's great gifts to the people of the North, and is one of the world's most nutritious and well-balanced foods. Scientific dietitians have concocted balanced foods for travellers and prepared them in handy tins, but though they have searched the world they have not found one single meat that they can serve by itself for their clients.

When the great herds of buffalo were fattened on the June grasses of the plains they would be rounded up in great "hunts." After the slaughter the meat would be dried on staging. Then it would be broken up and put into bags made of the green hides, and melted tallow of the buffalo would be poured over the meat until it was thoroughly saturated. When the curing was done in July or August a delicious berry [saskatoon] that grew in abundance on the plains would be added, and this gave the pemmican a relish that made it most acceptable.

As the trading posts increased so did the demand for pemmican. The traders bought tons of it from the Indians of the plains. The latter never stopped to calculate the great amount needed for their far-flung journeys and the long winter when the people of the forts were shut up for months. Seeing the storehouses of Fort Edmonton and other prairie posts bulging with sacks of pemmican, and hearing the traders, like little Oliver Twist, calling "More! more!" the Indians exclaimed, "Those pale faces must be very hungry people!" The traders at the prairie posts even went to the extent of employing "buffalo runners" to keep them supplied with fresh buffalo meat as long as possible so that they might send more pemmican to the outlying posts of the Company and assure the tripmen of their full supply. But gather the pemmican as they would, there were times when the employees of these trading posts faced starvation, and this was also true of men and dogs stormbound on their winter journeyings. Before the railroads entered the land and food supplies were imported in abundance the cry of the traders and tripmen was for "pemmican, more pemmican!"

When the tripmen came from York Factory with the trade goods from England they fed me with loaf sugar, which seemed to be the only kind of candy the Hudson's Bay Company imported. This was very acceptable to me, but I looked forward with greater eagerness to the coming of the brigades from the Saskatchewan who brought in the supplies of pemmican. I have often heard father picture what he thought was a little cameo of satisfaction and delight, which was the sight of a little fat boy sitting astride the prow of a "York" Hudson's Bay Company boat, with his face to the west, chewing at a chunk of pemmican. The end of the boat might be bobbing up and down as the water gurgled under it and the sunlight played upon the waters, and there may have been great activity going on behind the boy (for the voyageurs were busy unloading packs of furs and bags of pemmican), but that boy had his face towards the plains and he was wondering what kind of animals the buffalo were and what kind of a country produced such delicious meat!

11 The Fish Pond

The fish pond at Berens River was a source of great interest to me. It was fascinating enough for me to go with [Alex] Kennedy (the man about the house) whom father would leave with us when he would go away on his long trips. When supplies ran low in the house mother would instruct him to catch a sturgeon. He would select one in the fish pond, spear it, drag it ashore, and dress it by hanging it tail upwards to the limb of a tree. The dogs would come around eager to feast on what was cast away. The meat was cut up and put in the storehouse. Then we had sturgeon steaks and fish balls three times a day. The "spinal cord" of the sturgeon was considered by my sister Lillian and myself a bit of unusual delicacy. It was boiled until it was like calves'-foot "jelly" or "gristle." When father was around, his love of a bit of fun would induce him to set us little ones up like a pair of chickens with a fish worm, one end of the "cord" in my sister's mouth, the other in mine. Then at his word we would jerk to see who would get the longer end.

When mother had to serve sturgeon three times a day at our meals, week after week, she said that she was put to it to discover ways and means to make meals palatable and attractive. But hunger and fresh air are good appetizers, and there was plenty of both of these up North. The chief trouble seemed to be to have enough food, for there were always hungry Indians and dogs, as well as lively children, to feed.

But there was another way that that pond was of thrilling interest to me. One of the finest dogs father owned was a pure black curly-haired Newfoundland that we called "Cuffy." For some reason she had attached herself to my mother and was "her dog."[54] True to her breed, Cuffy was very fond of the water. In spite of her size, she was as quick as a terrier and was unsurpassed as a retriever. That fish pond seemed to have a fascination for Cuffy. She would go to the highest point on the bank, sit down there and watch the sturgeon playing in the water. But there was something very restless in her. Who can tell what ancient hunting instincts were stirred within her when her ancestors had to find their own food off the shores of Newfoundland? Cuffy would watch the fish until some big fellow — perhaps a sixty or ninety-pounder — would rest quietly on the surface, sunning his back. This was the chance the dog would be waiting for. Every instinct of the hunter or retriever would come into play. She would almost imperceptibly rise and creep to the edge of the high bank, with every muscle taut. She would spring upon the fish and sink her teeth and claws into its back. There would be instant upheaval and the big sturgeon would fairly churn the pond in its endeavor to shake off the dog. But Cuffy would cling tenaciously. She was not to be shaken off. Seeing that it could not rid itself of its enemy by this means, the fish would dive to the bottom of the pond. Though strong with teeth and claws and tenacious of spirit, Cuffy could not remain long under water and soon had to release her hold and seek for air. She would come spluttering to the surface, make her way to the bank and lie there, coughing and sneezing, until she got the water out of her lungs. Then she would crawl back to her observation post, watch until another fish appeared to tempt her, and the battle would be repeated, with the usual result. Cuffy retrieved every wounded duck or goose that she was sent after, but she never "landed" a sturgeon.

54 Cuffy (along with Jack, the St. Bernard) was a gift sent to Norway House by businessman and Methodist benefactor William E. Sanford, of Hamilton. Young, in *My Dogs in the Northland* (New York: Fleming H. Revell, 1902), 126–28, described the bond between Cuffy and Elizabeth Young.

12 The Big Bad Wolf

My father had the instincts, and apparently much of the ability, of a sportsman. When a student in Toronto, he played on a cricket team. He was placed at the "slip" and he said he "stopped many a hot one." However, although his mission work took him into a "hunter's paradise," he never turned aside to go pleasure-hunting. Nevertheless, sometimes a little sport offered while on his venturous journeys, and he did not side-step it. One of these experiences greatly interested me. While returning from a canoe trip that had taken him far away he discovered near one of his camping places a nest of foxes. On examining it he and his canoemen found that the wise foxes had dug for themselves several holes by which they might enter their den from different directions if attacked. Noticing that two of these holes were directly opposite to each other, father figured that if he had all the remaining entrances stopped he might drive the foxes from one hole by a long pole and bag them as they came out of the other. Since they were on their way home they had plenty of empty provision bags and would not have to keep the foxes tied up very long. The experiment succeeded and father brought home six little foxes. What happened to the mother we never knew. She may have defied the poking, she may have escaped before that operation began, or she may have been away hunting for food for her little pups.

What surprised my father and the Indians was that no two of these foxes were alike. The largest and strongest the Indians called a "Cross" fox. There was one real red, another almost white, another with a silver sheen, and one small one that was pure black. When he reached home father put these foxes in what we called the "bell tower." This consisted of a framework that had been erected to support a bell which had been given to the mission [by James Ferrier] after the church had been built. To strengthen this bell tower, and also to be a place to store things, the lower part of the affair was boarded in and a floor added. As the sides bevelled sharply, the foxes could not climb very far up the walls before they would fall to the floor. It was a bit of cruel fun for me to catch mice, drop them into this fox pen and watch the foxes devour them. We did not have them long, however. The Hudson's Bay Company officers bought them from father. The idea then of fox-farming had apparently not then been thought of, but fox-hunting was in full swing in England. So the little foxes were boxed up, shipped to England, and turned loose in that country to be "the sport of Kings."

Another example of father's ability as an outdoor sportsman is the following incident which took place in very different surroundings. At one of his later pastorates [in Ontario] some of the good men who took regular holidays to go "fishing" got their heads together and thought of their minister.

"See here," one man said, "our preacher has been working for us night and day, winter and summer, taking no holidays, and is more of a sport at heart than any of us." The others replied in good part, so they approached their minister and persuaded him to "take a day off" and go fishing. Father did not have any fisherman's fancy "togs" but he had old clothes, amongst which was a stout well-worn overcoat. As they were nearing their chosen fishing area father said, "Put me off there," pointing to an island in the middle of a river.

"There are no fish there," his companions told him. "The good fishing is farther on."

"You can go where you like," father replied, "but let me try around that island." And, to please him, they put him ashore, but thinking he had such little chances of success they left him neither bait nor fish basket.

His companions went on with high hopes to their favourite spot. However, luck was not with them that day, and though they tried hard they caught nothing. They were deeply chagrined at their ill-success, but comforted themselves by saying, "Oh, well, if we haven't caught anything it is certain the preacher hasn't either."

So they paddled their fine "Peterborough" canoe bravely up to the island with its lone fisherman and sang out: "What luck?" They did not see any signs of success on the part of their minister as they came toward the shore.

"What success have you men had?" father asked.

"None," they said. "And you do not seem to have had any either."

Putting his hand into one of the pockets of the old greatcoat, he brought out a fine fish. "Here's one," father said, "but as you left me no basket I put it into my pocket."

A basket was quickly handed to him for the fish. Then, digging into the torn lining of the coat, he produced one that made the men gasp with envy. Father went on, with a whimsical air, drawing several more from the pockets and broken lining of the old coat, saying, "How do you like this one?" or "What do you think of that fellow?" until there was a good basketful.

"You win," they said, like the good sports they were. "We'll believe your fish stories after this."

When he became a "famous author and lecturer" father was sometimes entertained by some English gentlemen at their shooting parks. As the rooks flew about, the sportsmen picked them off with their guns one by one. On one of these occasions father watched for his chance and got two with one shot. This brought forth exclamations of praise from his companions, to which he replied, "When your ammunition is short and you have to shoot your dinner you have to learn to make every shot count."

But though a good shot, there was one occasion [at Berens River] when his "quarry" successfully eluded him. It was a big grey wolf that nearly got me. It happened on the trail made for hauling wood. The winters were long and cold, and as the only kind of wood available was the "soft" variety, such as poplar, spruce or birch, a very great quantity had to be procured. Then, as the bush was cleared away the missionary had to go farther afield for the supply needed for the church and house. One winter, the place at which the wood was being cut was some five miles distant. A trail had been made along which the dogs would haul the loaded sled. Indians at the mission would remove the poles, turn the dogs around and send them back for another load. I was allowed to ride back and forth on the sled.

No wolf had been seen in the neighbourhood for several years, as the Indians had hunted them down. But as I was making one of these trips homeward on a load of wood a big grey fellow suddenly appeared out of the bush. He ran in the deep snow beside the load, jumping up and trying to get at me. For some reason the wolf would not run in the beaten trail, but would jump from one side of the trail to the other. The dogs fully realized the presence of the wolf, and, having a good trail, made fast time. The increased speed of the dogs did not make it any easier for me to cling to my perch, but I managed to hang on. When we reached the neighbourhood of the mission, and the wolf saw the Indians at the wood pile, he turned off into the bush.

The alarm of the presence of a wolf was sounded through the village, and at first it could hardly be believed. But night after night Indians' dogs were disappearing, and the traders at the fort lost fourteen. The wolf became so bold and daring that he was seen in daylight following dog teams. Father and his men tried again and again to shoot him. Indians who could put bullet after bullet into a tin can at four hundred yards could not hit this elusive fellow at less than half that distance. In fact some of the pagan Indians became so superstitious about him that they thought he must be a "Windegoo," while those who had adopted Christian phraseology thought he must be the very devil.

However, his boldness in following the dog teams brought about his downfall. A carpenter who had come to do some repair work at the mission one day saw the wolf following his team as he was on his way to work. Having heard that all efforts to shoot him had failed, he decided to try a different method. He ground up some glass, rolled it in a slab of deer meat and dropped it by the trail. When the wolf came to it he quickly devoured it and continued following. However, it was not long before he began to stagger and finally sank to the snow. The carpenter, taking no chances on his recovery, went back and shot him.

Father purchased the skin and used it as a rug in our home for many years.[55]

13 Dogs

When Mr. Grover Cleveland was President of the United States father was preaching and lecturing in Washington, DC. The President and his charming wife were present at one of the morning church services, after which the President remarked, "I wish that missionary had told us more dog stories." This led to father being invited to the White House for luncheon, where he told his distinguished host and hostess more about the sleigh dogs that had served him so nobly. Father was always delighted to have an opportunity to talk about his faithful helpers of the trail. There were the huskies of the North, hardy to stand the cold and wise as leaders, but full of thievish and

55 As the wolf's slayer, the carpenter would have had the rights to its skin: hence the purchase. When the English Methodist Mark Guy Pearse visited the Youngs at their Meaford, Ontario, parsonage in May 1887, he found himself standing on a fur rug — the pelt of that wolf, and so heard its story. Pearse, "Introduction," in Young, *By Canoe and Dog-Train*, 2–3. The wolf rug also seems to appear underfoot in photographs of the Young family (see fig. 4). In his 1962 reminiscences, Eddie told of how Little Mary skinned the wolf: "The carpenter made a frame for Mary so that she could stretch the wolf skin and dress it. They put this in the attic of the mission house so it would not be seen by prying eyes" — a needed precaution, given the troubles over Eddie's ermine skins.

mischievous tricks. Also there were those from the East, of St. Bernard, Great Dane and Newfoundland strains, strong, dependable and friendly — dogs that were given to father by Senator Sanford of Hamilton, Dr. Mark of Ottawa, and Senator Ferrier of Montreal. Father has paid fitting tribute to these valiant four-footed servants in his book, "My Dogs in the Northland." All these dogs were great companions for me and I moved freely and fearlessly amongst them. I was keen for every opportunity to ride behind them, either on the bare toboggan or in the cariole.

The construction of these sleds was of great interest to me. One end had to be steamed and curved like the letter "J" to form the head. The curved part was secured with moose-skin thongs and the boards fastened together with cross pieces. Along the outer sides holes were made for the tie ropes. To make the cariole an upright was tied near the rear end of the toboggan by ropes running from the upright to the curved head and to the ends. The sides were closed in with moose or deer skin and the whole thing painted or decorated.

The dog harness, also, was fascinating to me. The collars were round, well padded and decorated with tassels. The traces and back straps were made of strong moose hide. Some of the Chief Factors had beautiful "saddle cloths" of blue cloth decorated with bright beads for their dogs, and also silver bells. Such a turnout was a delight to see with the sunshine and snowy background.

But beautiful as "dog trains" appeared, they were not to be trifled with. The dogs of such equipages as a rule obeyed only their "master's voice." If anyone else attempted to drive them he did so at the peril of his life.

My mother had an experience with one of these fine teams, about which I never tired hearing her tell in her own sweet way. She and father had been taken to the fort for a Council meeting and party. While the men did business the ladies visited. When the affair was over the question was asked, "Who will drive Mrs.Young home?"

"I — I will," said the Chief Factor, jumping to his feet. He was a big, dominating man and was not to be denied. But he had been drinking freely during the evening, and the other traders, as well as father, feared the outcome if he, in the condition he was, attempted to drive his lively dogs.

However, the Factor ordered out his team and the handsome outfit, with silver bells and glistening cariole and lovely beaverskin robes, was soon at the door. Mother was tucked in, the big Factor cracked his dog-whip and started grandly away. He had taken the tail rope and attempted to keep his place on the sled at the back of the upright. To do this a driver must have all his wits about him and know how to keep his balance. At the rate the dogs dashed off over the snow, and with the swaying of the cariole, the Factor's pleasure and triumph at driving the lady home was short-lived. He was soon sent staggering off the sled and left sprawling on the snow. Away rushed the dogs, with father and the other traders running as hard as they could after them.

"Don't speak to the dogs," the men shouted to my mother. They feared she would undertake to halt them, but she had been long enough in the land, and had learned something already about the art of dog-driving. The racing dogs quickly left the running men far behind. As the dogs' heads had been turned towards the mission, they knew the route to the church well, and quickly covered the two or three miles. The road up the bank to the church curved near the mission house. As the dogs reached the top of the bank and turned towards the church, mother threw the cariole on its side, rolled out, scrambled quickly to her feet and ran for the house. She was safely inside before the dogs knew they had lost their passenger. The men who followed picked up the robes that were strewn along the trail, and found the dogs and overturned cariole at the church door. "All's well that ends well."[56]

The training of young dogs and getting them to work was always of interest to me. The "professional" way of the Indians did not meet father's approval. They seemed to have tremendous faith in their cruel whips, and when a dog proved a bit stubborn they did not hesitate to knock it about with a club. But father believed that a bit of kindness and a little patient teaching were better with the fine young dogs that he had raised. His favourite method was to use three of his best-trained dogs to help him. Two would be placed at the head of the "pupil" and one behind. Father would run beside the novice and do his best to encourage it to understand what was demanded. It was no use for the dog to try to stop, for the dogs ahead pulled him on and the dog behind was apt to nip him if he pulled back. Then, if he tried to

56 This happened at Norway House, as the route to the mission and church corresponds to the description given here. The factor was probably James Stewart; see Elizabeth's account of this incident, which is included in Part I.

run away the one behind knew its work and kept the traces straight by pulling back. It did not take many lessons of this kind for the bright, intelligent fellows to learn their "trade."

Sometimes an "incorrigible" was found. In the old days such a dog met with short shrift and was either turned into a dog feast by the Indians or into soap grease by the Whites. But I was given credit for saving at least one fine dog from such an end. The Indians wanted to destroy this fellow. He was a fine-looking, well-bred dog, and father was in despair. When I understood the situation I pled for him as a playmate. It was an excuse for father, anyway, to delay the death penalty, and so he was turned over to me and my sister.

Strange as it may seem, what those "professional" dog trainers failed to do, we children did. In our play we soon had the dog pulling things around for us, and then [he] pulled us also. He made an extra fine sleigh dog, and so we were "blest" for our success. He gave father the suggestion for his book, *Hector, My Dog*.[57]

Children love puppies, and so did we in the Mission house. To the annoyance of the "good housekeepers," we were constantly letting them come into the house. There was a great difference in the mother dogs. The queen of them all was a fine dog from Ontario that we called "Muff." From her size and beautiful colouring I think she must have been a St. Bernard.[58] There seemed to be nothing wanting in her as a dog. She was most efficient in all her duties, not only as a mother, but also as a leader, something that few "imported" dogs became. To us children she was the mother dog *par excellence*. She followed us around with eagerness to see that no harm was done to her precious little puppies, and if any made a mistake in the house she was quick to clean it up.

Muff's love for her puppies was almost her undoing. An important journey had to be undertaken, and there were not enough dogs to fill the traces without her. It was thought that her pups were far enough advanced to look

---

57 Published in 1905, *Hector, My Dog* adopted the device of casting the Youngs' experiences with dogs in the fictive voice of "Hector," who, in chapter 7, is rescued and tamed by Eddie's and Lillian's affection.

58 Muff was indeed a St. Bernard, the gift of Mrs. Andrew Allan of Montréal. Young brought the dog with him to Berens River in the spring of 1874 (*My Dogs in the Northland*, 195).

after themselves and that they would be all right with a little home watching. So Muff was called to lead away the second train of dogs. She was keen from the start to cover the journey, and was more so when the sleds were loaded at Winnipeg and her face was turned towards home. She tugged so hard at the traces, trying to hasten back to her pups, that she broke her collar-bone. The Indian dog driver wanted to shoot her, but father thought she was too valuable a dog to lose. So he rearranged the loads on his sleds and made a place for Muff. It meant more time on the trail, but he eventually got home and restored Muff to her pups.[59]

Perhaps the most exciting thing that happened over me and the dogs was a fight with "Jack." This fellow was a black giant that weighed about one hundred and fifty pounds. When standing on his hind legs he could look a six-foot man in the face and put his paws on the man's shoulders. He was a cross between a St. Bernard mother and a Great Dane, and seemed to have the best qualities of both breeds. He was the "king" of our kennel and acted as though he thought he was the protector of us all, especially father and me. He was very powerful and there was no dog around the place that would or could face him. And plenty of the Indians were afraid of him.

When that carpenter who killed the wolf came to Berens River he took a liking to me and would play with me. Unfortunately, he caught me up and tossed me in play when Jack was near. With a roar of disapproval Jack sprang at the carpenter and knocked him down. If father had not been there the dog might have killed the man. The carpenter wanted to pack up and leave. Father said he had to fulfill his contract, and that he had to win the favour of that dog. The carpenter said he would not go near him again and that father had to chain him up all the time he worked on the place. This, father declared, was impossible.

The upshot was that Jack was put in an outhouse and fastened with a strong chain, and the carpenter was to be the only one to go near him with food and water. If Jack showed fight the food was to be denied him. The first time the man opened the door Jack sprang at him like a lion. The carpenter dropped the food and ran for his life. Father told him he was a fool to show fear in the presence of the dog. He was strongly chained anyway, and could

---

59 Egerton Young related this story in more detail in *My Dogs in the Northland*, 201–9, and in *Hector, My Dog*, 279–82.

not get at him. I do not know how long, but it was days before Jack showed any signs of weakening and was ready to accept food from that man. But hunger is a terrible humiliator, and at last Jack was calm and let the man feed him. He was then freed, but was never reconciled to that man, and whenever the carpenter came near the hair on Jack's back rose ominously. The man seemed to be as much afraid of my presence, lest Jack should see us together and renew his attack.

14 Welcome Home

"Mother, Daddy won't play with me." That was a bitter cry from me, as father usually made the welkin ring when he returned home from tripping.[60] Where he was, joy reigned, if it was possible for him to make it so. But here was a day when he failed his little son.

Father was a man of great enthusiasm. He was truly "whole-hearted" in whatever he did. So when he became a missionary it was with "Apostolic zeal," and that of the best Pauline type, that he set about his work. He never heard of a band of Indians that he did not try to reach and deliver to them the Gospel of Jesus Christ. His fellow-missionaries said that he was trying to kill himself, but he was determined to leave no band unevangelized. He longed to be the first to proclaim to some the unsearchable riches of redeeming grace and to proclaim to men God's great love for them. In this way his missionary journeys, like Paul's, increased in extent. But he had to make all his own provisions for these journeys, do his share as a paddler of the canoe in summer, or as a dog-driver when winter held the land in its stern grip. So it came about that there were times when to reach his home alive he and his dogs had to fight their way through deep snows and bitter storms when every bit of food had been eaten and they had been tested to "the last ounce" of their strength, and missionary and dogs, more dead than alive, stumbled into the mission yard. The dogs would drop in their tracks and not wish to be disturbed, even by having their harness removed. On such occasions father was nursed back to life and strength by the loving care of

60 "Made the welkin ring" is a poetic expression, a "welkin" being the arch or vault of heaven (OED).

my mother. In his first exhaustion he did not wish to be disturbed, not even to have removed his leather and woollen travelling things.[61]

"Why won't Daddy play with me?" I asked, as I looked at him, lying like a log on the couch in the dining-room.

"He has been on a long, cold journey and is tired out," my mother replied. "We must let him rest and get warm, and when he awakes have something nice for him to eat."

"Who sent him on the long, cold journey and tired him so that he can't play with me?" I demanded.

"He went on the command of Jesus Christ, who told him to go," mother said.

"Then I hate Jesus Christ for sending my Daddy out and making him so tired and cold," I declared.

This declaration not only shocked my mother, but filled her with fear that she had given me a very wrong impression of Jesus Christ, and she took great pains to try to correct any misapprehensions. She got down the Child's Bible while father was sleeping and showed me the good and gentle Jesus, full of grace and truth, the Jesus who loved little children, healed the sick and loved the sinful. It sounded all very nice, but somehow, it was not convincing. That was not the sort of Master who would send anyone out on cold, long journeys and when he came home was so tired that he could not even greet kindly his own son!

But this same little mother was the unconscious, or indirect, means of bringing to me a very different picture of both Christ and her own part in missionary work.

My father and mother had little appreciation of what I did when I visited the bands of strange Indians who came with their furs to the trading post. I returned, or was returned, in safety to the mission House.

---

61 Eddie was probably remembering the unhappy time that his father did not get home to Berens River in time for Christmas, arriving instead a few days later, on 28 December. In a letter to his father, William Young, on 4 January 1876, Egerton described his hard journey home from Sandy Bar on the far side of Lake Winnipeg after an unexpected delay: "We made a tremendous *run* home in two days (44 hours) and the going very heavy on account of loose snow. I was so tired, for two days I could not hold a pen so as to write. I suppose I ran or walked at least one half of the time as the going was so bad. The Indians here all come to see me and to tell me how kind Ookemasquao (Libbie) had been to them and what a fine Christmas they had had."

As I had secured a "working knowledge" of their tongue, I proved to be a serviceable go-between. Many if not most of these bands were still pagan, and when not trading or loafing around the trading post they were dancing or engaging in some heathenish practices. When I visited some of these the Indians thought it sport to paint my face, stick feathers in my hair and teach me their dances. It was no wonder that after such visits Little Mary complained of the condition of my face and clothes! But father was not the least suspicious of what took place.

An Ojibwe Invitation, and Aftermath

One of these pagan bands was in camp and the tom-tom of their drums was heard every night. "I have been in this country for years," my mother said to father, "and I have not seen an Indian dance."

"Why, if you wish to see one," father said nonchalantly, "all you have to do is to send a present of tobacco over to the Chief of that band, and he will immediately invite you to see his young men go through their practices."[62]

"I wish you would do so for me," mother said.

Father did so, but he was not as curious of Indian customs as he was of Indian legends. It seemed to be the other way around with my mother. Anyway, father acceded to her request and sent over a little present to the Chief, intimating that he and my mother would like to go and see one of their dances. In a very short time two of his Indians in their best regalia came and said that the Chief would be glad to have them come that very afternoon.

---

62 This event clearly took place in the summer of 1875, when Eddie was six and had been at Berens River for a year. (By the next summer, the family was making preparations to leave for Ontario.) Eddie's 1962 reminiscences noted that this band of Indians had come down the river "and put up their big dancing tent in our back yard." Egerton Young had travelled up the Berens River (probably to Little Grand Rapids) in February 1872, following upon the visit of some of the upriver Ojibwe to the Norway House area the previous summer. Those whom he met in the winter of 1872 were reading the Cree syllabics and some were baptized (*Stories from Indian Wigwams and Northern Camp-fires* [New York: Eaton and Mains, 1892], 111–13). The 1875 visitors were probably from a neighbouring group that came down to trade. That same summer, a "Saulteaux chieftainess" also visited the Berens River mission, and Young visited her camp the following April (*By Canoe and Dog-Train*, 262–65). She may have been connected with the same upriver group, but Young provided no further details.

It happened to be a warm day and the edges of the tent were lifted. As the missionary and his wife approached the Chief's tent the sharp eyes of my mother saw the legs of the young Indians as they were going through their steps, and amongst them she noticed a pair of little legs that were familiar to her. As father did not recognize them she said nothing but held a bated breath, fearful as to what might happen. Perhaps she hoped that he would not discover the owner of those little legs.

The Chief welcomed his guests with great courtesy and some ceremony. He had arranged a pile of blankets like a dais for them. My father noticed that these blankets were far from clean, and knowing my mother's dislike of any uncleanness, and the suspicion of the presence of vermin, he hoped it would be a lesson to her and that she would never ask again to visit such a place. But whatever my mother thought of the blankets was never known. She had other thoughts and was also desirous of carefully responding to the courteous welcome of the Chief. He was doing his best for her and she was determined to equal him in courtesy.[63]

When the youngsters came in with their hops, steps and jumps, the missionary remarked to his wife that he did not know that such little boys were called upon to perform. This remark made my mother tremble.

My disguise was fairly complete, but in the gyrations of the dance there was a good deal of stamping.[64] The stockings I had on were dark brown and not unlike the colour of an Indian's legs. Fate, however, was against me, for in doing the extra stamping before the "honoured guests" a garter gave out and a brown stocking fell down, exposing a white leg! I caught sight of my mother's face and it was so full of dismay that I seemed to realize instantly that I was in the wrong place and immediately sought refuge at her feet.

63 In 1962, Eddie recorded his mother's hospitality to the chief and dancers afterwards: "In leaving the tent after shaking hands with Chief Sateau, mother said in good Cree, 'If you and your young men come to the mission house, I'll give you a slice of white bread and a cup of sweet tea.' They accepted the invitation and came. Mother was as good as her word. She was afraid the bread would not last out, but she succeeded in serving them all tea with devonshire cream and sugar also. They went away very much pleased." The Youngs had a cow, but we can't tell whether Elizabeth actually produced Devonshire cream: this may be an embellishment.

64 The 1962 reminiscences described the dance as a "Bear Dance" — mimicking bears and showing "how people could meet and defeat them when suddenly attacked in the woods."

My father's face appeared to turn all colours, my mother said; but whatever he felt, he knew that he was the guest of an Indian Chief and there was a decorum that must be observed.

[From the 1962 memoir: "The surprise of the missionaries was to see their boy come up to the dais and take his seat beside his mother. Chief Sateau and his father seemed to have great trouble making out what each other said. So father appealed to the boy, and said, "What did he say?" The boy promptly translated the Sateau language for him, for the dialect is quite different from the Cree. Mother smiled at this, but father was not sure, and then he would translate what father said in English or Cree for Chief Sateau, but father was not sure of this either. When and where did his boy learn so much sateau?"][65]

But, as soon as he could, he thanked the Chief for his entertainment, and, taking his wife by one hand, he seized his boy with the other and marched them as quickly as he could to the mission house. After securing a long birch rod he took me into the dining-room, the largest room in the house. Mother and Little Mary were asked to leave the room. He shoved the table against the wall and sat down in a rocking-chair, shook the gad at me and said: "Dance!"

I was somewhat relieved at the command, for I thought then that he only wanted to see the manner of the dance. So for him I went through the whole performance, and then said: "That's the way of it."

But he did not seem to appreciate my performance, and, shaking the rod ominously near my legs, he repeated the command, "Dance!"

Fear crept into my heart and I began to wonder what he wanted, but I went through the dance again. Still he said, "Dance!" and that gad played near my legs, both of which were now bare. Whenever I showed any sign of stopping he shook the rod and ordered sternly, "Dance!"

At last, tired out, I crumpled to the floor. He then dropped the rod, sprang to his feet, and, taking me into his arms, sank back into the chair. He held me passionately to his breast and I felt the beating of his heart. He just sat and rocked and held me as tightly as he could. I even forgot my own fears as I felt the beating of his heart and wondered at his silence.

---

65 The boy was, of course, Eddie. This account gives the chief a generic name, Sateau — properly Saulteaux, a term often applied to the Ojibwe and their language. Eddie evidently had learned enough Ojibwe to be understood locally.

"My boy, my precious boy!" he said, or rather murmured, at last.

Then his words came like a flood. He told me all about his early home, his conversion and success in his early ministry, how he and mother had left home, city church and loving friends to come out to preach the Gospel to the Indians, that they might be lifted from heathenish practices and degradation. Mother and he had endured all manner of hardships — cold, hunger and loneliness — all to do Christ's work. Had all those prayers, sacrifices and sufferings been in vain? God had given them a little boy who was more precious to them than their own lives, and instead of their lifting up the Indians, the Indians were dragging down their precious boy to their heathenish ways.

"Did Jesus Christ send mother to suffer like you?" I asked him.

"She has suffered far more than I have, I fear," he said. "I have had the excitement of action and mother has had to stay here and suffer at first alone until you came."

"And what did I do?" I asked.

"You brought great joy to both your mother and to me." "But," he added, "I fear that you also brought great anxiety to her, and you made it harder for me to go away from the house on my journeys. It was one thing more to bear for Christ's sake and the Gospel's."

"Why does Jesus Christ ask you to suffer cold and give up your friends?" I asked.

"It is just the way He did, my boy," my father replied, perhaps wondering at the persistence of my questions. "He came to this world to save us." Then he told me of Christ's life of service for mankind, what He had suffered, and that He had left it to His disciples to go out and work, preach, and suffer, if need be, as He had done to win the rest of the world for Him.

It was much more convincing than what my mother had said. I began to see that as they had suffered they were brave and good, like Christ, and were doing the most wonderful work possible to make the world more like Heaven, and Indian wigwams more like the home that my mother had made for me and my sister.

But that did not appear to me to be the end of that experience. My mother's health had not been good and the account of her condition had brought from the "home" doctor a declaration that if father wished to spare her life he should bring her home as soon as possible. He has always said that was the reason why he and mother relinquished the work that had taken such a deep hold upon them both. But, in spite of all such declarations, I have always had the suspicion that after what he had seen in that pagan Chief's tent he was almost as deeply concerned about me.

As far as I personally was concerned, that overflow of love from my father marked a very deep spiritual experience. I could never free myself of the impression made upon me by that beating heart. That he loved me like that! In fact, the change in my conception of my father was so great that he was, after that day, an altogether new man to me. All that went before seemed as nothing to what I then discovered in him. Both he and my mother were brave and heroic workers for Christ's sake, and they loved me with a self-sacrificing love.

Reminiscences of 1962 for the Years 1876 to 1898

Leaving Berens River, 1876

We all suffered from the cold that winter and spring. Mother became so ill that father sent word to his doctor in Toronto and told him. The Doctor replied that he must bring mother home as fast as he can, so father began making preparations for our return to Ontario. It was very difficult for me to say good bye to little Mary. Mother would like to have taken her home to Ontario but father said, "We cannot think of it. If anything happened to Mary, the Indians would not believe anything else but that we mistreated her." Father gave his cow to Timothy Bear when he promised that he would do his best to see that little Mary was well cared for.[1]

The last parting of Mary and her beloved protege was almost tragic. The parting had to take place, and father took his family and his big dog Jack and came back to Ontario. He brought Jack with him saying Jack had saved his life and it was up to him to take care of such a noble dog.[2]

I was home in time for my grandmother Bingham and Aunt Clara and Aunt Lottie and Uncle Joe to give me my seventh birthday party. We had lots of cousins in Bradford that day, but unfortunately for the peace of the occasion, those Ontario cousins began to call me "Indian," so I fought them.

---

1 Little Mary and Timothy Bear and his family later went back to Rossville. Mary and the Youngs continued to communicate at times: see her 1887 letter in Part III, sec. 14.

2 The family also regretted parting with Cuffy, the dog to whom Elizabeth was especially attached. Young, in *My Dogs in the Northland* (New York: Fleming H. Revell, 1902), 113, recalled that "Mrs. Young and the children pleaded that Cuffy should also be allowed to come," but he vetoed the idea as "the expense would have been so much the greater." Cuffy and the other dogs were left for the use of "our honoured successor," John Semmens, who arrived in Berens River in the fall of 1876.

To have peace my aunts put me into the sacred and holy place of their parlor with its horse-hair furniture. I did not weep or lose heart and proceeded to entertain myself. I dragged the sofa out of its place and put four chairs one ahead of the other. The sofa was to be my carryall [cariole] and the chairs were my dogs. By some means I got down one of the poles that held up the curtains at the window; I took the cord off too and tied the chairs for a harness. Then I took the pole and began to hurry the dogs along, so above the din of the kitchen my aunts heard Whack, whack, whack! They quickly took me back in to the kitchen and it was more profitable to let me handle the unruly cousins than to whack their parlor furniture. They returned the compliment by giving me the measles.[3]

School in Port Perry, 1876-79

When I was recovered from the measles, I found my parents and the family settled in the Methodist parsonage in Port Perry. Father had induced mother's sister, Clara, to come with them to help mother get settled. Port Perry was situated on the west side of Lake Scugog. It was a circuit of three appointments: Port Perry, Prince Albert, and another preaching place named after the steward, Mr Bates. On the east side of the lake there was a band of Ojibway Indians.[4]

He [father] had got a horse, a beautiful bay, and plunged into his new work with his usual zeal, and the demands for this double duty were heavy and trying. Sometimes when he would go pastoral calling he would take his big dog Jack with him. At some of these places the kind people would give Jack something to eat. He never forgot those places, and one where he was

---

3 Eddie also told this story in chapter 7 of "A Missionary and His Son," but there he placed it during the Youngs' visit to Ontario in 1873–74 (no birthday party mentioned). That date accords with Elizabeth Young's memoirs for 1873–74, in which she mentioned Eddie getting the measles at Bradford, and it seems unlikely he would get them twice. Yet, as noted earlier, a seven-year-old would have been more able to move heavy parlour furniture than a boy aged four or five.

4 The community, now known as the Mississaugas of Scugog Island First Nation, had been largely displaced by white settlement and the damming and flooding of what had been a shallow marshy lake. In that period, they occupied an 800-acre parcel of land on Scugog Island that offered very limited resources and no direct access to water (see "Origin and History" at www.scugogfirstnation.com).

particularly well served was the Ross farm in Prince Albert.[5] The public school in Port Perry was situated on the side of a hill, and at the top of it the sidewalk turned northward and passed Prince Albert. If father happened to be away, Jack would undertake to do some pastoral calling himself. His one meal at home was served between four and five o'clock, and he was always sure to be there on time to get it.

One day after school was opened [ended], the first children dismissed came running back from the gate crying that a black bear was coming down the sidewalk. The lady teachers in alarm hastened out, and seeing the big black animal swaggering down the sidewalk, called the children to come inside the fence and fastened the gate. When my room was let out I ran to the fence asking what was the excitement. I heard what they said and shouted, "That's no bear. It's my big dog Jack." I climbed over the fence to run up to him, threw my arms around his neck, and climbed on his back, for I rode him like a pony, and Jack walked past them while I swung my hand proudly over my head. As I passed the lady teachers I heard one say, "Oh, it's that young Indian. He's afraid of nothing." It was bad enough, I thought, to be called Indian by the boys and girls, but for the teachers to do so, it seemed to hurt.

But the two men teachers seemed to treat me very differently. The Principal treated me with real respect. He told the people of Port Perry that here was a boy born in an Indian village in the northwest and raised there and that he could speak better English than any people in Port Perry. The assistant principal was also kind to me, but from a different standpoint. He would gather the boys around the back steps of the school and ask me to tell them this and that in Cree language. It was all right when he was around, but it was different when he went away, for then the boys would point their fingers and say, "Indian, Indian."

One of those teachers had a beautiful riding horse and took great pleasure in riding it around the town after school, especially the little park in the centre of the town. One day after I had come home from school, my mother sent me on an errand and the shortest way took me through the park. When

5 The Ross farm was that of Mr. and Mrs. Aaron Ross, whom Elizabeth described in her memoir as "very kind and thoughtful." As she noted, her sister Clara Bingham married the Rosses' son William in September 1877.

I reached it, I did not see anybody but that lady teacher and her horse. She had fallen from it and was being dragged on the ground. The horse seemed to be getting more and more excited all the time. I hastened to it, stopped it and released her boot from the stirrup and helped her up. I was afraid that she might have hurt herself and offered to get the doctor but she declared that she was all right. She put the saddle back on the horse and tightened up the girths. I offered to lead her horse home but she said she could manage it all right, so I left her.

In that school I saw a rather remarkable thing, perhaps I should say from a boy's standpoint. There was a little room called the bell room. A rope came through the floors of the [bell] tower. At the side of the room there was a big bookcase with a glass door. The shelves had been taken out and a rod fastened in there from end to end. This rod was decorated with instruments of torture of various lengths. At the left were two long bamboo rods and a rawhide whip with leather straps of various length and thickness, some having several lashes. I don't think there was a cat-o-nine tales [tails] but I'm sure one had six tales and I wondered how soon I would be made to feel them, but I was soon tried out. I found that especially the lady teachers seemed to think that the pupil[s] had enough [punishment] when they cried. They did not seem to like me because I wouldn't cry for them. One turned me over to the assistant principal. I do not think Mr Rae liked his job for I had been always ready to please him when he wanted me to tell the boys something in Cree. However, discipline is discipline, and now it was up to him. He took down a bamboo rod and brought it down on my hand. It must have been there a long time for it was very dry and broke in several pieces. He smiled and looked at me. I wasn't sure what might follow. He picked up the bits of bamboo and said with another smile, "that will do to-day."

There was another teacher, a lady by the name of Christian who acted differently to her sister teachers. There were four of us boys who got into mischief. She would send us to the bell room also. She told us what she thought of us and said each of us should have eight slaps with the thick strap. I happened to be the last. It seemed to me that the other fellows cried very easily. They didn't have any little Mary to train them. I received my eight slaps and looked her in the face, so she gave me eight more and still I looked at her, perhaps a little defiantly or scornfully as I remembered little

Mary.[6] She then told me I was to remain in the bell room while she took the other three boys back to the room, telling her monitor to continue. She came back to me. She didn't stand up but sat on a chair and quietly looked me over. "I think," she said, "you would like to be a gentleman." That was something different I thought, than straps, and it was something that mother had tried to instill into me as Mary did that of physical endurance. Mother never missed a chance if an H.B.C. [man] came around, to draw attention to his manliness, except that trader in Berens River whom she despised. So I listened carefully and humbly to what she had to say and told her I certainly did wish to be a gentleman. My eyes moistened with my repentance, and after that if she caught me doing anything below par, she would say "that is not gentlemanly" or "that doesn't become a gentleman," and she knew it meant more to me than all the straps in the bell room.

I worked hard at my studies and made the top place amongst the boys in the room. There was one girl who had been the head of her class for a long time. She had a maiden aunt who had nothing else to do but look after her niece. She would walk to school with her in the morning and when the school was out in the afternoon, the aunt was at the school gate waiting. Lawra's name was always at the top in the school reports that were published in the local paper. One day a spelling match for the whole school was arranged. Lawra as head girl was chosen to lead one side, and I as head boy was to lead the other side. The pupils were then divided and the "spelling bee" began. At first the boys and girls fell down very fast, then slower and slower; they had to take their seats until just the two leaders were on the floor. The keenest of interest was manifested and the feeling was tense. The teacher offered a word to Lawra and she misspelled it. The teacher then offered it to me and I managed to spell it correctly. Then there was pandemonium. There was such cheering that I felt sorry for Lawra. It was not merely that I had come out champion in the contest, but the school children seemed to glory in the fact that Lawra had been defeated at last.

---

6 From earlier in the 1962 memoir: "Little Mary was always ready to serve me as quickly as possible but I would protest often very loudly if I were not quickly served. On such occasions father or mother would try to make me more reasonable, and if I did not cease my shouting and demonstrations they would whip me. . . . And so when Mary saw she could do nothing to soften their punishment, she would say to me, "don't let them know they hurt you when they beat you; then they will quit beating you. In this way she tried to make a sparton [Spartan] out of me."

Other Memories of Port Perry

One Saturday [when] I was down at the grocery store I met Mrs Bates the wife of the steward of the appointment. "If you will come and visit me some time I can show you something pretty nice," she said. "I'll go now," I said. So she hastened to finish her shopping, then she put me in the buggy and we drove up to the parsonage. Here she renewed her invitation to my mother for me. I could go up with her and stay with them and when father came up to the Sunday afternoon service he could bring me home. So mother let me go. When we reached the farm the cows were in the farm yard being milked. Mr Bates was standing at a high point from which he could see all that was going on. He believed and practiced the [saying], "the eyes of a farmer are worth more than his hands," but his hands were both strong and kind. At his right side, a beautiful white deer stood as it were at perfect attention. Down amongst the cattle moving freely was her son, a handsome fawn. His body seemed to be as big as that of his mother but he was not quite as tall, and two horns seemed to be pushing their way out of his forehead. Then he came up to my side. "He will take a drink of milk from you," said Mr. Bates. So I went to the house and asked Mrs Bates for a basin. I took this to a man who was milking and he put some milk in it. I then took it back to the place where Mr Bates and the deer were standing. I offered the milk to Billy for that's what Mr. Bates called him (and he called his mother Nanny). Billy took a drink of milk and then I offered it to Nanny but she shook her head and lifted up her right foot as if to say, "I'm not a baby, take it away." So I again offered it to Billy and he emptied the tin. Mr Bates said, "Nanny will take some oats from you." So I hastened into the barn, found the oat bin, and got some oats. I brought this back to Nanny and it was very interesting to see the dainty way in which she would take some grains of oats and chew them. Mr Bates decided to move his position but I thought Nanny would stay with me and feed on the oats. But to my surprise she followed Mr Bates, and when he stopped she was there at his side standing at full attention as though she would say to everyone, "This is the man that I honor." It seemed to me so strange to see a deer just as wild in Ontario as were those in the northwest, here standing beside a man with her fawn at her side, with not the slightest indication of fear but only held by love and honor. I was eager to hear the story of how this all happened.

One day in early spring Mr Bates had some occasion to go into his woods. As he drove near the edge, standing beside a tree was this beautiful white deer looking straightway at him and not showing any sign of fear or fright. A few quiet steps near her, and he saw what was the matter. Her fawn was lying flat on the ground, and her udder seemed to be deformed or torn in some way so she could not feed her baby. He gently picked up the fawn and brought it to the barn, and the mother followed him closely. He opened one of the big doors of the barn so she could be free to go in and out. He placed the fawn on the hay, and then went to the stable and got a tin and went to a cow and got some milk, and hastened back to the farm. With his finger he taught the little one to drink and kept rubbing its stomach till he was satisfied the fawn was all right. He went away and came back in half an hour and fed the fawn again. He shut the big barn door but left the little door open. It was fastened so Nanny could go in and out at pleasure. He continued his half hour visits to the fawn until it was dark and he was sure they were all right. In the morning he was at their side.

Billy was soon on his feet, and then Mr. Bates put a bar across the mouth of the little door so Billy could not jump over it but Nanny could go in and out at will. He did not want the fawn to be free until it was a little stronger. Soon Nanny and her fawn Billy knew all the movements of the cows, and they were there morning and night and were always made welcome. The deer would wander through the edge of the forest and look at the homes of other people but they would not accept anything from any of them. But the people rejoiced to see them and took great pride in them.

When harvest time was in full swing one of the neighbors brought in a man to help them. As soon as he saw these deer he rushed into the farmer's house, found his gun and went and shot them. He came in with a boast and [at] almost the first word, the farmer's wife cried out, "Whatever have you done?" "I shot two deer," the man said boastfully, "and you can have now some venison." "I do not know of any deer around here except Mr. Bates's Nanny and Billy, and if you have killed them, you had better get out of the country for the people here will mob you." He quickly fled. All the people along the line mourned the loss of Nanny and Billy, and the people said Mr Bates mourned the loss as though she had been a devoted daughter.

Things tragic also occurred in the parsonage. Mother's brother uncle Joe [Bingham] had paid us a visit and he gave me one of his trained canaries.

When I came home from school I could go into the parlor and shut windows and doors and let the canary come out of the cage and play with me. It would light on my finger and sing to me, and I would whistle back. I could put grain between my lips and the birdie would easily pick them out. We had a few nice days together, but alas, it was not for long. One beautiful sunny day, the servant girl had hung the cage on a nail on the side of the house. We thought it was so far in from the corner of the house that nothing could reach it. But a cat had climbed a nearby railing and jumped in such a way as to knock the cage right off the nail. It fell to the ground and the door opened. It was also a bad fall for the cat, and we wondered if it were possible that the canary [could] recover first and get out of the cage and fly away. Anyway, the only thing that we found was one beautiful yellow feather. Father got a bit of yellow paper and cut it in the shape of a canary and fastened it in the cage and hung the cage on the nail outside again. He got his rifle and put it just inside the kitchen door and told the girl to keep watch, and if she saw the cat creeping up to let him know. It was not long before she called him. They saw the cat climb to the railing. She opened the door. The cat jumped out but father was quick and shot the cat. But that did not bring back my birdie.

Bishop Taylor, a noted missionary bishop of the Methodist Episcopal Church, came up from the U.S.A. when he heard that father had come back from serving on the Indian mission field, and he personally asked father to come and join him in his missionary work in South Africa.[7] Father said he would love to go but he thought he had obligations that held him here in Canada. His wife was not well, he had a son and three little girls and he thought his duty was to look after them at this time. He [the bishop] spent a Sunday and Monday with us.

Because he was with us, family washing was not done on Monday. But the clothes lines of our neighbors were all filled. The afternoon was raining and the clothes were all left on the line overnight to dry. That night Jack was very restless, growling and tried to attract attention. Father thought it was because a stranger was in the house and told him to be quiet. In the

7 William Taylor, missionary activist in Africa, Asia, and South America, was elected Methodist Episcopal Bishop for Africa in 1884 and might have visited and issued such an invitation to Young in these years. However, Elizabeth's memoir of 1927 more reliably identified the visitor at the time of the theft as the Reverend George Young, who held positions in Ontario in the late 1870s before being reappointed to Manitoba.

Figure 1. Doll's laced cradle board decorated with beadwork, made for the Youngs' first daughter, Lillian, at Norway House, ca. 1872–73. Her mother, Elizabeth, recalled in her memoir "The Bride of 1868": "We had a dolls Indian cradle made for her, & an Indian doll put in it to her delight" (see "The Arrival of Lillian," in Part I). ROM 999.133.20 with permission of the Royal Ontario Museum (photograph copyright ROM).

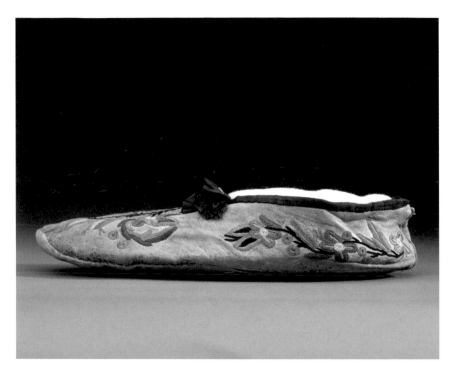

Figure 2. Moccasin, depilated skin, embroidered with silk thread, from Norway House, ca. 1870–73. Egerton Young noted in *Stories from Indian Wigwams and Northern Camp-fires* (1892) that "Little Mary" Robinson "made all our moccasins" (see Part III, sec. 6). ROM 999.133.17.1-2 with permission of the Royal Ontario Museum (photograph copyright ROM).

Figure 3. "Minnehaha and Sagastaookemou," Lillian and Eddie Young, Toronto, 1873. The photograph appears with this title in Egerton Young's *Stories from Indian Wigwams and Northern Camp-fires* (1892), opposite page 36. Young wrote that all his and Elizabeth's children born in the Northwest were given "Indian names": "Egerton, our first-born and only son, they [the Cree] called Sagastaookemou, which means 'the sunrise gentleman.' Lillian, ever full of mirth and brightness, they called Minnehaha, or 'Laughing-water'" (36). Although Elizabeth Young wrote of the beautiful outfits that Little Mary made for the children, they (unlike their father) were never photographed in their Cree garb. JSHB collection.

Figure 4. Egerton and Elizabeth Young and family, Bowmanville, Ontario, 1883. In the back row are Egerton and the Youngs' two eldest children, Lillian and Eddie (E. Ryerson). In the front are Elizabeth, holding William Joseph (d. October 1883), and their younger daughters, Winnifred, Grace Amanda, and Florence. Note the Berens River wolf skin under their feet (see Part II, sec. 12, "The Big Bad Wolf"), and on the left, a basket probably made by Rama or Lake Scugog Ojibwe women. JSHB collection.

Figure 5. Egerton Young and his St. Bernard dog, Jack, ca. 1877–78, Port Perry, Ontario. Jack was Young's outstanding sled dog at Norway House and Berens River, and the only dog that the family brought back with them to Ontario in 1876. The photograph also appears in *Young's My Dogs in the Northland* (1902), opposite page 66. JSHB collection.

Figure 6. E. Ryerson Young on horseback, ca. 1912–15, while he was serving the Methodist church in Bracebridge, Ontario, one of a series of three-year itinerant postings. JSHB collection.

Figure 7. Boy's leather jacket with porcupine quillwork band and sash, as worn by Eddie in the painting by J. E. Laughlin shown in the frontispiece. The jacket was doubtless made for Eddie, ca. 1875, by "Little Mary," of Norway House, who joined the Youngs at Berens River when they returned to the mission field in 1874, following their furlough in Ontario. ROM 999.133.8 with permission of the Royal Ontario Museum (photograph copyright ROM).

Figure 8. Leather jacket with silk-thread embroidery, probably made at Norway House, 1870–73. ROM 999.133.12 with permission of the Royal Ontario Museum (photograph copyright ROM).

▶ Figure 9. Moccasin upper with silk-thread embroidery. Again, this piece was in all likelihood the work of Mary Robinson, at Norway House, in the early 1870s. ROM 999.133.18.1 with permission of the Royal Ontario Museum (photograph copyright ROM).

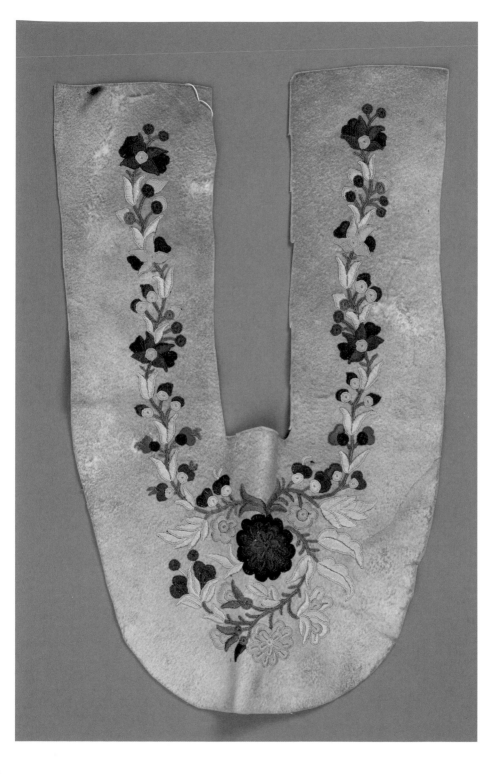

Figure 10. Man's cloth cap with floral beadwork. ROM 999.133.23 with permission of the Royal Ontario Museum (photograph copyright ROM). The image on page 195 of *By Canoe and Dog-Train* (1890) shows Young wearing this cap or one very like it, with a sash and pipe bag also resembling items in the ROM collection.

▶ Figure 11. Egerton Young in moose-skin coat, ca. 1889, photo by Perkins, Baltimore. The coat, doubtless made by Mary Robinson at Norway House, ca. 1872–73, appears in several of Young's publicity photographs and is now in the Royal Ontario Museum, ROM 999.133.1. The image shown here is also in Young, *By Canoe and Dog-Train* (1890), page 127. The tall fur hat may be what Young, in a letter to the *Christian Guardian* written 31 March 1873, described as the "best fur cap I have in the world," given to him by mission benefactor W. E. Sanford, of Hamilton. The decorated pipe bags and leggings are not in the ROM collection.

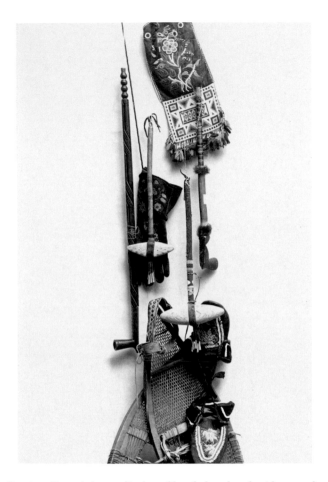

Figure 12. Egerton Young's home display of beaded and embroidery work, pipes, and other artifacts, probably photographed ca. 1900. Included are two artifacts relating to Norway House and now in the collection of the Royal Ontario Museum: on the left is, the catlinite pipe given to Young (see Part III, sec. 7) by Nelson House Cree visitors to Norway House in 1871 (ROM 999.133.27; the bowl of the pipe; the stem has been lost). The quilled band lying on the toe of the snowshoe matches the band shown on Eddie's coat (see frontispiece and fig. 7). The snowshoes, gauntlet, and pipe bag, which have evidently been lost, were probably also from Norway House.

▶ Figure 13. Egerton Young in moose-skin coat with hood, snowshoes, and pipe bag, ca. 1901. This photograph, taken at the studio of Charles L. Rosevear, Toronto, dates from about twelve years after the image in figure 11. The coat and hood with its tassel are in the Royal Ontario Museum, ROM 999.133.1.1 and 2. The pipe bag, which appears at the top of figure 13, is not in the ROM collection, nor are the snowshoes. A variant of this image appears as the frontispiece in Young, *My Dogs in the Northland*.

Figure 14. Egerton and Elizabeth Young, ca. 1873–74, she in her astrakhan coat, given her by Senator and Mrs. James Ferrier of Montréal, benefactors of the Berens River mission. The coat, she recalled, was "just what I wanted & needed" (see Part III, sec. 12). JSHB collection.

Figure 15. Four generations of women, ca. 1904. At the left, Clarissa Vanderburgh Bingham (1819–1906), on the far right, her daughter Elizabeth Bingham Young (1843–1934), and, between them, Elizabeth's daughter Grace Amanda Young Brown (1876–1934) and Grace's daughter, Elizabeth Brown (1902–90). JSHB collection.

Figure 16. Egerton Young and Harcourt Brown, his grandson, ca. 1904. Harcourt, born in May 1900, was a frequent visitor to the Youngs' Bradford home north of Toronto up to the time of Egerton's death, in 1909. He remembered his grandfather warmly, and took an active role in gathering and preserving the Youngs' papers. The photograph was taken at Charles L. Rosevear's studio in Toronto. JSHB collection.

morning we found that our baby carriage was gone from the verandah and the neighbors' clothes lines had all been stripped of baby clothes. Jack had done his best to arouse us of what had happened. The police were immediately notified and a search was made for the thieves on all roads. [With]in the day a man and a woman were found about twenty miles away. They were brought back and put in the locker. The owners of the clothes feared that theirs would be ruined by mildew [and] asked the privilege of taking out their clothes to dry in the sunshine, promising to put them all back again in the baby carriage. But the magistrate would not have any of it; it could not be done. The culprits had to be tried and sentenced before the goods could be released. As for us, our baby carriage was a wreck as the result of trundling those wet and heavy goods over rough roads.

If my father did not see his way to respond to the earnest call of the noble Bishop Taylor, the missionary secretary here at home in Canada was calling upon him to help them in missionary deputation work. He was as usual very unselfish in his time and service and undertook some deputation work. It interfered so much with his regular work that a young man from Victoria College, John W. Wilkinson, was appointed to help him.[8]

School Troubles and Father's Response

The matter of speaking Cree in the home was rapidly coming to a climax. Father and mother wished that there was some way that I might be helped to retain the knowledge of the Indian language that I had acquired. Father suggested that we use the Cree language in our morning devotion but I came to hate almost anything and everything that was Indian and my usage on the school grounds seemed to be more and more unpleasant until one day in the fight my school bag was torn and slate broken. That night at my bedside when I knelt and tried to pray everything seemed to be wrong.

---

8 Eddie may have misremembered the name and age of his father's associate. On 8 October 1877, Enoch Wood, general secretary of the Methodist Church of Canada, wrote to Young from Toronto: "The Central Board have requested your services on a Deputation with Bro J. A. Williams to New Brunswick, P.E. Island, and Nova Scotia. I think it will take you about six weeks. Assuming your willingness to go, a supply for your local work will be needed" — and Wood followed with a couple of suggestions. Young went, and the *Christian Guardian* published very warm reviews of his lectures and reception. John Williams (b. 1817) became a prominent Ontario Methodist in the period (G. N. Emery, "Williams, John Aethuruld." *Dictionary of Canadian Biography* online).

I knew tears were running down my face, but father said he heard me sobbing. I did not know that I was making a noise, but he heard, and thought he had better come up and see what was the matter with me. When his footsteps were heard on the stairs, fear sprang in my heart. I knew he didn't like this fighting and I was afraid he might whip me, but when he reached the top of the stairs I decided to tell him all that had happened. When he came up beside me he did not utter a word of rebuke or reprove or threat; he simply leaned over on the cot, looked at me, squatted on the floor and listened. At first my mind and soul seemed very full and bitter; where was all the peace and love of the Holy Mountains and the peace of Christ? And I wound up by saying, "It seems very strange that the more a fellow tries to do right it is harder to do right."

Then father lifted up his head and said, "Do you know what is right?" "Why," I said, "of course I do. Haven't I [you?] been preaching and telling Indians that they must learn how to do the right as Christ has taught us and live the Jesus way of life?"

"Oh that's all right," said father. "But you have a lot to learn yet. See where you are at school; you are in the very lowest room. If you do your work well where you are, they will promote you to a higher grade, and if you do your work well there, then you will be promoted to a still higher grade, and so on until you go through the public school. Then you will go to the high school and it will be the same there, grade after grade, and then if all goes well, perhaps we will be able to send you to the University. So just now you go on the way you have been doing, keeping Christ before you and trying to be like him."

Then father knelt down beside me and prayed that I might be kept faithful to the ideals that I had and especially to Christ. Then he helped me into my cot, pulled the sheets over me, kissed me on my forehead and quietly slipped away. My, I thought, no rebuke, no threat, only quiet understanding and inspirations. If my earthly father could actually speak like that, whatever must our heavenly father be like? So with my heart renewed in peace and love I went quietly over "Our Father who art in heaven," etc., and then I went to sleep.

My father went to a harness and saddle shop and had the man make a school bag for me out of pig-skin leather which he said he didn't think any school boy would tear, but they tore the braces from the bag until they were fastened by rivets. That bag lasted me throughout my school life and the days I rode on the saddle when in the ministry (see fig. 6).

Grace Amanda and the Death of Jack

In October [1876] my baby sister Grace Amanda was born, named after my father's mother, Amanda Waldron. She was soon a joy in the house. Her merry face shone with intelligence and she was always saying bright things. One day [when] we were picnicking at the lake shore I had dug out a hole in the sand. She looked up at her mother's face: "I think this water would be nicer if Lizzie would bring a dipperful of warm water."

As soon as snow came, father had a sled made for me. He had brought home Jack's dog harness. The runners were set wide so as to run in the regular cutter track. I had a wonderful time that winter with him [Jack]. He became the joy of the people of Port Perry, especially after he began to do shopping for mother. For a time I would walk down with him as he carried a big basket with a strong cross handle, and we would go to the butchers with mother's order for meat. The butcher would fill it and put in a bone for Jack and then we would march back to mother. Once when I was not around and mother was in a hurry, she thought she would see what Jack would do. So she wrote on a piece of paper what she wanted, put it in the basket, and told him to take it to the butcher. The butcher read the note, filled the order, put it in the basket, also a bone for Jack and told him to take it home. So he took the basket and laid it down at mother's feet. After that he could be depended upon to do the shopping.

In the spring time a band of gypsies paid an annual visit to Port Perry. They installed themselves in the park. They had a large dog of whom they were very proud, and their jealousy was aroused when they saw Jack. When Jack visited the butcher shop part of his walk was along by the park. They saw Jack come with his basket and they suspected he had something good in it. So they set their dog on to bark at him thinking that Jack would set down the basket and they might be able to steal it. But Jack was not so minded; he let the gypsy dog snarl away and he walked home. He found mother, set the basket at her feet, wheeled and jumped over the garden fence and came to the park. The gypsy dog was inside their fence and Jack jumped the fence and attacked the dog. There was a savage fight but Jack got him by the throat and killed him. The angry gypsies attacked Jack with clubs. One must have had a golf club with a metal end, and it broke the skin on Jack's shoulder. Several young men gathered and told the gypsies to quit pounding Jack. At first they would not listen, but when the young men began taking off their coats the gypsies left Jack.

We appealed to the Vet in the town, but he was afraid of Jack. He only put a little tar in Jack's wound and when father came back from one of his missionary deputation engagements, he found his brave Jack dying of blood-poisoning. Father did what he could for him and when he saw that the end could not be far away, he took Jack down to the old [William] Young farm near Trenton. On the trip down the train met with an accident. A rail had been broken and down a sharp grade, the train was brought to an abrupt stop. The door of the express car in which Jack was being carried was snapped open, and with a roar Jack sprang out. He broke the rope with which he was tied, then free outside, he rushed around to find father and frightened many people. Then he caught sight of father who had come out of the last coach, and he dashed straight for him. Father knew what to expect and braced himself. The dog sprang on him, one paw on each of his shoulders, sending his black fedora flying with the first lick of his tongue. With one hand father tried to protect his face, and with his other he hugged his big loving dog whose heart was beating like a trip hammer. Father would say, "It's all right Jack, it's all right." He was finally quieted down and taken to the farm where he died and was buried at the root of a large maple tree.[9]

Colborne, 1879-82

In June 1879 father was stationed at Colborne.[10] There was no Indian tribe attached here but there were two outside appointments. We had said good-bye to friends in Port Perry. Aunt Clara had married William Ross and we left them in a fine home. Because father had not finished his five-year term at Berens River, he had to bear part of the expenses of his homecoming. Mother's legacy, which he had loaned to his brother in Trenton, had gone

9 In *My Dogs in the Northland,* 119–21, Egerton Young recalled Jack's escape from the baggage car and vociferous greeting in connection with a different occasion, when he and Elizabeth were on a train from Trenton to Toronto. But he and his son both told the same story about Jack's injury, death, and burial at the foot of a beautiful maple tree on William Young's farm (122–24).

10 E. Ryerson Young dated the dictating of the previous section of his memoir to 3 February 1962. This section, which he headed "Colborne," was composed two days later, on 5 February.

when his business had been closed up by creditors.[11] In his deputation work he had received only his expenses.

There was no more talk about trying to keep up Cree in our morning prayers and nobody called me, in school or out, "Indian." Perhaps there were more women in Colborne like the one who said, "We do not want the returned missionaries here. They have lived so long among the heathens that they do not know how to appreciate the amenities of civilization."

I had told my father that I would do all necessary work to take care of a cow if I might have all the milk I wanted to drink. Father took me at my word. The minister who had occupied the parsonage before we came had a cow and father had asked [him] to leave her. So when I came I went down to see my new bossie. I got a pail and made a nice meal for her and gave it to her. She seemed to appreciate it. Then I got a milk pail and a stool and sat down beside her to milk her. The next thing that I was conscious of, I was sitting with my back to the wall behind the cow with one leg pointing one way and the other at right angles, and milk seemed to be sprinkled about everywhere. So I got up, found my pail and stool, and went and tied the cow's head tight to her manger and sat down again to milk her. I pressed my head so tightly in her flank that she could not lift her leg to kick; then she leaned her body on my head and I thought my neck would break. I got up and found a board that fitted very neatly between her ribs and the side of the stall. Then I sat down again to milk. When she found she could neither kick nor press her weight upon me she slid down on her left side to the floor. Disgusted, I came back to the house and asked, "What kind of a cow is that out there?" The oldest daughter of the minister who had preceded father and who owned the cow, Minnie Cullen, was there. When she heard my words she laughed. "Why," she said, "that cow will not let a man milk her. It's a woman's cow."

"Is that so," said I, and Minnie laughed again as though she enjoyed my defeat and discovery. Turning to mother I asked, "Please lend me your scrub

---

11 The legacy had come to Elizabeth from her father's brother, William Bingham, who lived in England. On 1 July 1874, William died, leaving £300 with the instructions that, following his wife's death, the sum was to be distributed evenly among those of his brother's children who were still living. William's wife died on 18 March 1886, and Elizabeth acknowledged receipt of her one-seventh share at Meaford on 31 March 1887 (JSHB collection). When, or before, the business of Egerton's eldest brother, James, failed, the Youngs evidently loaned or advanced him that amount, which was then lost.

skirt," then I went again to the stable. I put on the scrub skirt, sat down on the stool beside the cow, and milked her without any more trouble. Then I took off the skirt and hung it up in the stable. After that I put it on at milking time. After things had gone smoothly for some days I thought I did not need it any more. But to my surprise, Bossie did not think as I did, and so to please her, I put on the skirt again.

The parsonage was backed by the livery stable. They threw their horse manure just behind it. The room in the parsonage allotted to the minister for his study had only one window, and that was on the side facing the livery stable. Father asked the trustees if they wanted their sermons fumigated with horse manure. They took the hint and immediately looked for another parsonage. Then came a change that was a short paradise for us children and all in our family. A man who had a fine farmhouse within city limits and land beyond had sold his extra land, keeping the part that was around his house in the village. This consisted of the house, orchard, and garden. The orchard had all sorts of apples, pears, and plums. The house was rented to father from April 1880–1882. With the house there was also a fine brindle cow and thirty chickens, and father bought these and I entered into my heritage. Father sold the cow he [had] bought from Mr Cullen. We might have done something in the way of gardening when we entered the place, but the only thing I remember was [that] father had dug a deep trench in the middle of the garden and planted celery sprouts intending to fill in the land on each side of the little plants as they grew. It was the old hard way of growing celery. It was the best we ever ate when it came to our dinner table.

The rooster was one of the prettiest and smartest little chaps that I had ever seen. He was beautifully colored and had a wonderful long tail. He was called a "spanish-hamberg." As I had ideas of larger poultry for the table, I bought a young plymouth-rock rooster. When I set him down, my little rooster took a dive at him and the plymouth fled until he was well out of sight outside of the flock.[12] I said to myself, "Be careful little fellow, chickens grow fast"; and it was not many days when I came out one morning and found my little king S.H. with his beautiful crown cut in two, blood streaming down head and neck and his fine long tail feathers broken. He looked straight up

12 A Google search indicates that the first rooster was probably a "Silver Spangled Hamburg," a small breed, the roosters weighing about five pounds. Plymouth Rock roosters are a larger, long-lived breed.

at me as much as to say, "See what that rascal has done to me," and the big plymouth was in the midst of the flock of hens perfectly happy and indifferent to the fate of his defeated rival. I had pity upon the brave little fellow and soon ended his misery by cutting off his head and handed him into the kitchen so they might make a delightful pot pie.

Father still looked after the horse but I began to take an interest in him. I would go and visit the livery stable once in a while to see how they [the liverymen] looked after their horses and polished them up. One thing they did was to take them down to Lake Ontario and add a line to their halters. The man would walk along the wharf that stretched into the lake and he would swim his horses. It wasn't long before I did the same with Tippo Sultan; we called him "Tip." So I took the clothes-line and fastened [it] to his halter and led him into the water as I walked onto the wharf. To my surprise, as soon as he was in deep water he was kicking up his heels and plunging and having a right royal time. It was something that I never saw any of the livery horses do. When I got him out of the water I would scrape the water out of his hide. I would fold his blanket and put it over his back, strap a cirsingle [surcingle] tightly about him, get on his back, and ride right through the town. It was not long before people were coming to father to tell him that I would fall off. Father would reply, "When he does, please bring him home." He knew how I rode the horse bare-footed and put my feet under the girth.

As the only boy in the house, mother had duties for me. I was to see that the lamps were all supplied with coal-oil and the glasses were kept shining. On Saturday I had quite an array of boots to keep black, and in those days even little girls as well as the grown folks wore boots that had to be blackened, and they all had to be cleaned before midnight Saturday.

Then when a music teacher who came from England invaded the village, mother wanted me to take lessons. This man, Mr. Wilson, had established music classes in the villages like Colborne along the railroad line. He was sure that people on each side of Bowmanville must be musically inclined, for near them in Bowmanville there was the [Dominion] Organ and Piano factory. He was a tall athletic Englishman, and one day when he came to give me my lesson he acted a little sheepishly and strangely confidential to one as young as I. "I'm afraid," he said, "I will now have a bad name in this town. I have just thrashed a man down on the main street."

"Who is the man?"

"I think they call him Woods. When I first met him, he asked me to lend him two dollars. I always keep a few shillings in my vest pocket," he said as he patted the left side of his vest, "and I handed him eight shillings. To-day I stepped into the bar-room to have a glass of beer and the man was there. I asked him when he was going to return the two dollars, and for an answer he swung his fist at me. I caught his wrist and spun him around toward the door and struck him with my cane across the shoulders. He turned and tried to take another swing at me. I caught his other wrist, held it, and said, "You'll treat these men in this bar-room or I will thrash you." "Not on your life," he said.

"Then I gave him another blow on the shoulder and he fled out the door. He ran up the street, and I laid on him blow after blow for I could almost walk as fast as he could run. Whatever will the people here think of me?" he added.

"I think the people here will think you are a fine fellow and [have] given Woods a little bit of what he deserves, for he is the village bully and nearly everybody here has suffered in one way or another at his hands." This cheered Mr. Wilson very much and we proceeded with the lesson.

When I registered in school I had good reports from the teachers in Port Perry, but I may have been unfortunate when I presented them to the teachers in Colborne. My deafness may have been more noticeable as they declined to promote me. I felt very bad as my sister [Lillian] received her promotion and got a step closer to me in school standing. However, I determined to study harder and to read the advanced lessons. The principal, a Welshman by the name of Flewellan, had one favour for his pupils. On Friday afternoons he had a "what and where" question period, and as the pupils answered, they were allowed to go. Almost invariably, I was the first out. In spite of all the work I had to do, I seemed to find time to do a great deal of outside reading.

One day father bought a load of hay that had been standing at the market place, and when it was delivered father was here to receive it. When the men declared they had put the load in the hay mow, father thought they had reserved too large an amount to feed their horses. He had hardly spoken when one of the men standing at the edge of the door of the hay mow tossed his fork into the hay still on the wagon and there was a sharp squeak. Father said, "You had better uncover that pig there." The men saw that their trick was exposed; it didn't take much shoving of hay aside to show they had a big hog in there. "I'll go back with you to the weigh scales and we will have this pig weighed and the price deducted for this load." The young men were very angry, but father was firm and said it was very sad to think that we in Canada could not trust our young farmers to be honest.

The Christmas of 1879 we accepted an invitation to spend with father's parents in Trenton. Father had secured a sleigh to accommodate our family. The road was excellent for driving. The horse had been freshly shod. Though it was sunny, a little snow was beginning to fall. All were in good spirits and Tip the horse did his best and I held the lines. Colborne was nine miles from Brighton and it was another nine miles from Trenton. There was only one pitch-hole, and that was so severe that each one got a jar. I seemed to escape, but father was so shaken that he had his fist up to find somebody to blame and my head caught his blow. He had no business to hit me but he did.

We made Trenton in just one hour and half after we left Colborne. It was snowing harder every minute, and in the night it seemed to come down in bundles. We had a happy visit with our relatives, but in the morning men said we could never reach home because there was now so much snow on the road; we would be stuck and frozen on the way. But my father said he had to get home for his church business meeting, so we started. Though father walked, the horse could hardly make any progress even at a walk. Snow was almost up to his knees and the drifts were as high as his thighs. We struggled along and it was night before we reached Brighton. Here were two families who were related to us: one that father called cousin Fanny Young, who was the wife of the school master Wm. Begg.[13] She had two boys, Will and Magnus. I was sent to her. In another house was a sister of my father's mother [Amanda Waldron], aunt Flora [Laura] Waldron Bowles; she had a large house that took care of them [the rest of us].

The next morning things were just as snowy as ever, even worse for a terribly cold wind was blowing, but father was as determined as ever to get home as quickly as he could. All the men whom he met advised him not to try it till farmers with their horses and sleighs had opened the road.

13 This was actually Peter Begg, whose wife, Fanny, was the daughter of Matthias Young, a brother of the Reverend William Young. They also had a third son, Andrew (Wilson Brown, family history files; and census data, Brighton, Ontario).

However, as father wished it we made the effort and reached home without anyone being frozen.

In this new house [in Colborne], I remember, we had some of our best family gatherings. Father would be busy reading, mother would be sewing or reading, and the children with their school books would be studying around the dining room table. Because I had to repeat a grade, I had more time for outside reading. Sometimes I thought my sister Lillian considered herself very important and advanced because she had been promoted and I had not been successful, and occasionally arguments would be a bit heated. Father would say on any such occasions, "Hold on, keep cool; it's the loser that will be the winner," for in the end of the debate, the winner does not add to his or her knowledge, but the loser does. Generally father's words were heeded, but on one occasion my sister was so wrought up that, on being beaten in the argument, she seized my double slate. This affair was a double slate that we could use something like a book; we would take two slates of the same size, bore holes through the wood, and insert shoe laces to act as a hinge; in this way we could carry our sums home without being rubbed out. We found it very useful, and my sister found a new use for my double slate. On being overcome in the argument she seized my slate, and with all her force broke it over my head. I do not remember father saying anything to her except that, that kind of argument never solves a problem. So we went on with our work.

Florence started school and seemed to be doing quite well. One day, somebody told Lillian that Florence was to be whipped for something. Lillian made haste in her forceful way to the teacher and demanded to know for what she was to be punished, saying that Florence had never done any wrong intentionally. So the teacher reconsidered her intention. Florence was a little deaf and that may have been the only shortcoming in her class work.

Grace was a little younger than Florence and was not sent to school with her older sister, but Grace asked Florence to go over the work that she had received at school, and it seemed to her parents that she grasped the work better than her older sister. She begged to go to school with her. However, my parents thought she ought to wait another year.

In church, father expected his children to be very respectful and listen carefully to his sermons, and he didn't want them to be restless and look-ing around. However, one Sunday morning he thought that little Grace was doing too much looking around. On coming home, he had picked up a gad by the roadside and questioned her as to what she had heard of his sermon, but before he punished her, he thought he would test her [and] asked, "What was I preaching about this morning?" Grace promptly answered, "Little man up a tree. Jesus said, 'come down in a house and have dinner.'"[14] Father was taken by storm and dropped his gad. Grace turned as if to leave him, then turning back, she added, "and I know how many rafters there are in the old church too." So he realized that in looking around, she was not star-gazing but trying to solve a mathematical problem.

We had some games — checkers, Halma, go-bang, that was played with colored buttons. As many could play as could get around the board. We also had carpet balls.[15] It was quite a treat to have father with us for he was usually too busy with his church work; he had not much time for games. Grandma Bingham and Aunt Lottie visited us and they liked games too.[16] We were amused one night when Grandma said, "I always like to play with Egerton for he always lets me win."

Our cordwood was cut by Lawrence Reynus. If the weather was fine when he was working, Lillian would come out and sing for him. One time the fellow was so impressed that he told father he would saw his wood for nothing if he would only let Lillian come out and sing. Poor fellow, he seemed to be eager to please either father or Lillian. Father was a wonderful hand with an ax and he could knock to pieces a pile of wood as quickly as any man I ever saw, and I would pile it in the wood shed.

When sap was flowing I visited the farm of Mr. Cochran. He had several sons, most of them older than I, and also had a large grove of maple trees. In the midst of them he had a brick furnace with pans so he could siphon down the sap as he boiled it. One of the boys had trained a young bull to pull a big

14 Evidently Young had preached from Luke 19:1–10, the story of the wealthy but short tax collector who climbed a tree to see Jesus as he passed; Jesus called him down, and he became a follower.

15 There is a game known as carpetball, which is played on a long carpet-covered table, but this game was probably something simpler. Halma was a checkerboard game, usually for two players, with nineteen men each. Gobang, a British name derived from the Japanese word *goban* ("chessboard"), was a strategy board game, the aim of which was to get five pieces (coloured stones) in a row (*OED*).

16 Aunt Lottie was Charlotte, Elizabeth's youngest sister, who, on 31 August 1882, married George Pim in Toronto (Wilson Brown, family history files).

barrel on a stone-boat between the trees,[17] and as they came to the tapped maple trees they would empty the pails of sap into the barrel and when full [it] would be brought back to the furnace. The bull knew his work so well that he was guided by the voice of his master.

When there, I met Mr Cochran and he told me that he had a sow that had given birth to twenty-two piglets, and if I would carry one home he would give me one. I told him I would take it. So when it came time for me to go home I got a bag and went after my pig. Then I started away, but I had not gone very far when a couple of his boys with horse and buggy picked me and my piglet up and took me home. Father was greatly surprised and wondered where I could find a place for it, but I soon showed father that I had looked far ahead. There was a corner where we stood forks and shovels, etc. I put these up on pegs on the wall. I built a neat little pen and trough with an upstair platform and to this I fastened a board covered with cleats so the piggie could run up and always find a dry place to rest. It would also be a place for exercise running up and down. The piggie was very happy there.

When the flowers were beginning to come, the family of Senator Keeler decided upon selling the estate of the late Senator and father was interested in buying a new cow.[18] The auctioneer of the village was the saloon keeper, Mr Jacques. He and father were always banging at each other, father with his temperance sermons and Jacques when he had an audience at his auctions. Mrs Jacques and her boy that was called "little Jacques" attended our church. The boy was very faithful to the Sunday school but he always absented himself when the temperance lesson day came around. He didn't like to hear his father's business denounced, and he never went to the barroom except on an errand. When Mr Jacques saw father in his audience he was always sharp to notice what interested him, and when he saw father betting for the cow he was soon in his glory. He would say, "Parson, you want to be careful. This cow has a bad reputation for opening gates. It is often found in the Pound because it had found its way into strange places. You will have to keep your sacramental wine locked up away from her"; and with such

17 A stone-boat is a wooden sledge used for moving heavy items such as stones or hay bales.

18 Joseph Keeler was a member of parliament, but not a senator, and was active in grain, lumber, and other businesses in Colborne. He died on 21 January 1881.

remarks, his audience was kept in a merry mood. However, father held his ground, so the betting went on, and it seemed to me that the more people laughed the less bidding was done. Finally with a flourish of one, two, three, the auctioneer said, "I sell this cow to parson Young for twenty dollars." The Keeler young men were very much annoyed when someone said "to think of that fine cow going for a price like that." However, Jacques was busy for the next thing that was to be auctioned off in the house. The Senator's books and manuscripts were offered for sale. There was one bundle that looked like large magazines, wrapped in paper which was badly torn and tied with tape. The auctioneer said, "How much am I offered for these old magazines?" They consisted of nine parts of an edition of William Shakespeare's writings. A prompter said these were not magazines but [a] fine edition of Shakespeare's works. But Jacques kept up his calls for bidding for old magazines. He had noticed that father was one of the bidders and after a flourish, said, "Sold for six dollars to parson Young." When I got this treasure home father was very careful to show me how to handle them. The engravings were the most beautiful that he had ever seen and the books were so large that I had to put them down on the parlor floor and lie down to read them.

When we got home with the cow we soon found that what the auctioneer had said was perfectly true. The cow was a lively young Durham and very strong. One time I found that she had got out of our yard and had crossed the road. She first tried to open the big gate but it had been too tightly tied for her. Then she went to the other end of the gate and put her horns between the bars and lifted it off its hinges. The gate fell inward and she climbed over it into the field. I was soon over the fence and drove her back and made her get out of the field over the tilted gate; then I drove her home.

A circus visited the town with its parade of animals and a steam organ and a free exhibition of a lady walking a tight-rope to the main tent to attract people to come see. We children were not permitted to attend the circus but we determined to have one of our own. It was then that Lawrence Raynus [Reynus, as earlier?] was our big shot. Beside a rail fence we had several booths fixed up with sheets and we charged other children two pins for each exhibition and Lawrence would crawl under the sheets and he was an elephant here and a lion in the next tent and so on. And Florence declared she could walk the rope like the circus lady, so I tightened the clothes line up for her, put the step ladder by the tree and held the rope in one hand. She took off her shoes and I gave her the clothes pole, and I walked underneath so as to catch her. I am pretty sure she made it six good steps before she fell on my head and shoulders and crushed me to the ground. Neither of us were really hurt, but she declined repeating the stunt.

There were musical ladies in the town and they organized a concert for the children of the town. This was a great joy to us young people and I think the ladies had all in our family taking part. I know they had me. I sang a solo. I was in a duet, and sang a sailor song and was responded to by a girl named Nora. There were dialogues, etc. I am sure Lillian and I were called upon to play many parts. In the pantomime I was dressed like a robin with a hook on my nose to scatter leaves on the babes in the woods. There were a couple of boys who repeated long recitations. It was a very popular entertainment.

When the apples began to fall, Daisy the cow was out helping herself and one day after school as I came home through the gate that faced the front street and which was quite high from the barn, men were coming in and I passed a man with a board that had holes in it and a solid rubber rope with a kind of a ball at one end. And when I was far enough in I could see down towards the barn there was a company of perhaps one hundred and fifty men, women, and children and in front of them was Daisy the cow, terribly bloated and apparently in agony. I pulled off my school bag, dropped it on the ground, and ran through the crowd. I threw my right arm around the cow's neck and with my left hand I grabbed her throat. My hand was so taut and I felt something move slightly and realized that she had an apple in her throat. I pressed again and again and finally an apple shot out of her mouth, and with a tremendous belch the cow came back to normal size and the crowd shouted, "Oh, Eddie has saved his cow." Somebody had sent for the Vet and he was the man that I passed when I ran down to the cow.

One day a farmer who had delivered a load of hay in Colborne visited Mr Jacques's bar and was homeward bound. He had evidently got too much liquor and was jerking his horses and they seemed to be wild and not knowing what to do, and unfortunately they came past the school house as we boys came out on the run. The farmer was pulling the horses one way and they made a jump that sent one of the big loose boards flying. Little Jacques was one of the first boys out and the board caught him in the back. Father happened to pass at the same time and stopped to see what he could do. He told me to take the horse and buggy home while he took the boy to the doctor. Word was sent as quickly as possible to the boy's father and when he came down to the doctor's, he saw his boy lying on the doctor's office table, the doctor working at one side and father with his coat off working on the other side. Jacques wanted to have the boy taken at once home, but the doctor said he was not to be moved for some time, till they can find out how much he had been injured. "Well," said Jacques, "as soon as he can be moved let me know, and I'll take him home." He hurried home and told his wife what happened and she went to work to prepare a room for him. It was several days before the doctor would let the boy be taken home. At last he was placed safely in the bed his mother had prepared for him. Father would visit him whenever possible, at any time of day. He would not enter the front door of the hotel, but go to the back door. Jacques, however, would see him coming, and when father was in the room he would stand at the door and listen to the conversation. One day, his wife caught him there and told him to go in and meet the minister; "he would be glad to talk to you." "Just see how the parson makes little Jacques forget his pain," said Jacques, and then he slipped away.

One morning I went downtown with my aunt Lottie. She was having a dress made; it was in a tall brick building on the third floor. I had left her at the market square and was interested in seeing a farmer trying to take up a big load of cordwood. He had to go through a gateway and up an icy bank. He was not able to make it so he had secured a second team of horses. He hitched them in front of his team and then started again. Seeing me, he asked me to take the lines of his own team while he drove the first team. We started well. As he passed the gate, he stood in between his horses and the load, and I tried to slip by as the load was going through the gate. But it was my ill luck to be caught by that big load as it skidded. I was thrown to the ground. My aunt saw me fall, from the dress-maker's window and came to help, while men who were in a drug store close by came to aid me. They carried me into the drug store and laid me on the counter. They did their best to stop the flow of blood from my nose and mouth. I was kept there until it stopped, then my aunt helped me up to the dressmaker's. Here she made me comfortable and there I rested until she was ready to go home. Before we started, they noticed that I was very pale and so the ladies rubbed rouge on my cheeks. My aunt said we should not say anything about what happened when we got home.

However, the next Sunday in the Sunday school the superintendent in his prayer thanked God for saving one of their boys from death. My sister Lillian asked her friend, "What boy is being prayed for?" "Why," said her friend, "it was your brother." So when Lillian came home she told the folks about it at the supper table. The accident happened on a Thursday, and here they were looking at me when my chair might have been empty.

February 4th 1881, another little girl was born to mother called Laura Gertrude Winnifred Young.

In October of that same year my piggie had assumed a good size and [it] was thought the time to butcher him. When dressed he weighed about a hundred pounds. Father said, "We can't eat all that meat." The girl house-keeper who came from a farm said, "Don't sell a bit of it, you have a big family to feed." Father sold half to the butcher, and he was glad to get a hold of a milk-fed pig. Father was very much surprised to find our half was gone inside of one week.

Entrance examinations brought a minister's son from Grafton to stay with us. After the tests he invited me to go to Grafton to stay for a few days. Grafton at that time had a big saw-mill and a pond behind it full of saw logs. One day we were out with the boys of the town. Instead of going down to the mill, they stopped opposite the village and ran across the logs. I tried to walk the logs but fell in between them. When I was in the water with my head beneath the logs, I heard a voice inside of me say, "Look up." I opened my eyes and looked up and saw an open space, shot up my right arm, and put it around a log. That stopped my sinking into the wooze, and I put my left arm around another log. These two lifted me so my head was out of the water. I could see the boys on the other shore but they could not see me. One or two of them ran to the foreman of the saw mill and told him what had happened. He came quickly, pulled me out, and carried me ashore. Mrs. Wilson, my friend's mother, quickly had my clothes off drying, put me in a warm bath, and then to bed, and then in the morning I was sent home as fast as the Wilson horse could take me.

Father was always zealous in arranging his missionary meetings at his different appointments. He wanted his people to know the needs of the christless world. From his own experience he knew the fullness of the meaning of "go ye into all the world and preach the gospel to every crea-ture," and so he tried to inspire as many other Christian people as he could.

At one of his appointments called "Wicklow," he had a special series of services there. They thought the people with warmed hearts were ready to respond to Christ's call. Two of his ministerial brethren were so stationed on the railroad they could come in on an afternoon train and return on the midnight express. On the day appointed these ministers came to Colborne and asked the livery men to let them have the fastest team of horses available; they were going to an evening meeting but wished to be back in time for the midnight express. So they appeared at the meeting and everything seemed to go in the best of spirits. The church was crowded. The ministers gave informative and inspiring addresses. To that meeting father took me so I could take care of our horse, Tip. I always wanted to be free to be one of the first on the road home, so I found a spot a little distance from the church so I would not be bottled up by the other teams, so when the service was over I was ready for father to come, and we would be off for home.

The other ministers were shepherded by the livery man himself, and soon we saw them on the road behind us. Father seemed to be depressed and disappointed and I'm sure it was on account of the poor financial results. Anyway, he sat back in the buggy and left me to do the driving. The liveryman came along smartly and was not far behind. I shook the reins over Tip's back, wake up, wake up, Tip, they are coming! However, the team came on. They gained on us until their horses were beside our buggy. Then it was nip and tuck for some distance. The horses seemed to tire; they could not keep up the pace with Tip. On and on he went until they were well behind. When we reached Colborne we could hardly see them. We dodged down to our street and put Tip in the stable and ran out to meet the team as they were coming in. I waved my hat and said, "Hurrah for the preacher's horse," as they passed by.

The next morning before we finished our breakfast, the liveryman said to father, "I want to buy that horse." "Well," father said, "I need him yet; if I sell him now, I would have to buy another." So father promised to give the liveryman the first chance to buy when he was for sale. Tip was sold [for] $210.00 [at the] end of June.

Bowmanville, 1882–85

On April 1st 1882, we had to surrender the most delightful parsonage home we ever had. It was a terrible scattering. Lillian was sent to the home of Uncle Sam [Young] and aunt Annie of Trenton. Florence and I were sent to Uncle James [Young], father's oldest brother. Mother and father were taken care of by some friends in Colborne until conference time. We saw very little of one another until we were settled in Bowmanville in July 1882.

Father and I came first to the parsonage. The lady across the street from the parsonage (Mrs Lyle) brought father the key of the house. It was a fine brick parsonage but had been shut up for many days. Inside we found everything scrupulously clean. The carpets had been taken up, cleaned; the carpet for each room had been folded and left in the middle of the floor. Mrs Lyle returned with a jug of ice cold lemonade. It was a very hot July day and much appreciated. In the evening mother and the girls appeared and with them their baggage. Finally, some of the church people appeared and arrangements were made for our care that night. There was no garden or orchard; it was just a parsonage behind the church. Some time after, the chief steward Mr Younie, who had recently been appointed, came to look things over at the parsonage. We children happened to be in the yard and as he looked around, he said in a kindly way, "There doesn't seem to be anything here for you, not even a swing"; and so I said, "it is so different to the lovely parsonage we had just left." He went away and returned that same day with material for a swing.

Two weeks after, people began flocking to the church, some of whom had never taken much interest in the affairs before. Now with new enthusiasm they came with full baskets to give a real reception to our family that had been sent to serve them. There was an unfortunate split in the congregation, and for some time the majority of the people had little to say in the management. Now the people had suddenly arisen to assert themselves, and soon there were new officials in control and a new day of better understanding.

There was a fine high-school and I had my first chance at continuous school work. I passed my entrance. The principal, Mr Tamblyn, met my father and asked if his boy was deaf. Father was shocked. He knew that I had often suffered colds and [was] not as bright as other boys. "Why do you ask?"

"Well," said Mr Tamblyn, "when we are dealing with subjects that do not need his ears, he is one of the brightest lads in school. But when his ears are needed he falls right down. I'd advise you to see a Doctor."[19]

It was not long before father took me to a specialist in Toronto. When I was examined, he said, "You have a very deaf lad, and the worst of it is, the deafness of this kind cannot be helped." Father felt very bad for he recalled that many times [he had] given me a clout and said, "Wake up, don't be stupid." Now he could hardly believe, and made further inquiry. He found another doctor who thought perhaps this deafness was caused by a clot of blood, so he lanced my ear and hung leaches there, but all his efforts were in vain. Both doctors advised better health for better hearing. The teachers were very considerate, so I made better progress the three years I was in Bowmanville school.

Christmas 1882, the congregation celebrated the fifteenth wedding [anniversary] of father and mother and presented them with a beautiful set of moss rose hand painted china. In 1883 a little boy [William Joseph] was born but passed away in a few months. He died in June [October] while father was away at a conference.

Meaford, Brampton, and a Family Reunion

In June 1885 we were moved to Meaford. There was no high-school and no parsonage. We children were scattered amongst the people and were so for some weeks. I went to the public school to fill in time. A piece of good luck came to sister Lillian. Some friend held a scholarship fully paid for one year in Hamilton [at] Wesleyan Ladies College. This was given [to] father, and Lillian had the privilege of spending the next year there.

A house was found and served as a parsonage and home for us. At the new year, I was sent to Collingwood Collegiate. The spring of that year I had a setback. Collingwood is a great shipbuilding centre, and some of us students were down examining ships when a wild wind storm filled the air with sawdust. For the first time I discovered my right eye useless. I could not see. My friend took me to my boarding-house and I took the next train to Meaford. Father and mother were shocked at my discovery.

19 This was William Ware Tamblyn (1843–1912), who had become headmaster of Bowmanville High School in 1882 ("Educationist Passes Away," obituary, *The Toronto World* [Hamilton edition], 19 November 1912, 3; the issue can be viewed at www.news.google.com/newspapers).

The doctor cleaned the eye out and told me to go back to my studies. Father thought I was too nervous.

In June 1887 we were transferred to Brampton. Here we had a good high school, so I determined to work hard and in 1888 I made the University of Toronto. And mother and the children were established in a home in Parkdale while father accepted a call to England to relate his work for the Indians. Father had a book published in 1889 [1890], "By Canoe and Dog Train," and Sir Charles Tupper, then Commissioner for Canada to England, said, "Mr Young, you are the best known Canadian outside of Canada."[20] In 1888 my four sisters were sent to the Wesleyan Ladies College, Hamilton. I was put in a boarding house, and mother joined father in England.[21] Between father's lecturing engagements, they were very kindly entertained by friends in England. Then in 1890 they returned to Canada. We were all united in a cottage in Grimsby Park, Ontario.

Robert Helme, a son of one of the lovely families that had entertained father and mother when in England, was on a world tour in Australia returning through Canada and was advised to call on my father and mother while here. When he reached Toronto he telegraphed father and was immediately invited to come to Grimsby Park. While visiting us, the "Love Bug" hit him and my sister Lillian, and he took Lillian back to England for a year. Then they returned to Canada and were married in 1891.[22] She was twenty years old. They went right back to England and made their home in Lancaster.

20 Sir Charles Tupper served as Canadian High Commissioner to the United Kingdom, 1883–95, and may have made this comment in 1894–95, when Egerton Young spent an extended period lecturing in England.

21 This account of the Youngs' travels is out of sequence. On 11 September 1888, Young left Parkdale for a four-month lecture tour in the United States (he had stayed only one year in Brampton, not the three that the Methodist church doubtless expected). His scrapbook contains accounts of his speaking in Philadelphia, New Haven, Wilmington, Brooklyn, Washington, DC (where President Cleveland heard him preach), and Baltimore. In early and mid-1889, he spent some months lecturing in Great Britain, where he returned several times in following years; he and Elizabeth made their most extended sojourn there from September 1894 to April 1895 (1888 diary; Harcourt Brown, biographical and family files).

22 Egerton R. Young files, a newspaper account of the marriage that he performed, 10 March 1891, in Trinity Methodist Church, Toronto. JSHB collection.

Four Decades in Methodist Church Ministry, 1892–1932

In the fall of 1890 we found a new home at 73 Avenue Rd., Toronto. I attended the University of Toronto 1888 [to] 1892, and that fall I went to Victoria College as a student minister. After my graduation I was stationed as assistant minister at the Scarborough circuit. [Then] 1894 at Hillside mission, Muskoka; 1895 at Windermere mission, centre of Muskoka. Ordained in 1896, Trinity Methodist Church, Toronto. 1896–98 stationed at Bracondale Methodist Church; St Clair Ave West; 1898 Lambton Mills. Also in 1896 I wrote the report of the Toronto Conference. In 1898 I wrote the report on the General Conference [for] Dr Curtis, Dr Burwash. Then I was appointed assistant Editor of the *Christian Guardian* that same year, 1898, resigning in 1900.

In 1901 Coppercliffe; 1902–6 Port Carling. Went in there a free man and emerged a married man. [Married] May 27, 1903, to Edith Ella Allen. January 29, 1905, Ryerson Allen Young was born 1906; William Edward Young was born, died 1909. In the year 1908, Harold Egerton Young was born at Malton, November 5th.

In 1906 I moved to Malton; 1909 Chatsworth; 1912 Bracebridge; 1916 Orangeville; 1920 Islington; 1924 Newtonbrook; 1930 Barrie Central Church. In 1932, retired. Forty years in the ministry. During that time I wrote thirty-three annual reports on Conference.

In my Ordination class there were eleven:

Isaac Bowles.
Isaac Couch.
Philip Brace.
Henry Fish.
John Wellington Graham, L.L.D.
Arthur Ingram: Ordained 1896.
Herbert Magee.
Andrew Paul.
Thomas Edwin Egerton Sh[i]re, B.D.
Sydney Smith, Ph.D.
Egerton Ryerson Young, B.A.

This is February 10/62. I am 92 years old and the only living Minister of my class. . . .

In 1891 the Official Board of Trinity Methodist Church recommended me with two other young men to the ministry and so we were put on trial. Our pastor, the Rev. Dr. Hugh Johnston, issued our assignments to preach in portable churches and other places. My first assignment was to the men in the central prison. The doors of the cells were close to a wide counter, and on the other side of the counter the prisoners were free in the wide room. The prison guard had a chair at my left hand. I spoke sincerely and earnestly to the men. I was surprised at seeing so many young men there, and after I was through my address, I thought I would give them a chance to speak their thoughts to me. To my surprise, nearly everyone had a grouch: the law was too hard; he was not understood, and it was always someone else to blame for his being there. At my right hand was one elderly man, the only grey headed man in my audience, and he said, "I have been a Christian for forty years — off and on."

My second assignment was to the Mercer [Women's] Reformatory. It was a large room. It had been cleared of all its furniture, and in the left-hand corner the matron had put some boxes where I could stand on, in the suggestion of a pulpit. The women were gathered in the corner diagonally opposite. There were some chairs there, but not enough seats for all; some were standing in the doorways. From my box pulpit, I spoke to my audience. I was not aware that the matron and the women were having some misunderstanding, so in my ignorance I got closer to their difficulties than I knew, accidentally.

In my address I spoke about my mother, a young woman raised in a lovely Ontario home, sent to meet the most primitive conditions amongst the Indians. Here you have a warm and comfortable home, soft beds to lie on and all the varied foods to eat. Out there the weather was very cold and rough for the larger part of the year, houses drafty, and most of the Indians living in log houses no better than sheds or tents. And for food, the staple was fish — fish for breakfast, dinner, and every day during the week the same. Sometimes even fish were scarce. The Indian women looked to her in all their difficulties, and sometimes the men also. When she put up a civilized clothes line between the kitchen and a dog kennel, she warned an Indian who was cutting wood to supply the kitchen stove to keep away from that line. Indian-like, he didn't think he needed any advice from a woman. It was wash day and mother had her tub full of washing and an Indian woman helping. The man got his ax tangled with the line and got his head cut, and mother had to sew him up. I then referred to Christ and the kindly way he always spoke to women, even to those who had gone astray. When I was through, I stepped down to the floor. The matron came and thanked me warmly for my remarks, especially about my mother and her fish-food. She informed me that the women had threatened to go on a hunger strike because they thought they were getting too much fish. So I was quietly led out of the place.

Most of my assignments were in portable churches that have since been replaced by handsome churches. In one portable, so many additions had been added that I thought I was in a shooting gallery. [At] another place where the pulpit was in the middle of the portable, the opposite wall was so close that it seemed to throw my words back into my face. At one morning service I delivered a sermon that I had worked very hard on to say something acceptable and effective, and when I looked at my watch I found that I had spoken just eight minutes. After the service, I apologized. One woman kindly said, "Ah, well, it was good what there was of it."

At a home for elderly and lonely ladies I had another kind of experience. The room where I spoke was an enlarged parlor with easy chairs and chesterfields where these women were kindly cared for. At one end the nurse had placed a small table with a bible on [it]. From here I began my service. We sang a hymn, read a passage of scripture and led them in prayer; then the sermon. Then the top of my front collar button flew off and the ends of my collar opened out. Immediately I tried to loosen the collar to take it off and lay it on the table. The nurse came quickly to my aid. She had a safety pin and took the ends of the collar and fastened them to the shirt, straightened my tie and quietly returned to her seat. I proceeded with my sermon.

The other two young men had received assignments similar to mine. There was just one more thing we had to face before our reports had to be presented to the last quarterly meeting of the year. We were to preach a trial sermon before a Wednesday night prayer meeting. About two hundred people gathered that night in the Sunday school room. Dr. Johnston was in the chair. Before he called upon us, he gave a short address to the people. He reminded them that the Methodist Church was a church of the people. Their ministers were their own sons, and they were responsible in selecting these young men and sending them out to preach the gospel. These young men have passed through a certain amount of trial and testing. Now they are to speak to you and you should listen very carefully and judge with care and honesty to see if you think they are suitable men to go into our ministry.

Then we were called one after another. One young fellow came from a city home. He was rather tall and a very gently mannered young fellow. He spoke in a quiet and earnest way and then took his seat. The second young fellow was a sturdy and strongly built young man. He stood straight before the audience, planted his left foot ahead of the right one, and he didn't seem to move any muscle except his lower jaw as he shot out his address to the people. He was the son of Dr. Johnston. Then it was my turn. I didn't find any embarrassment in speaking to the friendly people.

Then Dr. Johnston took the floor again: "I am sure you have followed these young men with interest in what they said and how they acted before you. There is one rule in passing all judgment upon other persons and that is, that you would ask yourself, could I have done any better if I was in his place? So if any of you here to-night think you can do any better than they, you are permitted to come up here and try." We were all passed unanimously. So we were reported to the quarterly board and they passed [us] up with kindly recommendation to the Toronto Conference. However, before the Conference one of our men died. Hugh Johnston turned aside the ministry and entered the medical profession, and I was the only one of the three to reach ordination [in 1896].

At the close of the General Conference [in 1898], Dr. Curtis, President of the Newfoundland Conference, said, "The report of the General Conference this year is the best report to date." [But] Chancellor Burwash took me to task. "I do not understand you, Young. Though you sat at my feet in the lecture room, you said you could not hear my lectures but here in the conference room you report me perfectly."

"I do not think, Dr., that is too hard to explain" [I replied]. "In the lecture room you sit in your big chair; you sit back in your big chair and sometimes you close your eyes and your lectures are really Spiritual Meditations. Here in the conference, what do you do? You stand up and your voice is tense. In the heat of the debate, your voice is shrill and assertive and so your words get over the hill of difficulty into my poor ears."

"I guess you are right, Young," the Dr. admitted kindly. "I am always under a great handicap but I do the best I can. Thank you for your kind words."

A Poem by E. Ryerson Young, on his Blindness

"As Darkness Steals upon Mine Eyes"

Oh God, while silence sits upon my tongue,
While darkness steals upon my helpless eyes,
Blotting for me the light of earth and skies,
And dumb despair my staggered mind has wrung,
Pardon, dear Lord, my songless soul, but give
Me grace to know the spirit is not blind
Or any faculty of heart or mind
Where truth and love and faith in Thee may live.
Send me again dear Lord, to thine own school.
Teach me the zeal and meekness of a child,
That fingertips, as eyes, may be beguiled,
And power to read again, my mind shall rule,
Then light, through trained and quickened fingertips
Will bring new songs of praise upon my lips.[1]

1 E. Ryerson Young wrote this poem probably in the late 1930s, while he was learning Braille. For some time, as his sight was failing, he kept on using a typewriter; the typescript at hand has been corrected, probably by his assistant. It was enclosed in an undated letter that he wrote to his sister Grace's daughter, Elizabeth Brown, sometime before the mid-1950s, while he was still living at 96 Cranbrooke Avenue, Toronto; she had written to ask him for a copy. JSHB collection.

III

*Supplementary Documents
and Excerpts*

Part III presents a number of texts, arranged in approximate chronological order, that supply useful context for the memoirs published in Parts I and II. These texts include stories, short manuscripts or excerpts from manuscripts, and letters that provide information and background on events, observations, persons, and topics mentioned in Elizabeth Young's and E. Ryerson Young's memoirs. Some items speak for themselves and need no introduction; others are introduced by brief comments. Unless otherwise indicated, the documents from which these texts are drawn are from the JSHB collection.

1 Resolution, Quarterly Board of Hamilton City East Circuit, 4 May 1868

In view of the unexpected departure of our dearly beloved Pastor and wife from our midst, to go into the far "North West" as missionaries of the Cross: We the members of the Quarterly board of Hamilton City East Circuit cannot allow them to depart without an expression of our high appreciation of their Services amongst us. Therefore moved by brother Whyte and Seconded by bro Dunnett and carried unanimously. That whereas our pastor the Rev E. R. Young, having been called to leave us and go to a distant part of our mission work, we desire to record our entire confidence in his piety, ability and usefulness during the period in which he laboured amongst us. His faithfulness, zeal and affection have endeared him to all our hearts, and we pray that in the land to which he journeys he & Mrs Young may be equally successful in winning souls to

Christ, and when they cease to labour on earth they may have an abundant enterance into *our fathers house on high*.

Resolved that a copy of the foregoing be furnished bro Young as well as inserted in the Circuit minutes.

Signed, Tho[ma]s Morris Circuit Steward of Hamilton City East

2 The Rope from Hamilton, by Egerton R. Young

Among Egerton Young's papers is a typescript of 118 pages titled "In the Red Man's Country." Most of its chapters appear in his 1907 book, *The Battle of the Bears*, but that book begins quite differently from the typescript, which was probably written not long before. Near the opening of the typescript (pp. 4–5 and 9–13), Young described a gift received in Hamilton and its usefulness in a terrific storm that the Youngs and their fellow travelers experienced on the night of 3 July 1868 beside the Red River. It adds vivid details to Elizabeth's account of the storm in her memoirs (at the start of the section headed "Sojourn at Red River").

> Many and varied were the gifts which we received [on leaving Hamilton in May 1868]. The most of them were very suitable either for ourselves or for the poor Indians among whom we were so long to dwell. Some that at first we hardly knew what to do with, and yet were loath to refuse, came in very serviceable in some unexpected emergency. The following is an example:
>
> "'Tis but little I can give you, but I want you to take this fine rope which I have made for you. Maybe it will come in handy in some of your wanderings in the wild country to which you are going." Thus was I addressed by a big, large-hearted rope-maker on the eve of our departure from Hamilton. He was far from being a rich man, and so he had brought me as a gift this great coil of rope, which he now threw down before me.
>
> We could not then see how it would ever be of the slightest use to us, and in addition we had no desire to add more to the weight of our already heavily-loaded wagon, in which we were to travel for thirty days over the prairies after we had left all railroads

and steamboats behind. Still, to have refused the rope would have wounded a dear friend's kindly heart. We accepted the rope and found a place for it in our wagon.

For days that coil of rope seemed an eyesore. It was always in the way. When our wagon was unloaded on the prairie, it was over "that rope" somebody stumbled. If something was wanted in a hurry, it was always that heavy, awkward rope that was in the way or on top of the thing desired. Thus it came to pass that that big, useless rope belonging to Egerton Young began to be talked about as a nuisance and they said that it ought to be thrown aside. But there was work for it to do ere our journey ended. . . .

On 3 July 1868, the party camped near a settlement of "French half-breeds" just south of Red River. Egerton noticed how the smoke from their log houses was rolling down the roofs to the ground. "As it was evidently so much heavier than the air," he observed, "the latter must be very much rarified, and I was certain there would soon be a storm." The evening was so beautiful that the others laughed and dismissed his predictions. However, Egerton wrote, "I decided to follow my own convictions." Once the Youngs' tent was pitched in the usual way, Egerton took his axe into the nearby woods and cut a dozen or so extra tent pegs which he pounded in to secure it more firmly.

My persistent hammering and pounding . . . considerably annoyed some of my brother missionaries and their wives, who had already retired to rest, and they were not slow in shouting out their protests against the noise and the unnecessary precautions I was taking. However, I heeded them not; and it was well I did not, for I was even then preparing a shelter from the storm for nearly all of them.

When I had pounded the stake-like tent-pins to my satisfaction, I went to my wagon and pulled out and uncoiled that long rope. Fastening one end securely to a stake, I passed it over the tent and then back again. Long as it was, I utilized every bit of it in lashing down that tent solid and secure. I was well satisfied with my work, but I knew that I would be laughed at the next morning, if no storm occurred, by all who were clever enough to get up before I had removed the rope. . . . I lay down and was soon fast asleep.

"Egerton! What is that?" It was my wife who had awakened me.

"Only the wind sighing in the tops of the forest trees," I sleepily replied.

"Egerton!" again cried the wide-awake, excited wife, "it is more than that!"

Yes, indeed, it was more than that. It was a first-class western cyclone that was coming. Like a great monster, howling for its prey, we could hear it as it was rapidly rushing down upon us.

Others had now heard it, and from the veteran leader of our party, the Rev. George McDougall, who had dashed out of his tent, there were heard some brief commands. But all were apparently useless, for the cyclone had now struck us. It seemed as though everything must go down before its irresistible power. Tents, wagons, buckboards, blankets, sheets, shawls, pillows and other things movable went flying through the air.

My tent, however, stood the terrible strain, but it had to pass through a fearful ordeal. The storm shook it till it trembled like a leaf. Then, as though maddened by his failure, the cyclone tore loose the side curtains and, pouring in great blasts of air, tried to lift it up like a balloon and carry it away as other had already gone. But that rope, woven by the hands of love, and therefore every strand and fiber good and true, did its work and successfully stood the tremendous test. Screech and howl, struggle and blow as it would, the cyclone could not break the rope, and we knew that so long as it held our tent was safe.

A cyclone soon expends its dangerous fury. So it was in this case, but the wind continued to blow furiously, and soon the heavy rain came down. Now my tent was indeed "a shelter in a time of storm."

All the destitute, tentless ladies of our party were quickly sheltered under its impervious canvas, while the men were all busy in the dawnlight searching and securing as many as possible of the various articles which had been blown away. Some were found more than a mile distant, while there were other things that were never seen again.

3 Adventure with a Bull at Norway Ho[use], by Egerton R. Young

Egerton Young included this story on pp. 6–10 of the manuscript of chapter 5 of *By Canoe and Dog-Train* but omitted it from the book. The book manuscript has not survived, but these pages were kept, possibly for use elsewhere. The fragments of text at the top of page 6 and the bottom of page 10 show that the story, had it appeared in the book, would have preceded the second paragraph on page 56. His account of the incident, which evidently occurred on 30 July 1868, adds colour to Elizabeth Young's brief reference to the episode in her memoir (in the "Settling in at Rossville Mission" section). Young may have omitted the story from the book because it did not flatter a brother missionary.

> A singular adventure the next day [after our arrival] came pretty near putting an end to my Missionary career. While walking through the village with Mr. [Charles] Stringfellow and getting acquainted with some of the Indians, he and I had occasion to cross an unoccupied common where a savage bull was roaming about. Not dreaming of danger, for I had never in my life been molested by these animals, we moved along the foot path and got near the bull. Then I noticed that my nervous brother had quietly taken the other side of the path, thus placing me between himself and the furious animal which was pawing the ground near the foot path ahead of us. Absorbed in the conversation about the Mission work, I paid no attention to the bull, as I had no fear, when a sudden start from Brother S. caused me to look at the bull and I saw at that instant he was about to charge. Fortunately for me I did not lose my presence of mind, and so did a good deal of thinking in a very short space of time. Hastily looking around, I saw that no stick nor stone, as weapon of defense was within reach. I saw also that flight would be useless. I also observed that this bull had very wide horns and the thought came, rather than take either horn of this dilemma, better try and get between the two.
>
> No sooner said than done; so as with a savage roar the bull charged me, I turned myself sideways and moved so that he struck

me fair between his horns throwing me perhaps twenty feet, in such a way that I lit on my feet uninjured: quickly as possible he charged again, and I received him exactly in the same way with the same result. The third time as he charged again I was not quite quick enough in getting into position, and so one of his sharp horns made an awkward rent in one of my garments. But fortunately for me, he threw me this time on a pile of stones, and as the battle had thus far been on one side, and getting rather monotonous in its methods, I was glad of an opportunity of assuming the offensive. So seizing some of the stones and striking him severely over the head, he gave up the contest and retired in disgust.

From my *coigne* of advantage on the stone heap I was amused at seeing my Brother Stringfellow about a hundred feet away with hands uplifted and face white with terror.[1] Hurrying over to quiet his fears, I found him almost incapable of speech, and when I laughingly said to him: "Did you think I had lost my presence of mind?" his queer answer was, "I think you were, I think you were." As my coat was a long one I buttoned it close around me and we hurried back to the Mission house. When we reached there Mr. S's bloodless face excited the suspicions of the good wives that something was wrong, but all the poor man could say for a time in answer to their inquiries was, "The bull, the bull, the bull."

We had thought that possibly we might, in the wild missionary life before us, be at times in perils oft from savage men, and in the dreary forests perhaps from wild beasts, but this unceremonious attack in the heart of the village, had never been imagined or thought of. However, we were thankful it was no worse; and that the danger of its repetition might be averted, there was a big feast [doubtless the New Year's feast described by Elizabeth] soon after and the principal article offered was the not very tender meat of this savage bull.

---

1 Shakespeare, *Macbeth*, act I, scene 6: "coign of vantage," a position affording facility for observation or action (OED).

4 Letters of Clarissa Bingham and Sarah Bingham
to Elizabeth and Egerton Young, 1868–69

While Elizabeth Young headed to Rossville mission in the summer of 1868, her recently widowed mother, Clarissa Vanderburgh Bingham, remained in Bradford, running a boarding house and supporting her younger children as best she could. Two of Elizabeth's sisters, Mary Ann and Nelly, had married, and their brother John had died in August 1867, the same month as his father, Joseph. Four were still at home: Sarah Louise, aged about fifteen; Joseph, aged about twelve; Clarissa Jane (Clara), aged ten, and Charlotte (Lottie), who turned nine in December 1868.[2]

The Youngs preserved a small collection of letters sent to Elizabeth by her mother and some of her siblings in 1868–69; the original letters are now in the United Church of Canada Achives in Toronto (Young fonds, box 1, file 9, "Correspondence from the Bingham family," 1868–69). Later letters have not survived, nor have those that Elizabeth and Egerton sent to the Binghams. The excerpts that follow document the challenges that Clarissa faced, taking in as many boarders as she could with few resources and very little assistance. Sarah helped out, amid her schoolwork and music lessons. Clarissa Jane (named as Kit in the letters) and Charlotte (Lottie) doubtless helped, too, but they were still very young. For health and other reasons, prior to his death, Joseph, their brother, evidently spent considerable time living with his married sister, Mary Ann, and her husband, James Strong.

A constant theme in the letters is Clarissa's missing of "Libby," who must have been a major source of support before she left home, as is evident from her repeated questions about when and how soon Libby and Egerton would be coming home. The long gaps between letters from her daughter fueled Clarissa's worries about their well-being and fears about whether they had even "gone to that spirit land." As of November 1869, she had heard about Eddie's birth five months earlier, in June, but not about his name. Trusting he was still living, she wrote, "I hope you have chose a name by this time."

---

2 Wilson Brown, family history files. The Bradford 1871 census generally confirms the children's ages; it also shows that Clarissa was still running a boarding house as of that year.

Clarissa's letters provide a few close glimpses of a Bradford family in the 1860s. They are also evidently the only surviving documents in her hand. Their idiosyncratic spelling and freedom from punctuation tell us something about her educational background — a level of literacy probably higher than that of many in rural Ontario, yet not on a par with that of her daughter and son-in-law. Some of her letters are quite long; passages referring to local news of friends and neighbours not identified are omitted here. Mother and daughter had a close relationship. Elizabeth's love and respect for her mother and her hard work are strongly reflected in the Berens River episode later recorded by her son and quoted in Part 1, in the section headed "Where Are My Quilts?"

From Clarissa Bingham
   Bradford, Sept. 25 [1868]

   My Dear Children
   We have just received your verry welcome letter of the 20th of
   August we were getting very anxous to hav another letter from you.
   Sarah and I ware takeing our dinner after the boarders ware done
   and she just turned her cup and in thare was as prety a cup as ever
   I saw thare was a place it seemed a long way off and a strait line to
   the top of the cup and 2 dobts at the top and I told her thare was
   a letter comeing from Libby and Egerton poor Sarah could hardly
   believe it tonight when one of the boarders came in with a letter
   for her "now Ma you told me I was going to get a letter from Libby
   wright strait" and the girls from the shop came in with their cups
   and I laught and told them things I saw in their cup some of theirs
   came true tonight and they all think I can tell fortunes now, well
   enough of the fortune telling I am glad to hear you have a girl [to
   help] but I don't like to hear of Egerton going away so long from you
   we are getting along pretty well. I am paying my rent and keeping
   ourselves without drawing on the interest. . . .
      This is the 10th of October I was verry poorly on Sunday
   and Monday with a dizziness in my head I could not walk across
   the room without holding on to something but I am quite well
   now and the children except Kitty has got her bad headache and

Steve has just come in and brought some figs and maple sugar
he come in often to see how I am getting along. . . . I wonder
sometimes if my Libbie and Egerton wont be back next summer
you remember George Chantler he was here to see me poor
fellow he has berried 2 wives in 8 years . . . he was asking about
you and Mary Ann and Elly he thinks you wont stay thare long
it will be sutch a change for you, you will pardon me for not
sending this sooner but you wont think hard of me for I am so
tired at night that I cannot sit up late and get up early to get the
mens breakfast by half past 8 [6?].

My Dear Children I am just going to send this in the morning
whether I get it finished or not you will see that I have had several
tryes to get it ready we have been getting the stove pipes fixed today
and I am verry tired and it has been snowing all day. . . . I have
been thinking about you today more than common when I see the
snow I wondered how it is whare you are do write all the particulars
and tell me when you think of comeing home you will say you have
barely got thare. . . . it seems as though I cannot get to say good by
but I must say farewell with a mothers love and best wishes for 2
Dear Children that are ever in her thoughts and prayers as feble
as they are. . . . Libby and Egerton pray for your Mother that is
lonely and needs you pray some time I think I shall have to give up
keeping boarders for I cannot get a woman to help me when I want
and then I have to work to hard myself you will be tired of reading
this good night again.

Bradford, October 26th, 1868

Dear Children
I am geting verry anxious to get another letter from you we think
everry day will bring one we are all well except myself I have a bad
cold and we have been fixing the house up for cold weather I have
had the stove pipe run up by my room door and the door moved to
the other end of the hall and the pipe runs from the kitchen through
the dineing room into the one that goes in my room so I think it

will be comfortable. Joe has come down to spend Sunday with us and brought me some eggs and 2 geese and some pumkins . . . he is afraid I will work to hard. . . . Sarah is getting along with her music verry well Mrs Ambrose says it would be such a pity to stop her takeing lessons for she is getting on so fast James [Strong] thinks it is to bad for her to take lessons and me to work so hard but she must have some incouragement for she has to work very hard as well as me. . . . Kitte is home with us know and goes to school and getting along in her studyes very well some times I think I will have to keep her home to help for we have a great deal to do we have 8 boarders and there is 3 more wants to come as soon as I can make room Miss A[??] is giveing up the shop and I am going to make a petition [partition] across whare the counter was and carpet it and it will be more comfortable than going up stairs. . . .

poor Nelly I think she is worse than ever she is freting about me getting up to light the fires but I do not for I get Sarah up in good time to light them it seems so unfortuniate for me to be living so far from all of you that are married. . . . I have got butter in for the winter there is not many potatoes in yet people are digging them now perhaps they will be less the cheaper after they are gathered they have been froze there has been hard frost here.

It is well for you that you can get your washing done for you for that is more than I can get all the time Sarah and I had to wash week before last. . . . Kit is writeing and she is running over the paper so fast it would be a pity to stop her going to school for she bids fair for a good schooler if she has a chance I am trying to get the Children fixed up for winter I have made Sarah a tippet and muf out of that fur and it looks verry nice they say she looks like Libby you don't say anything about your melodian or (w)ringer I hope you wont neglect your music. . . . thare is a gentleman in this evening that plays on a guitar and it makes me think of my Libby in years that is past and I live in hopes that I shall have the privelage again of listening to her voice again.

Bradford – Sept. 15th, 1869

My Dear Children,
You will think Ma is getting careless but that is not the case I
intended to answer my Dear Egertons letter as soon as I possibly
could and one week after another has gone untill 3 has gone by since
I received your letters. . . . kit was reading about those that were
murdered [Red River troubles] and she says it is time for Egerton and
Libby to come home before they come there to hurt them we are all
well and getting along as well as we can I am beginning to dred the
winter for it is so cold for me to get up and light the fires. . . .

    I often think how long will it be or will I ever see my Egerton
and Libby again do not make up your minds to stay there many
years when I think I have Children and a dear little nephew
[grandson] away off in the far far West but it is really true but I must
stop or this will be a gloomy letter tell us your prospects as regards
provision for the winter I hope you will be better provided for this
comeing winter please God our crops are good except potato the
rot is comeing pretty bad it has been a wet season all through. . . .
Egerton can do most anything could he not take that babys picture
and send it to us for the Children don't know how they can wait. . . .
Kiss that dear babe for us. . . . hope to hear from you soon and it be
good news your affect[ionate] Ma

From Sarah Bingham
Bradford Sept. 30th 1869

Dear Libby and Egerton,
I suppose you think I have all moust forgotten you but I have not it
is a shame that I have not written before this. . . . I wish that I could
see that little Nephew of mine Eg[erton]. And I would have some
fun. . . . I would like to have its photograph but I suppose I cannot
until you come home. We expect Nelly home soon I wish you could
come to and stay all winter but we cannot think about that. I hope
we will see each other some day. I am taking musick lessons again.
Mrs Ambrose was wishing that I had a pianio but there is no youse

of wishing that. How is your melodian getting along you never say anything about it. I have been trying to teach Kitty but she is very hard to learn.

I suppose you offen wish for some good apples we have to bye all ours. . . .

I have been getting my picture taken to send to you it is not very good of my face but it is very good every other way. . . . Ma has been drying some raspberrys for you if she can get a chance to send them. I must stop now I cant send another half sheet with this letter

Give that baby a lot of kisses for me

From your dear Sister Sarah to her dear Sister and Brother

From Clarissa Bingham
Bradford Nov. 6th, 1869

My Dear Mishionary Children it is know 3 months since we have had any word from you the longest that we have been since you left us and I am thinking something must be wrong or we would have word I am trying to keep up heart and hope for the best but it is hard work as the weeks pass I think I surely will get a letter but none comes I think Egerton is away and something has hapened him and Libby don't like to let me know or Libby has taken cold and she is sick or gone for death is on our track Old Mr. Stephensan is dead and Old Wille Hardman Mr. Hardman was found dead in the field he went for potatoes for dinner and Old Mr. Stephenson give away to drink since his wife died and it caused his death. . . . sometimes I think perhaps you are comeing home and we dream of seeing you. . . .

I am verry mutch confind at home I have had a bad cold but am better I have been to Mary Anns they are well I left Sarah and Kit to keep house they done for a day but I would not leave them over night we have 7 boarders 3 girls and 4 men I have to keep Kit at home Sarah is not strong and it is to hard on me and we can not afford to keep a girl if we had a house of our own we might last year was a hard one we hope for a better one this but it bids fair for a long one. . . .

I often wonder whether you are liveing or no if you are liveing do come home soon as you can do write and give us some encouragement about your comeing home again this is the 3 letter since none has come I must wait as patiently as I can and hope for the best and say good by once more except of our kindest love and kiss Dear little boy for us all for we often wish we could see him and we hope nothing has hapened serious may the Lord bless and spare your precuious lives till we meet once more this side the grave.

From your ever affect Mother to Egerton and Libby and baby Young.

November 15th

Still no word from my Dear Children. . . . we are dreaming of seeing you. . . . I feel some times as if it is no use to write Libby and Egerton is gone to that spirit land and then someone says something to cheer me and get me to fell a little better and trying [to] think all is well. . . . winter is coming pretty fast we have had some verry cold weather and a great many have not got their potatoes dug it makes me think of you whether you have plenty.

I am foolish enough to think perhaps you are coming home then it is tooe mutch to expect I must say fare well once more hopeing to hear from you soon kiss that Dear Dear babe if he is liveing

Still hopeing to hear from my Dear Children from your affec. Mother Bingham

To Libby and Egerton Young and baby I hope you have chose a name by this time.

From Sarah Bingham

My Dear Sister and brother,

I am all moust ashamed to sit down to rite I have put it off so long. We have seven boarders and it keeps Ma and I very buissy. You must not think for a moment that I have forgotten you for as buissy as I am with my music and work I often think of you and Egerton and wish you hear with us. I have got two new pieces of music called Nora O'Neal and the reply they are very pretty pieces. Would you like to have them sent to you if you would I will try and send them to you. I have had the tooth ache for three days and could not do

anything to help Ma so I had to have it drawn I never had anything
hurt me so. The Doctor sed I would never die with consumtion
I made so much noise. Egerton I have not forgot that piano yet.
I hope you will excuse my scribbling. Goodby for this time

I remain your affectionate sister

Sarah L. Bingham

To her dear sister and brother — write soon.[3]

5 "A Great Surprise to the Missionaries Wife": Moss

In the set of memoirs titled "In the Land of Fur and Frost," a typescript
prepared by E. Ryerson on the basis of his mother's stories about mission
life, he quoted her as recalling that moss was "made as soft as cotton wool"
and provided "one of the best dressing for babes in the world" (3). Elizabeth
also composed the following description of moss, handwritten on a single
sheet of lined paper.

In place of carpet-sweepers, Electric sweepers, Dusters, floor
polishers, and all the civilized devices, Moss, Moss, was gathered
from the woods bye the Indian women, picked over & made free from
stems, Thorns, dried placing it on the rocks when dried gathered
up for drying and cleaning purposes. One important use it was to
perform, as Indian mothers make a frame like a shoe, and decorate
it with beadwork, or any kind of leather or cloth and lace it up with
leather laces made of Indian deer-skin, and when about to put the
Papoose in they put a layer of this beautiful soft moss in, lay the
little rosy cheeked Papoose in on top and cover him up with it to the
face or chin & lace him up, and as there is a bow shaped top and to
it a strap that goes around the mothers shoulders, she carries it in
summer and in winter throws a blanket over it to keep it warm & the
child comes out piping hot. The next thing the moss is used for, as
floors need cleaning there as in civilized countries, this moss is used
for drying purposes, it is very useful. When the floor is dried up, it is
then swept out and burned, for all cleaning purposes it is most useful.

3 This brief letter was probably written in November 1869 and enclosed with
Clarissa's letter of 15 November, above.

0

6 Women's Work

Tanning Moose Hide

Egerton Young took an interest in tanning — which, in Ontario, was men's work — partly because he was familiar with the process: his father-in-law, Joseph Bingham, was a tanner. In his *Stories from Indian Wigwams and Northern Camp-fires* (1892), Young set down a detailed description of the processing of a moose hide, based on his observations of Little Mary's work. Following intensive scraping, cleaning, and stretching of the hide, "deer" (caribou) brains "are carefully rubbed in, after which the skin is subjected to an amount of rubbing, pulling, and scraping that would wear out the patience of any white tanner. However, the result is a skin so tough and enduring that nothing can tear it."

Next, the skin was smoked. "Mary, the old Indian woman nurse, who made all our moccasins, used a large kettle, in which she placed pieces of a peculiar kind of rotten wood, which, when ignited, made a most pungent smoke but no flame. Over this she would fasten the mouth of the skin, which she had sewed up into the form of a sack. The dense smoke poured into this baglike affair, and, not being able to get out, soon permeated the whole concern, and the skin was tanned." If several skins were being tanned, the burning wood was placed in a hole in the ground, and the skins spread under a tightly secured tent. In this, Elizabeth recalled, "the leather is tanned to a lovely fawn color" ("In the Land of Fur and Frost," 4).

Young added, "For nine years I wore a coat made out of moose-skin tanned in this way. It was then still considered to be good enough in which to appear before enthusiastic crowds . . . in America, and also on the platform . . . in London, and in many other places in England. It is good for at least nine years of hard service yet."[4] Figures 11 and 12 show Young in what he called "my trusty suit of moose-skin."[5] Elizabeth, in contrast, was never portrayed in "Indian" dress.

4 Young, *Stories from Indian Wigwams and Northern Camp-fires* (New York: Eaton and Mains, 1892), 263–64.

5 Ibid., 281. See also the portrait of him wearing the coat, opposite that page.

"To Tan Deer Skin"

In "The Bride of 1868," Elizabeth described the labour entailed in preparing a "deer" (that is, caribou) skin for use:

> The Indian women like to keep this a "secret." After dressing the skin and making it perfectly clean and white, they sew up all the holes if there are any, which they sincerely hope there are none, then make a bag, and then with rotten wood they make a smudge smoke & put the mouth of the bag over it: Constant care is necessary to keep the smoke regular and steady.
>
> In drying the skin, a very still fire is needed and two women one each side of the fire, pull & stretch the skin, until it is soft and dry. Then the tanning process takes place. Moose skin is done in the same way. When it is all ready to be made into moccasins, leggings, mens jackets, moose skins make very good warm coats for travelling in the cold weather, on which there is a capote [hood? word smudged] for the protection of the head which is easily drawn over the head. [See figs. 11 and 12.] The Indian women make beautiful silk work for the moccasins, leggings, coats, & caps. The Patterns for their silk work is drawn from fancy prints of which their dresses are made, the leggings are decorated down the outsides of the leg. This is done with Silk & Porcupine Quills. The vamps of the moccasins are decorated [see figs. 2 and 9]. And the surround of the Caps [see fig. 10]. The young Indians think they are quite swell when decorated thus."

"Silk Work on Leather, Deer Skin," by Elizabeth Young

> To encourage industry, soon after reaching our mission, the callers were so frequent at the mission for food, clothing, a thought occurred to me as they were handy with the needle making moccasins, leggings, bead work, &c, so spoke to some of the Indian women. They were quite willing & happy. At once I gave them, leather, silk thread, thinking this [was] all at present or until the work was finished, but no, epacis Pacquashacan [*pahkwêsikan*] a little flour & tea to keep them while they do the work, and some soap to keep my hands clean. This was all just now. The work and

everything went on as usual. To my surprise I was called on again in a few days for a little more soap to keep my hands clean, and so on and in a little while some more tea, and in a few days some more Pacquashcan. So now I began to think the Venture was expensive & a failure, at last the silk work was done, and other ventures tried. But it was all the same. Their wants were all the same.

We were always glad when parcels, bundles came from England or Canada, so that we could be Almoners distributing to the needy ones. We were more than happy making the poor people comfortable.

The above text is written in ink on a single loose page. At the top are some notes in pencil, seemingly by E. Ryerson Young: "Dress making — Leather & then cloth. Coat & moccasin making. Leggings." Below are written some women's names: Mary Murdo, Nancy Kennedy, and Mary Robinson. Elizabeth referred to Mary Murdo in her 1927 narrative, noting the help she received from Mary when she was first learning Cree. Nancy Kennedy was probably the mother of Alex Kennedy, often mentioned as the Youngs' dog driver: see his letter of 1890 later in this part. Mary Robinson — who was described in pencil on another page as the "best sewer" — was, of course, "Little Mary," so important in the Youngs' family life in their mission years.

A paragraph on another single page is headed "Rabbit Skin Blankets." Here, Elizabeth wrote: "An Indian woman will take about 30 or 40 rabbit skins, dress & cure them & cut them into strips of about two inches in width while they are still 'green' & weave them into a blanket. When dry, the skin tightens & there is a perfect surface of fur on both sides. This makes a beautiful, warm blanket."

"Dressing Up Their Men"
"In the Land of Fur and Frost" (4–5) also preserves reminiscences from Elizabeth regarding the sophisticated craftwork of Cree women (for examples of their skill, see figs. 2 and 7–10). As she recalled, this labour was rarely dedicated to the women themselves:

The women take great pride [in making garments]; there is keen rivalry amongst them in their skill in decorating their work and dressing up their men. And some of them [the men] are real dandies with beaded caps, beautiful silk work on their leather shirts, leggings neat and gracefully decorated down the sides and the moccasins with front and vamps beautifully decorated with silk or porcupine quill work, with horse-hair or bead work, or a pretty combination of several of these. The skill of the women was lavished upon the men. They seldom bothered much about their own dress, unless very young and very aggressive, which was little seen in the women at Norway House.

7 Sandy Harte

In September 1869, Egerton Young travelled north by canoe from Norway House on a missionary trip to Cree people in the Nelson River area. The Norway House Wesleyan Methodist Register of Baptisms (UCA, Winnipeg) holds records of his visit: entries 1457 through 1463 list names of seven males whom he baptized there. All were adults except for the first, Alexander, aged "about 12 years," son of "John Harte," the chief. In fact, Young baptized many more than those seven. At the bottom of the page, he added, "N.B. I have baptized 110 at Nelson River. As I was unable to find out their ages, or the names of their parents, I have not entered them here. E.R.Y."

Number 1457, Alexander — or "Pe-pe-qua-na-peu," his Cree name as Young later transcribed it — was Sandy Harte, who was taken into the Young family and of whom Young, Elizabeth, and their son, Eddie (E. Ryerson), were all to write so warmly.[6] Young recorded Sandy's story most fully in

---

6 Egerton Young recorded Sandy's name in an old notebook as "Alexander Sandy Harte. Pe-pe-quá-ná-péu. (Indian name)." Underneath he translated the name as, "One making sweet music." Jeffrey Muehlbauer has interpreted the name as *pipikwan-nâpêw*, 'Eagle Flute Man,' or *pipikwêw-nâpêw*, 'Flute-playing/Flute-having Man' (e-mail, 19 June 2013). The name may have been conferred at Rossville where, Young recalled, Sandy was "a sweet singer [who] sang in his own musical language" and at times "would burst into song," singing hymns in Cree (Young, *On the Indian Trail and Other Stories of Missionary Work Among the Cree and Saulteaux Indians* (London: Religious Tract Society, [1897]), 119, 121). No use of flutes was mentioned, but perhaps he sometimes played Elizabeth Young's melodeon, a wind instrument of another sort. The origins of the name "Harte" (sometimes spelled "Hartie") are unknown.

his book *Indian Life in the Great North-West*, telling how he found the boy lying in the chief's lodge, crippled by an accidental gunshot wound to his leg. Young had with him copies of biblical texts printed at Rossville in Cree syllabics and found the invalid greatly interested in learning to read and write the Cree characters. He wrote that, at the boy's request, "he was given the English name of Sandy Harte." Sandy's father, whom Young described as "a fine-looking man," must have sanctioned the baptism, and Young published a drawing of him (artist unknown) on page 17 of *Indian Life.*[7]

Young was impressed at Sandy's intelligence and interest in the syllabics and wrote that, when he was leaving Nelson River, he commented to some people that if Sandy had an education he could be a teacher, even if he could never be a great hunter. The next summer (1870), some of the men he had met there turned up at Rossville — bringing Sandy in a canoe. They were acting, they said, on Young's suggestion that Sandy be educated and had brought him for that purpose.

Of course, we can't tell how Young's words at Nelson River were translated, understood, or remembered by his listeners. In any case, Sandy's coming was a surprise to the Youngs, and a challenge as well: their resources were very limited owing to the troubles in Red River and the many needs they faced at Rossville. However, they rose to the occasion. As Young recalled, he talked the matter over with Elizabeth, asking divine direction. Elizabeth evidently provided the guidance he sought: "The noble woman said, 'The Lord is in it, and He who has sent the mouth to be filled will surely

---

7 Young's first-hand account of the episode varies considerably from its more simplistic reading by his younger colleague, the Reverend John Semmens. Although, in *On the Indian Trail*, Young alluded to a "prevailing custom" (often asserted by missionaries to exist) of killing helpless persons, writing that "they had postponed the killing of this lad because he was the son of the chief" (103), in *Indian Life in the Great North-West* (Toronto: Musson Book Company, [1899?]), he wrote more warmly that he "was the chief's son, and so he was cared for." (14). Semmens, however, in his *The Field and the Work: Sketches of Missionary Life in the Far North* (Toronto: Methodist Mission Rooms, 1884), cast the episode in a darker light: "To his pagan father's mind there came but one thought. He would end the life of his sick boy." Semmens also simplified the adoption story, stating that Young, seeking "to preserve the boy's life . . . volunteered to take him back to his own home at Norway House, doctor him, educate him, and send him back again to his people. . . . All this was readily agreed to by the selfish father, who saw no advantage in the education offered, but . . . a present escape from caring for a helpless invalid" (133–34).

supply all our additional requirements.' So we cheerfully received Sandy into our home, and made him as one of our family."[8]

Young wrote a further twenty or so pages about Sandy in *Indian Life in the Great North-West* and devoted chapter 6 of *On the Indian Trail* to him as well, providing a good many more details. Elizabeth's account of him, written probably between 1927 and 1931, complements her husband's descriptions, providing insights into her own responses, her challenges in dealing with the new arrival, and the strength of the bond that developed:

> Very Early in the Spring not long after Mr Young's Visit to the Nelson River Indians, a Strange Canoe & Strange Indians our Indians know so well when any stranger[s] arrive, they gather around them. So these Strangers came to the Mission with this cripple boy, saying, "we have brought Sandy as we promised you." Of course this was all news to me, but after it was all explained to me, I sincerely acquiesced & felt very much interested in the poor lame boy who was forced to use crutches. Of course it was another mouth to fill & another one added to my care, another one to keep, etc.
>
> I little knew how much it meant to me to take the poor boy under my care as I already had all I could do to care for the mission & the innumerable callers I was receiving constantly. But here was a poor cripple boy, needed care. If it had not been for the missionaries appearance at his father's home just when he did, the poor lad would have been disposed of. Thanks to the missionary & a kind Providence he is alive, & now I have an opportunity to help him by caring for him, & with God's blessing I am going to. He is left to us & his friends have gone. The poor boy will feel strange so far away from his own people, & it beho[o]ves us to try and make him feel at home, & happy.
>
> We do just the same for him as for our own dear Children. First to be clean about his person & his clothing his room; but of course

8 Young, *Indian Life in the Great North-West*, 15–21. His consulting with Elizabeth parallels his account (quoted in the introduction to the present volume) of her role in accepting the call to mission work back in January 1868 (*By Canoe and Dog-Train Among the Cree and Salteaux Indians* [London: Charles H. Kelly, 1890], 28). See also chapter 10 of *By Canoe and Dog-Train* for Young's description of his second visit to Nelson River.

not all at once, only just a little at a time, he goes to school, in a very short time the Teacher announced that Sandy was playing truant this of course could not be allowed & when it continued the missionary one day found him standing on a prominent point looking directly towards home & brought him to the mission and had a good faithful talk with him; we found out he was not willing, not only to attend school but did not want to obey Okimasquao [Muehlbauer: *okimâskwêw*, 'the master's wife']. S. M. Young informed him, that Okimasquao was working for him, every day, cooking for him, washing for him, making his bed, and home nice for him. So he must be obedient & if Okimasquao asks him to help her, he must do it.

Just at this time I was very much tried in finding the bed & bedding were running away with vermin, not only the bed but they were marching up the walls. So the missionary just put it straight, but very kindly, & firmly Sandy boy just get your clothing & bring them to me. Now the boy was *frightened* thinking he was going to be sent away, but the missionary just said, here is some soap, take these clothes to So & So & [an] Indian woman, and ask her please to wash them and bring them to the mission, & then you come for me.

In the meantime there was some fumigation going on, in the mission, some scrubbing some cleaning & when the clean clothes came home, we had a consultation & a love feast, & a reconciliation, & Sandy was now my boy clean happy & satisfied having really found out who cared for him. So now I had one sincere friend & it was Sandy. The missionary had precious meetings going on in the church with the Indians & our Sandy boy was one of the first to give his heart to God. After this he was such a kind loving boy a real comfort & help, helping me in so many ways, with the children, with the work, making snow shoes, cleaning fish, helping with the fires as well as studying.[9]

9 In a three-page manuscript titled "The First Visit of a Missionary," in which Elizabeth described Egerton's trip to Nelson River, she supplied further details about Sandy's presence at Rossville. He helped to look after the dogsleds and dogs and, "although he had to go around on crutches it was wonderful what he could help [with] in the school, in the church, in the house and around the mission, and when Mr Young was away he was a great comfort to me . . . [also] making Bow and arrows for our son Egerton, paddles." JSHB collection.

One day an old Indian woman came in calling. I was very anxious to see some of their fantastic steps. So I asked her if she would show me some, if Sandy boy would Tum-Tum for her, ah, ha. If I would give her a new pair of moccasins, my answer was ah, ha, and away she went, and sure enough it was hard on the moccasins.[10]

Our boy Sandy's friends came to visit him and now we invited them into the mission, set the table and gave them the best we had. When all was ready we all sat down with them, Sandy said "Chesquaw" [Muehlbauer: *cêskwa*], that is in Indian Wait, & Sandy asked the blessing. Then all were helped but not one touched anything until the missionary did, then they all joined & really & truly were most polite. Sandy boy talked & prayed with them ere they left.

And when our time came for leaving Norway House we left our Sandy boy, a fine young man, & a very sad young man knowing full well he was loosing [a] good friend, of course he went home. A little while after we heard he was a *local Preacher*, & schoolmaster, married, & a good man & Indian.[11]

Egerton's writings from the period 1871–73 shed further light on the Youngs' relations with the Nelson River people. They help to date the feast mentioned above, at which the Youngs and Sandy welcomed his friends and relations, to the early summer of 1871. They also record a gift of great significance that marked the occasion. As Egerton later reported to his Toronto superiors, the visitors from Nelson House, numbering about twenty-five, presented him with a "splendid redstone pipe" as a sign, he said, of their turning to Christianity.

10 E. Ryerson Young made some pencil notes on his mother's telling of this story. The woman demonstrated her dancing, described as "a shuffle & gliding," and Sandy made "music" for her — "sticks on wood — to keep time." Then, indeed, she "needed [a] new pair" of moccasins.

11 This text is transcribed from pages 10–14 of a fifteen-page handwritten memoir by Elizabeth Bingham Young titled "Daily Reminiscences of Norway House's Living," the original of which is in the UCCA, Toronto. Although previously misattributed to Egerton Young and filed in series 4, it is now in series 5, Records of Elizabeth Bingham Young, box 10, file 3.

This pipe travelled far, both before and after 1871. Its bowl, which now resides in the Young collection in the Royal Ontario Museum, is made of catlinite, a fine-grained, red stone that may have come from a western Minnesota quarry long used by Aboriginal people as a special source of pipestone, or from a smaller quarry on the Bloodvein River, in Manitoba. The Nelson River Cree must have acquired it through trade or travel some years before Egerton's mission visit to them in 1869.[12] Egerton saw its giving as a symbol of conversion: his Cree visitors told him that "nearly the whole tribe have given up conjuring, &c." Sandy's people, however, would have attached their own meanings to the pipe, which, Young wrote, "they almost worshipped as a god" (he was ill-equipped to grasp their spiritual understandings). Their gift of it signified their regard for him but also surely expressed with great power their recognition of the Youngs' care and love for their chief's son, Sandy. The Youngs, in turn, valued it in their own way, bringing it to Ontario, where it joined several other treasured objects on the wall of Egerton's study (see fig. 13). Sometime after his death in 1909, his daughter Lillian Helme brought it to her home in England, whereupon it passed to her son, Egerton Helme, who took it to his new home in South Africa. Late in his life, having some notion of the pipe bowl's importance (the stem had been lost), he found a means to return it safely to his uncle (Egerton Young's son, Eddie) or his family around 1962, ninety years after its giving.

In the summer of 1872, several Nelson River people travelled to Winnipeg for the first Methodist church conference to be held in Manitoba. The next summer, before he left Norway House, Egerton Young recorded a sequel to that event:

> Macedonian Calls. The Nelson River Indians called again on me
> today to have a talk. The first question was, "Has a Missionary come

---

12 Young, 29 July 1871, to *Wesleyan Missionary Notices*, 1 February 1872, 212. The catlinite pipe, the bowl of which is now in the Egerton R. Young collection at the Royal Ontario Museum, appears on the left side of figure 13; the pipe stem was lost to theft while the treasure was in the hands of the Lillian Young Helme family in England. A shipping label kept with the pipe bowl reads: "Helme . . . Cape Town. To Miss Elizabeth Brown. New York. To be returned to the Rev. E. Young." Elizabeth Brown was the daughter of Grace Young Brown, E. Ryerson's sister; he had probably died before its return. Correspondence regarding the pipe is in the JSHB collection. Thanks to archaeologist Perry Blomquist for information on the Bloodvein as a source of catlinite.

for us yet." The *Bishop* Dr [Enoch] Wood told us when we saw him in Manitoba last year, "That something would be done for us. We carried that good news home with us to our fathers and it was like the sunshine to them. When we were leaving our home this year with our furs, our father said to us, 'You had better take another boat with you to bring back the Missionary'" [but they lacked means to do so]. . . . They were very sorry that there was no supply for them.

When the rumour which was [earlier] current among the NH Indians reached them that in all probability I would be removed from Norway House they came and putting their arms around me and urged and besought me to go and live with them and be their Missionary.[13]

As Elizabeth noted, and as Egerton wrote (see sec. 11, below), Sandy and the Youngs parted with great sadness in the summer of 1873. Sandy stayed for most of the following year at Rossville, studying and working for the Reverend John Ruttan. On 23 March 1874, he wrote to Egerton, in English, of feeling "grief in my heart because of the loss of my brother" (at Nelson House) but finding comfort "from those good books I am learning and reading now. I am very comfortable with my new Master who is kind and cares for me. I am learning very much at the school, and hope that I may be useful to my people at Nelson River."

His next letter to Egerton, however, was very different. Late that spring, the Reverend John Semmens was delegated to start a mission at Nelson House, and Sandy accompanied him, at least initially. Things did not go well. The letter, written in Cree syllabics, is hard to decipher in some places, as well as challenging in its older and sometimes obscure usages.[14]

---

13 Young, on pp. 63–64 of an 1870 diary used for later writings (copy in JSHB collection). Missionaries frequently invoked "Macedonian calls" to inspire mission work, evoking Paul's vision one night of a man of Macedonia praying and saying, "Come over into Macedonia and help us" (Acts 16:9).

14 In 1984, a University of Winnipeg student, Donna Hartie (the widow of a Nelson House Cree, although she had never heard of Sandy Harte) and Cree-speaker Joe Mercredi produced a preliminary translation for me. Then, in 2013–14, Jeffrey Muehlbauer took up the task, labouring hard to achieve the best translation possible of a very difficult text. My warm thanks to him and his Cree consultants for all their help and efforts. Happily for Young, he would have received the letter at Berens River, where his Cree associates could read it for him.

In it, however, Sandy referred, rather obliquely, to conflicts with Semmens regarding a shortage of food supplies; it also appears that Semmens may have drawn him into selling furs at the fort, which missionaries were not supposed to do. Linguist Jeffrey Muehlbauer has worked intensively to arrive at the translation that follows. The words he has placed in parentheses provide alternate translations of Cree terms, while bracketed texts represent Muehlbauer's and his consultants' best efforts to surmise the meanings of the Cree syllabics, which pose problems of both legibility and interpretation.

I am writing to you, Mr. E. Young, so that you should know I am still doing well through God's compassion. So then, that is how I am hoping it [this letter?] should find you of course. There is nothing much that I will be able to tell you about, but I will tell you that I did not accompany the prayer chief [Semmens]. He sent me out, like they would send me away before. That's what he did to me. So then, I will tell you the reason I left. Probably at the moment the fishing season is the reason. Mr. Semmens did not give me a little bit for us to make food with. So I worked for them. So my father was there, also my brother was there where I fish. I was happy that we are going to tell them about God's religion. So then, I thoroughly (already) told to you why he allowed me to sell beavers at the fort. It was not intentional. He was not supposed to have done that. He got nothing. Similar to that, that's what I want to tell you, him [me?] being poor on earth. Truly, I was not able to grasp it (i.e., I frown on it), what's happening to me now. I cannot tell you who should do it; me myself or Mister Semmens. So I will not swear to you responding much to me. Of course I will be able to swear the truth that God knows if [I sold things]. [So then, I will have to think a little better about Mr. Semmens.] [Untranslatable text follows.] I myself do not remember when I stopped accompanying you. I hope you will tell me what you're thinking. It is me, Sandy, who is writing you, Mr. Young. Truly, I knew that I loved you and my father to such an extent. So then, you should tell me about God's religion. I myself have never forgotten. So then, I hope that you should pray for me. These are the only things I will say to you. Try and write me if you are able. I greet all of you, all your children, also the chief woman [i.e., Elizabeth].

Although Semmens's Nelson River relations with Sandy got off to a bad start, his later writings made no reference to the difficulties, which we hear of only through Sandy's letter to Young. In 1884, Semmens recalled in his memoirs of the North that when he started the Nelson River mission, Sandy Harte, son of the chief, was his "companion, assistant, and fellow evangelist. Without delay, he began his work of faith and labor of love. Teaching with him became a passion. Early and late, and at all hours, he was at it. . . . He taught his fellows Zion's sacred melodies. He made them acquainted with the Evans' characters. . . . To this day, without ostentation and without remuneration, he esteems it a privilege to speak to the people concerning the salvation of Jesus the Christ."[15]

Sandy's father, John Harte, continued as chief at least until 1900. Writing to Egerton Young from Winnipeg in 1900, Semmens reported that "John Hartie sits by his fire-side awaiting the Master's call while Sandy his son still talks of the great love of the Father Divine."[16] The Reverend Samuel Gaudin and his wife served at the Nelson House Methodist mission for many years, starting in 1891. In 1900, when they were leaving on their first furlough, "an old Chief, John Hartie, came to say Good-bye. . . . The Chief was a sincere Christian respected by the entire community. . . . When he came to say farewell to us, he said in a very beautiful way, 'May you find the hand of the Great Father stretched out to you as I have found your hands reached out to me.'" On his death a few years later, he received many warm tributes.[17]

---

15 John Semmens, *The Field and the Work: Sketches of Missionary Life in the Far North* (Toronto: Methodist Mission Rooms, 1884), 135. On p. 113, however, Semmens noted that his stay at Nelson River was brief: "We were not long in making the discovery that we were entirely useless in this locality. We had no interpreter," as the Hudson's Bay Company had reneged on supplying one. This is a puzzle, as Sandy could presumably have served in this role, but he may not have been hired or paid as such. The "we," unidentified, may be a royal "we."

16 Semmens to Young, 16 November 1900, UCCA, Young fonds, series 1, correspondence (copy in JSHB collection).

17 S. D. Gaudin, *Forty-Four Years with the Northern Crees* (Toronto: Mundy-Goodfellow Printing, 1942), 97–98.

Postscript

On 1 April 1935, the Reverend A. C. Huston, the United Church missionary at Nelson House, responded to a letter that E. Ryerson Young had evidently sent him inquiring about Sandy Harte and his family. Huston provided further valuable details:

> Sandy Harte has a brother living here by the name of Joseph and
> a grandson by the name of Angus Bonner, from them I learned
> Sandy was the oldest of the family of six boys and six girls. The
> father's name was John and his wife's name Charlotte. They could
> not recall her last name prior to her marriage to John Harte. . . .
> John Harte was by what they say the first chief, having been chosen
> before the treaty regulations. . . . He died about thirty-five years
> ago. They said your father took Sandy back to Norway House after
> one of his visits here and when he returned to Nelson House it was
> to carry on as a local preacher till his death in 1910 or thereabouts.
> He had married a girl by the name of Jane Hunter and had three
> daughters and one son. They are all dead now. Sandy was shot
> in the thigh after his return from Norway House but recovered
> [misdating the injury that happened before Egerton Young's visit in
> September 1869]. He must have been about sixty years of age at the
> time of his death. He was buried here on the reserve.

8 Egerton R. Young's Illness with Typhoid, 1872

Norway House, Aug. 29th 1872

It is with great weakness I write you this short note.[18] Shortly after leaving Winnipeg I was seized with diarrhoea. I was exceedingly sick the last six days. We had a very disagreeable passage of twelve

---

18 At the top of the page on which he transcribed this letter, Young wrote "From a *private* letter," but the name of the person to whom the letter was sent does not appear. In all likelihood, though, it was addressed to the Reverend Enoch Wood, who, at the time, was the superintendent of missions for the Wesleyan Methodist Church.

days. I think if I had not got home when I did, I never should have reached here alive. The disease is not yet cured. If I use any strong remedies to stop it I am thrown into a violent fever, and then break out into the most profuse perspiration. I am so wasted away you would hardly know me. I cannot check it gently and restore nature to her natural work. I am so depressed and sad in spirits. I enjoyed the Conference in Winnipeg exceedingly. I felt the continued comforting presence of the Holy Spirit but now I am under a heavy cloud and seem to have so very little faith or power to pray. In the midst of my gloom I can only keep saying: "Peace! doubting heart; they God's I am!" I know you will pray for me. I never was so sick before. I never had such fierce attacks from the devil. "Oh God, forsake me not!" Will you be so kind to give my apologies to our honored President, Dr. Punshon, for my not having written, as promised, an account of Indian children's habits, amusements, etc. My sickness has unfitted me for everything. My people were glad to see me back; but alas! I cannot minister unto them. Timothy [Bear] is pushing ahead at Beren's River.

E. R. Young

Around the end of September, Young wrote a sequel to the above letter. The following excerpt is from a typed transcript of that letter:

I think I wrote you a letter when very sick, about a month ago. I had a bad attack of typhoid fever. I was very much depressed, mentally, and had some dark and gloomy hours; but the cloud passed away, and now, with a glad heart, I can exclaim, "The Lord is my light and my salvation," &c. I am very much thinner than when I was in Manitoba, and am still very weak; but I feel well, and am now able to attend to my labors. One great drawback here to rapid recovery of wasted strength, is the difficulty of getting any of those little dainties, such as beef tea or chicken broth, — which the sick crave. We had in the house pork and pemmican; but at this season there is no fresh meat of any description.

9 Schooling in Rossville: The "Infant Class" and Miss Batty's Thoughts on Shawls

The most detailed accounts that the Youngs left of Rossville mission schooling are found in two chapters of Egerton Young's book *The Battle of the Bears*. Chapter 9, "Indian Boys and Girls at School" describes the Youngs' teaching arrangements. The Sunday school, in particular, was important to their efforts to reach a broad cross-section of the community. There, Elizabeth "had charge of the infant class, which consisted of all under the age of eight or ten years." The regular day school teacher, Peter Badger, "had the intermediate pupils, including all . . . up to the age of sixteen years." Badger was a fluent Cree speaker and writer, "a man used to writing his language," as David Pentland has observed.[19] Egerton Young had charge of the older people who came to the Sunday school. As he wrote, "Many of the older people would at times come in, and often . . . they would strike a light, and have a good smoke out of their long pipes, while listening to the lesson for the day."[20]

In chapter 10, "The Old Indian in the Infant Class," Young shed further light on the "infant" Sunday school class taught by Elizabeth. It was "the most popular one. Many grown-up infants wanted to be in it, and as the reasons they urged . . . were strong ones, we had to yield in some cases, and let them sit down with the little ones." One was a Cree man of about seventy who arrived from some distance and began to attend all the services and the Sunday school, where "he would always go into the infant class." When Young invited him into his class, "he would shake his head and refuse me most decidedly." His argument was that he had "seen many winters, but my mind is just as a newborn child in the knowledge of the Good Spirit. . . . So I must sit down and learn with the young ones, who are of my own age in these things."[21] His reasoning was surely genuine, but Elizabeth's manner of teaching and her efforts to communicate in Cree were also surely factors in the popularity of the "infant class."

19 David H. Pentland, "The Rossville Mission Dialect of Cree: Egerton Ryerson Young's 1872 Vocabulary," in *Essays in Algonquian Bibliography in Honour of V. M. Dechene*, ed. H. C. Wolfart (Winnipeg: University of Manitoba, 1984), 44.

20 Young, *The Battle of the Bears* (Boston: W. A. Wilde, 1907), 134.

21 Ibid., 150.

Young also set down a vivid description of the pupils' school dress. Among the boys, it was quite diverse; some had items of Western clothing, but a good many had leather garments that varied widely in quality, fit, and ornamentation. The girls' dress, however, had one common element, namely, "the great blanket which each one wore. It was amusing to watch the girls' efforts to keep their faces hidden, with only one eye visible, while in many cases the girl was so small and the blanket so large, that much of it was trailing in the snow or on the floor of the church."[22] The Youngs evidently made no effort to standardize dress other than to try to furnish warm clothing and encourage cleanliness.

In September 1873, the Reverend John H. Ruttan took charge of the Rossville mission. Peter Badger, who had taught there for several years, continued in his post. In June 1875, Badger left, however, to become teacher and catechist for the numerous families leaving to settle at the White Mud River, and in early August a new schoolteacher arrived from Ontario — Clementina Batty. Miss Batty made some changes in the school regime. A few months after her arrival, she wrote a letter for the Methodist publication *Missionary Notices*, dated 6 January 1876 and directed to schoolchildren. Describing the Cree people in largely negative terms, she detailed her campaign to change the girls' dress and demeanour:

If you had come with me the first morning I opened school, you would have been surprised to see twenty or thirty girls sitting, each with a shawl over her head, though it was a warm summer day. Every time one was spoken to she would draw the shawl over her eyes and mouth, making it quite impossible to hear what was said. . . . so it is little wonder if I could not understand them, especially as they could not speak a word of English and I could not understand a word of Cree.

Mr Ruttan told me he had been waiting for me to come and take these shawls off, so I thought I would do it. I went round to one, shook hands, and said, "What cheer?" for I had learned that much "Cree" or rather sailor's English. I waited until we were a little acquainted, and then showed them I had no shawl on, and asked them to fold theirs up.

22 Ibid., 134.

Poor girls! They were astonished at such an unheard-of proposition and only hugged their shawls the closer. I had to laugh at their dismay, but at the same time took off the shawls one after another with my own hands, for they seemed quite paralyzed. There was a great hiding of faces and a great many half-terrified half-bashful looks, and for several days I had to take the shawls off myself. It was amusing to see how awkward they seemed, especially when strangers came in; very much the same as you would, if you should find yourself in church some day without a hat. But they are getting over it. . . . I will tell you one good effect it has. My poor girls, I'm afraid, seldom combed their hair while they had their heads covered, and you would have been almost horrified to see such rough-looking heads as the removal of shawls revealed. They nearly all comb their hair now, and I keep a comb in the school for those who have none at home, or forget to use it.[23]

Wittingly or not, Miss Batty was challenging Cree protocols that mandated shyness and a degree of concealment for girls and young women in the presence of strangers and men — protocols that the Youngs and Peter Badger had simply accepted.[24]

23 A handwritten version of Miss Batty's text, titled "Cree School Children. By C.B.," appears in Egerton R. Young's Berens River notebook (UCCA, series 2, box 2, file 3), 188–94, but it is not in his hand. Her account was printed in *Missionary Notices of the Methodist Church of Canada*, 3rd ser., no. 6 (March 1876), 100–101 (thanks to Anne Lindsay for finding it). The issue of the *Notices* also quoted a letter from the Reverend John Ruttan dated 28 September 1875, which warmly praised Miss Batty's "earnest manner and kind heart. . . . Though she has much to discourage her in the capacities of her pupils, yet neither diligence nor piety is wanting in her work of faith and labour of love. The children are learning the English, or . . . how to use the English, quite fast" (86). For further information on her, see the postscript "Mission Wives at Rossville," in Part I.

24 As anthropologist John Honigmann noted in 1953, in the Cree community where he lived in 1947–48, "an unmarried girl in the presence of a young man typically hides her face in a shawl with signs of pronounced shyness and confusion": "Social Organization of the Attawapiskat Cree Indians," *Anthropos* 48 (1953): 812.

10 "Thanks to the Kind Ladies of Canada": Egerton Young to the *Christian Guardian*

The following letter, dated 8 October 1873, appears in Young's Berens River notebook (UCCA, Young fonds, series 2, box 2, file 3), 176–77. By October, Young was on his way to (or was already in) the Toronto area and so may have delivered the letter in person.

Dear Bro, — Mrs Young and myself desire through the columns of the Guardian to return our very sincere thanks to the kind ladies of Canada who sent, through our friend Mr [William E.] Sanford, of Hamilton, the cases of warm clothing for our poor Indians at this mission. The names of the good ladies we did not receive. We found out either by parcels in the cases or by letter the following names, which we gladly place upon record: Mrs. Jackson and Mrs Sanford of Hamilton; Mrs Cox, of Ottawa; Mrs. Lewis, of Queenston; Mrs Morren, near Barrie.

If our dear lady friends could only have seen the tears of joy, and smiles of gladness, and heard the hearty words of thankfulness, and observed the marvellous change wrought in the appearance of our Indians, they would have felt amply repaid for all their trouble and sacrifices. May they ever realize in their own souls the blessed fulfilment of the Saviour's promise. "Inasmuch as ye have done it unto one of these my brethren, ye have done it unto me" [Matthew 25:40].

There was a marked improvement in the personal appearance of the congregation the next Sabbath after the arrival of the cases. Some, whose best coat had been an old one made out of a threadbare blanket, were enabled, through their gifts, to appear in God's house clothed in broadcloth, which although a little worn, will be carefully preserved and kept, exclusively, for Sabbath use for many years.

I noticed that one old Indian, who is called Rabbit Hunter, to whom I had given a second hand black coat, still persisted in wearing his old ragged one. I asked him why he came to church looking that way, when he might have been so much more decently clad. "Where is the nice black coat I gave you? I said a little sternly. "Now, minister," he replied, "don't be angry with me and I will tell you all about it. You know I never had such a fine coat as that in all my life, and I was afraid if I wore it to church I would be thinking about it, and so not be able to listen well to the sermon; and then, you see, some of the young fellows would like to get that coat, and they might ask me to trade coats, even on God's holy day, and so I thought I would leave the coat at home in the box for a while. Please don't be cross with me, I will put it on and wear it as soon as the big glad thought of getting it settles down in my heart." Pretty good logic that for a poor Indian, and an answer from which much can be learned.

Our kind lady contributors will not be offended at the length of time which has elapsed since these cases were sent, and our acknowledgment of the receipt of them, when we inform them that, although sent more than a year ago, they only reached us a few weeks ago. Japan is as near Toronto or Hamilton as are these isolated m[ission] fields.

Egerton R. Young

11 Transitions, 1873–74: Letters from Egerton to Elizabeth Young

The following letters were published by Harcourt Brown, a grandson of Egerton and Elizabeth Young, in *Manitoba Pageant* 17 (1971): 2–11. The letters, together with the full text of his preface, are available on the website of the Manitoba Historical Society (www.mhs.mb.ca/docs/pageant/17/youngletters.shtml). Egerton wrote the first two letters in August and September 1873, from Norway House, and the two others, one apparently incomplete, in April 1874, from Berens River. The text of the letters has been rechecked against the originals for accuracy, and one passage that was omitted in the published version of the first letter (in the second paragraph below the "August 11th" heading — from "Do you really believe it" to the end of the paragraph) has been restored here. The letters record the strong bond of affection between husband and wife, the warm attachment that the

Rossville people felt for the Youngs, and the logistical challenges of a mission family's life and travel.

At least one letter between the second and third is missing: at the start of his letter of 6 April 1874, Young mentioned sending "my last to you" from the Stone Fort (Lower Fort Garry), before leaving there for Berens River in late March. The letter of 10 April 1874 is unsigned, seemingly lacking a final page or pages. The first letter was originally kept among diaries and other documents held by Harcourt Brown; the second and third letters were among the Young papers held by the Reverend H. Egerton Young, in Toronto. All are now in the UCCA, Young fonds, series 5, box 10, file 5. A note that Egerton Young wrote in his Berens River notebook (UCCA, Young fonds, series 2, box 2, file 3) may serve as introduction: "Parting words: 'We shall be so glad to see you darling, but do not come to us until your work is well arranged and you can come without anybody saying with any reason, "What doest thou here, Elijah?"' Libbie's parting words on the northern shore of Lake Winnipeg, July 31st /73."[25]

Norway House,
August 4th, 1873

My darling Libbie,
We watched your receding boats until they went out of sight near Montreal Point.[26] That my heart was sad and lonely I need not stop to say. A great large vacuum, all at once, seemed to have at once taken the place where my heart was supposed to be. As you faded out of the vision of your husband's eye, he earnestly prayed that the all-seeing eye of the *One,* who beholdest all things, would ever be upon you and on our darling little ones. I was in no mood for shooting that evening and so we remained upon that sandy shore until sundown.

25 The quotation is from 1 Kings 19:11–13: God was critical of Elijah for being in one place when he should have been fulfilling responsibilities somewhere else.

26 Young (with Sandy Harte) accompanied Libbie and the children as far as Warren's Landing, at the north end of Lake Winnipeg, saying goodbye on 1 August. Montreal Point is the most northerly point on the east side of the lake itself.

We parted on that shore, Love,
You for our childhood home
I to the field of toil, Love,
Where the red men do roam.

As the mosquitoes were thick we went out to a little rocky
island which was destitute of trees and spent the night. My bed
consisted of an oil cloth, one blanket and a pullover. I rolled myself
up in the blanket and oil cloth and slept well, although my side was
a little sore in the morning as the rock was a rough one. At Prayers
both morning and evening all prayed. It would have done your heart
good to have heard Sandy [Harte] pray. I was amazed at his fluency
and earnestness. Poor fellow, he mourns over your departure in a
way that shames my *apparent* indifference.

We spent the day in shooting, called at Johnny Oig's in the
evening and saw the dogs.[27] Tell Eddie Shunias [Money] and Robin
and Lothair and all the rest, even Poquashikum [Flour] and Koona
[Snow] are all well, and were glad to see me. We reached the
Mission about dark. Mary had returned before us. Everything is
neat and tidy. Poor Timothy [Bear] is very feeble. He eats with me
and I think it was the best arrangement we could have made. Times
are hard. The nets yield us but little. We have eaten up the dried fish
and must live on Pemmican as there are no sturgeon. We had a nice
mess of green pease yesterday. I am teaching the school while Peter
[Badger] is away at Red River.

Yesterday I packed up my tools, medicines, and two Cases of
Books. Harriet Badger is making me some moccasins and Mary is
working at the gloves. I have sent Willie and four others to cut hay.
We have a little boy to bring in the cows, and Chloe milks them.[28]

27 For a substantial biography of Oig, see "John 'Johnny' Oig, c1817–1889," www.
redriverancestry.ca/OIG-JOHN-1817.php. He had local importance in the Cree community of Rossville, although he was said to have Chipewyan background.

28 Chloe was the daughter of Timothy Bear. John Semmens recorded that on 16 April
1874, at Rossville, Timothy Bear invited him to the wedding of Chloe to James McDonald
(*The Field and the Work,* 70).

I have not got Martin [Papanekis] of[f] yet. I am annoyed that he is so slow, and begin to think that the better way would be to go and board at Mr. Flett.

If I only knew that I was to go on to join you in *Ontario*, I would soon decide what to do but this uncertainty is what perplexes me. Depend upon it I will come as soon as I honourably can, but not before even if I never come. No one shall accuse me of deserting my Post and running Home without authority. Still I am well convinced that I could serve the Church better this year at Home, than out here. But you will say there is a good deal of *concate* [conceit?] as Pat would say, in that last sentence: well scratch it out then if you like.

The Indians all miss you very much. They come and sit around, and look so sad that I have to get out of their sight to keep from having the blues. We have had two fine showers hope they did you no harm. We all hoped you got to Beren's River for the Sabbath and for fresh milk for the dear little ones.

As a few days have dragged their slow length along since I wrote the previous sheet, I will now commence another one.

This is Saturday. I have been trying to get up my work for tomorrow, but the thoughts do not seem to flow with their accustomed freedom. Perhaps because it is that my thoughts are far away. The wind has been contrary for you for the last few days, still we hope you have managed to get to the Stone Fort ere this.

I have packed up most of the books and tools and medicines. The women have well cleaned the house from top to bottom. I think they have made a good job of it.

I have looked over the *old Letter* Box and have sorted out a great pile and burnt a still greater lot. I read and read until the brain got in a whirl, and the memory of other days drove the present out of thought.

The day is cloudy with any amount of higher winds. Slight showers have been falling but the ground is very dry. The wheat is a complete failure this year, and I don't think we will more than get our seed potatoes back again. We are having plenty of green pease but very few young ducks to eat with them.

Tell Eddie and Lillie their little *pussies* are able to run around the floor a little. The men are away at the hayfields. They have to cut it all under water then gather it in boats and take it to the shore and spread it on the rocks to dry. Very slow and very expensive work.

I think I have about packed up everything that is to go from here. It is a little *wearing* on the nerves, this being in a state of such great uncertainty as to the future; however, "God reigns on high." All will be right, and we shall yet praise Him.

August 11ᵗʰ

I have decided to hire Martin [for Berens River] and have given him a hundred dollars advance. This will put the Mission on a good footing at once, as his son Donald will keep the school. I will be able then to come on to Ontario as soon as possible after I get word.

I have been at the *old Letters* again. Oh dear what a time. Do you really believe it, I waded through our *correspondence* of the *Golden* time. Don't you think we were a little *soft*, or *spooning*, or *moonstruck* or something else? Perhaps not, you are just as dear, and as much beloved as ever and, if I get in a hurry and don't know what to write why I think I will just slip in one of those old *Love* letters and say, multiply it a thousand-fold and accept it from your beloved.

We are nearly all starving. Out nets yield nothing and there is precious little else and that is not very *satisfying*. However we will get through. Poor little Mary is really so ambitious to do well, and, for her, she does well. She tried to make a little porrage for my breakfast this morning, but she burnt it dreadfully, and then she was so vexed about it. The bread is very good, considering the bakers.

[Charles?] Paulette was married today to Ellen Memotas. William's relations are hopping mad about it. When I scolded some of the Scotchmen for not coming to church, their answer was that the church seemed so sad and drear without Mrs. Young's sweet strong voice that they felt better at home. So you see even those poor fellows miss you.

They are so very kind and friendly at the fort that I would if I dare leave the extensive Mission premises, go over and stop there a great deal. But I have a great deal to do, and must stand by the stuff. I am teaching the school which I find not very pleasant for the olfactory nerves this warm weather.

Enormous fires are raging in the woods all round us. The air is full of magnificent smoke clouds. The wind is blowing a gale, and the Lake is lashed into foam.

A large number of boats under reef sail have shot by in the distance. They have come up from York and I am a little nervous that perhaps the Red River boats may be among them and so you will not get this letter. However if I can hire a couple of men to brave the raging waves I will send this letter across to Mr. [Roderick] Ross to forward it to you.

This is the 14th of August. Two weeks ago today you left your Northern Home, the birthplace of your children, the home still of your husband. God bless and take care of you and our little ones. I will not disguise the fact that I am very lonesome, still I am not downhearted as I believe your going was for the best. I will feel anxious until I hear from you.

John Sinclair has written up another of his miserable letters. He now accuses Dr. T. [Lachlan Taylor] of having been on the spree and of having done incalculable injury by his constant drinking before the poor Indians &c, &c, &c.[29]

Sandy and Isaac Keeper have gone to the old Fort to try and get us a few ducks. I would have gone with them only I am busy getting Martin ready and in keeping the school. Now darling I know of nothing else to write about. I hope you are well and that you have met with no misfortunes. If you cannot get a lock for

---

29 Lachlan Taylor visited the Oxford mission (as well as Rossville) in the summer of 1873; for accounts of his visit, see Part I ("The Birth of Nellie and the Pitfalls of Hospitality") and George Young, *Manitoba Memories: Leaves from My Life in the Prairie Province, 1868-1884* (Toronto: William Briggs, 1897), 256–57. John Sinclair, the lay preacher then in charge of that mission, was to be replaced by the Reverend Orrin German, whose arrival at Norway House is noted in Egerton's next letter, of 8 September 1873.

the big Trunk, get a good needle and thread and completely sew together the *canvas* cover. This would be a good way to fix the ones you do not wish to open. I hope you have found plenty of dear friends to aid you in your affairs. I felt a little uneasy about your purse as it was in that big casette near the top. The HB Company's bills are in it also, they are of one pound each. They will pay your board bill if you are at [sentence unfinished].

As I have not yet heard about the arrangements made by Conference of course I can give you no advice as to the future. Be influenced by your own feelings and health and that of the children and also by the judicious advice of friends.

Give my love to Mr. and Mrs. Flett, Mr. Armstrong, Mr. Semmens, Mrs. Young, George, and all the others you meet including the Mr. Stewarts.

I will close this and then go and see if I can find anybody willing to go across with it. Kiss the dear ones and tell them Papa sends lots of love to them. God bless you my dearest. May he ever have you in his holy keeping and save you from all harm. So prays as ever

Your affectionate husband
Egerton R. Young

Mrs. E. R. Young
Stone Fort, Manitoba

Norway House
September 8th, 1873

My darling,
Our successors have arrived and entered upon their duties. I think they will do well. Mrs. Ruttan is very young and will have much to learn. The Lord help her.[30] They have a beautiful organ, so our

30 On meeting Ellen Ruttan in January 1875 at Rossville, George Young described her as having come "right from the Wesleyan Ladies' College, Hamilton, only a few weeks elapsing from the day she left her studies till she entered upon her duties in this far-off mission" (*Manitoba Memories,* 295).When she arrived at Rossville in early September 1873, she was about nineteen years old, having married earlier that year. (The

dear little melodion [melodeon] has its song put out.[31] I must leave it here for the present and also the pictures. They are not as well supplied with clothing &c as I should have liked to have seen them. They are well off as regards provisions &c. They will live well.

Mr. [Orrin] German is two days late for the last Brigade and so must go in a Canoe. I am to go *today* with Big Tom [Thomas Mamanowatum] to my new field [Berens River].

I hope to be with you about the middle of October. I was so dreadfully disappointed that Mrs. Ruttan had no letter for me from Libbie. But I suppose you were too busy. Well darling, this is the last letter from Norway House. The place of many joys and more sorrows. The birthplace of our children, the battle ground of many a victory.

Yesterday I preached to the Indians in the afternoon. Mr. Ruttan in the morning and Bro. German at the Fort.

I never thought the poor creatures loved us half so well. There was weeping and crying all over and my own heart was deeply moved.

Mr. and Mrs. Ruttan are wonderfully pleased with the mission. The Lord give them prosperity. We are to make arrangements today about their servants, &c &c. Mary refuses to stay. She has done nobly for me.

Well so *at last* our career here is ended. Well, let us thank God we have not labored in vain or wept or suffered for nought. Love to Eddie and Lillie. Kisses and loving words to them I send: our little treasures who saved [us] from many a weary hour. I do not think I will have another chance of writing. Love to all the dear ones.

God bless you my dear good faithful loving wife. So ever prays

Yours lovingly

Egerton

1891 Canadian census showed her still in Manitoba and gave her age as thirty-seven: www.bac-lac.gc.ca/eng/census/1891/Pages/1891.aspx, search "Ellen Ruttan"). For more details, see the postscript to Part I, "Mission Wives at Rossville."

31 The Ruttans evidently kept up the musical side of mission work. On 30 August 1875, Egerton wrote to the Reverend Edward Hartley Dewart, editor of the *Christian Guardian*, that Norway House had been "handed over to Bro. Ruttan, a veritable singing pilgrim, and, if the people will not be preached into heaven, they will surely be sung into it, by him and his devoted wife" (Egerton R. Young scrapbook, clipping, p. 55).

In the Berens River notebook (UCCA, Young fonds, series 2, box 2, file 3), Young wrote: "Left Norway Ho. Mon. 7th [8th?] Sept. 1873 at 10 o'clock at night. Slept on the river at the crooked turn. Started again at daybreak. Lots of Indians followed us for miles. Last thing I saw were the uncovered heads of sorrowing Indians. . . . Said Bros. Ruttan and German, 'Bro Young, your letters brought us here. We thank God we have come.' These words uttered after they had witnessed their first Indian service."

Egerton subsequently journeyed to Ontario, where he remained for roughly five months before returning to Manitoba, arriving at Berens River at the end of March 1874. Elizabeth and the children (Eddie and Lillian), who had preceded him to Ontario, could not make the return trip until midsummer.

Ferrier Mission, Berens River
April 6th 1874

Dearest wife:
One week has passed since I reached this place. As there is to be an extra packet sent in towards the end of this month, I will not delay until the time for writing is limited, but will commence now.

My last to you was written at the Stone Fort. We left that place a few hours after the letter was sent off. The day was warm, the snow soft, the sun brilliant, and so we suffered. We had not gone half a mile, ere one of Mr. Semmens' new dogs slipped himself out of his harness and started off on a run for his home, a place twenty-five miles away. We spent about an hour in trying to overtake him, but it was all in vain, so we pushed on without him, much to Bro. Semmens' chagrin.

At an Indian's house a couple of miles down the river, I found Donald Papanekis, who had come in as one of the Indian lads for me.[32] He had injured himself by running too much,

32 In the latter section of his first letter (dated 11 August), Young refered to hiring Martin Papanekis, mentioning that Donald, his son, will "keep the school." Martin's father, William, and his three sons — Martin, Samuel, and the Reverend Edward Papanekis — were close associates of the Youngs in Rossville. Martin and his family moved from Rossville to Berens River late in 1873, where they provided important assistance with the Youngs' mission there.

and was very sick. He and most of the Indians thought he had not better attempt to return to Beren's River, but I thought differently, and carried my point against them all, and *carried* the lad in my cariole, all the way back to his anxious father and mother who were overjoyed to see him with them again. He is far from well, yet still he is better than when we left Red River. He rode in my robes and blankets every step of the way. So you can imagine that the trip was not as pleasant a one as I had anticipated as I had to walk much more than I had fondly hoped would have been my lot.

After we had left the settlement and the river we at once reached the bitter cold, which made us shiver. The fierce north winds blew against us every day, with but one exception. The bright sun on the dazzling snow blistered our half frozen faces, and partly blinded our eyes with its brilliancy. When we came to where the boys had *cached* the fish for our dogs they were not to be found, and so we had to take our fresh beef and bread and share with our dumb and patient companions, the dogs. Fortunately I had purchased a hundred weight of fresh beef, fondly hoping I might have it to use here with the white fish, but alas the best-arranged plans sometimes get all astray.

Mr. Semmens fell and badly hurt his knee just as we were starting and the result was he was in misery all the time. His dogs were small, one untrained, and one (the one purchased to take the place of the rascal that slipped off his collar and ran away) was wretchedly poor. Sometimes a fit of stubbornness would come over them and they would be thrashed until the good brother inflicting the punishment would get a little riled in spirit and flushed in the face. When the battle was over, and the dogs were once more thrashed into line, he would shout out "Bro. Egerton, do you believe in Christian perfection?"

"Yes, my brother, I do."

"Well, do you believe we can enjoy it, and live it, when training and driving stubborn obstinate dogs?"

"Yes, my Brother. Firmness and decision in conquering dogs are not sins, and if we ever expect these Esquimo dogs to be of service to us in carrying us to proclaim the glad tidings of salvation to bands of Indians, who can in the winter months be visited in no other way, we must teach them obedience and give them a few proofs of our power to enforce it."

"Bro. So-and-So," says he, "never gets ruffled. What do you think of such an experience?"

"Well, perhaps there is not depth enough in him to make a ruffle," I answer. "Our Saviour was ruffled, when he cleaned out the temple of money-changers. Stephen was ruffled when he delivered his splendid address, closing up with: 'Ye stiff-necked and uncircumcised in heart and ears &c.' Moses was ruffled when he saw the golden calf, and as the Sabbath school child said, 'smashed all the Commandments at wonst.'"

"Let us push on my Brother Semmens, the night is advancing" (for we had been travelling on the frozen lake throughout the long cold night). "See the Bear is fast completing its circuit around the North Star, the little stars that have been shining so brightly through the long night now like little children are the first to retire out of sight. The glorious Milky Way that all night long like a great white bow of promise spanned our sky sinks into oblivion. We are getting tired out with this walking and running and riding, and our dogs also seem weary, and as we are nearing this well known point let us turn in and make a fire and have something to eat and drink."

We dug a hole in the snow, spread out some boughs, opened out our camp bed, and then after eating, and then not forgetting our faithful dogs, wrapped ourselves in our blankets and robes and went to sleep. It was a fearfully cold night or rather morning.

So it went on day by day. Saturday night found us forty miles from home. What should we do. We had been accustomed to rest on the Sabbath day, but now our circumstances were different. I had a sick lad in my cariole. Our dogs' fish had been stolen and they were not at all satisfied with the fresh beef we could afford to give them. So I assumed the responsibility, and said we would push on. We travelled thirty miles that Saturday night. Sunday morning found us ten miles from the new Mission field. We had breakfast, then on we pushed. A fearful headwind arose. The lake smoked with the blinding snow, and the storm roared like a dozen Niagaras.

"Cannot face it," says one.

"Yes we can," I shout, push on, we cannot compare [?? illegible] green willows. Bro Semmens cries out, "It is a judgment of God against us for travelling on the Sabbath." "No such thing," I shout back. "It is from the Devil, who is angry at our coming to rout him from this place where he has so long had his seat."

Gallant Jack and Cuffee, with the new dogs Boxer and Muff, answer nobly to my words of cheer and pushed along barking with delight at the fierce elemental war. Sometimes so dense was the blinding snow, that the lead dogs of the train would be invisible but success crowned our efforts, and the whole four trains safely reached the shore. We were close to the little humble dwelling of Martin Papanekis ere we were seen. Martin rushed out to meet us and I saw his face was full of anxiety about his boy, but his respect for the ookemou caused him first to shake hands with me, and then I threw off the robes and told him his boy was better. A great big lump came up into my throat, as with tears of gladness in his eyes he stooped down and so lovingly kissed the poor sick fellow. I felt so glad then that I had brought him out with me instead of leaving him in Red River, as the others proposed.

Well, we were so thankful to get into a house again. But what sights we were. Our faces are blistered and burnt out of all recognition. A week has passed since I arrived here, and I spend a portion of each day in picking off the dried skin which comes off like fish scales.

I am living in my end of the little house which has been fitted up for me by Martin. It is small, cold, cosy and I am not uncomfortable. I have so much to do that I can eat anything eatable, and then when night comes can sleep anywhere. But I must leave for another time and sheet a description of my work.

Ferrier Mission
Beren's River
April 10th 1874

My darling wife,
I must write you a letter on this glad day. I have had as pleasant a
day as I possibly could under the circumstances. I arose early, had
white fish and flat cakes and tea for breakfast. Then chopped wood
for a while — then wrote letters until noon, after doing which I
went over to Mr. Flett's for dinner and remained there until after
tea and now just as the glorious sun is sinking to rest behind the
western snowy expanse I am again at my table in my little room,
with my pen writing to my heart's treasure on this the anniversary
of her natal day. I can only say the Lord bless thee, my darling and
spare you to see many happy returns of this glad day.

I went out last Monday to the big Island with the men. I had
my own dogs and worked like a good fellow, hauling the timber,
logs, &c, &c, out of the dense forest to the shore. We had over four
miles to go with some of them, and I assure you it was hard work.
The men had made a little log shanty in which to live, and if you
could only have seen us in it, and observed the rough way we lived
you would have been amused and amazed.

The *flat cakes* were made on the lid of an old packing case.
When they were taken off the box, Cuffy or Jack would go and lick
up what flour was left. Then when dinner was ready, that same box
served as my chair, while my table was a rough work bench with
a dirty old flour bag as a table cloth. For breakfast and supper we
had fish and flat cakes and tea. For dinner we also had a little meat.
We slept on the rough boards in a bed composed of a blanket and
buffalo robe, and slept well too.

This was the way, my dear, I spent my birth day. I am feeling
strong and well, and have so much to do that I keep up in spirits
splendidly. What is there to cry or fret about, when all nature
is rejoicing and the world is bright and sunny. The Indians are
very kind and respectful and I have bright hopes for the future
of this place. Tis true there are not many here at present, but they

will crowd in as fast as it is possible to make them welcome and comfortable. Mrs. Flett got up such a nice *dinner* and *supper* in honor of the day. You must really feel grateful to her for her kindness to your faraway beloved on this happy day.

A nice pound cake has been sent up to me by Mrs. Flett. It must go a long way, and last a long time. It was made on your *birthday*. Am I not highly honored?

Mrs. Flett has another son, a fine little fellow a few weeks old. His name is Donald *McTavish*. So you see they have their hands full without boarding me. I am *going in* for the fruit &c, &c. So if you come out we must have a fresh supply. I expect to leave here as early as possible so as to be in Winnipeg early in June. Shall I meet you there? Take good care of your dog; if he is going to be large, perhaps somebody coming by the Dawson route will bring him for you. Don't try to bring him by cars. It would cost 25.00 or 30.00 dollars.

The barking crows are flying. So spring is coming.

Our new house is to be more of the style of Mr. Geo. Young's of Winnipeg as it will cost less than Mr. Ferrier's den would, be more easily heated and more convenient.[33] Only it will have a good large bedroom below.

12 Elizabeth Young's Second Account of Ontario and Berens River, 1873–76

The following text is transcribed from the first six pages of a memoir by Elizabeth Young, handwritten on twelve loose-leaf lined pages preserved in E. Ryerson Young's papers. Elizabeth's reference to her son's serving as a

---

33 Young refers here to the successful Montréal businessman James Ferrier, whose elegant home — which evidently included a luxurious den — the Youngs visited during their Ontario furlough (and where Eddie had his rooftop adventure, described in chapter 7 of "A Missionary and His Son"). He and his wife, Mary, were strong advocates of Methodism and made considerable donations in kind to the Berens River mission, which Egerton Young sometimes referred to as the Ferrier mission. In her 1927 memoir, Elizabeth spoke gratefully of the Ferriers' support, crediting them with "making the bell, carpenters tools, & many other things a donation to Berens River mission."

minister in Newtonbrook dates the memoir to about 1928 (see concluding pages of his memoir outlining his career). These pages provide details not mentioned in her other memoirs:

> Now we are on our way, Winnipeg is our first stop. Then we proceed. Port-Arthur, Collingwood, Barrie, Bradford to my mothers.[34] Here we staid until Egerton came & then we went to Trenton, to visit Grandpa and Grandma Young & the Young folks, & on to dear Auntie Bowles at Brighton. We had not been home very long until the children soon began with the children's diseases first the measeles. We were visiting at this aunts with Lillian when she took the Measeles, & here we had to stay until it was safe to proceed. At the same time my dear boy Eddie had them at Grandmas in Bradford. So here I was between two fires. I just had to rest content that he would be well cared for. I could not leave Lillian so had to trust to the dear ones for his care, and pray for Wisdom and Guidance. As soon as we dare to push on we went to Trenton & from there leaving Lillian with her grandparents [William and Maria Young] there I went with Egerton to Montreal. There we met some very warm kind people, who made us happy & comfortable. Our friends were [the] Ferriers. They gave me a beautiful black Astrichan Coat, which was very much appreciated & enjoyed, for didn't I have to go back to that cold country, my, it was just what I wanted & needed.[35]

34 As of 1873, Port Arthur (now part of Thunder Bay, Ontario), was known as Prince Arthur's Landing and was the starting point of the Dawson Road or Trail, a very rough land and water route to Manitoba. Elizabeth, like most other travellers at the time, probably went from Winnipeg to Moorhead, Minnesota, and then by rail to Duluth, embarking on a steamer, which would also have stopped at Prince Arthur's Landing before crossing Lake Superior.

35 "Astrakhan" is "the skin of newborn or very young lambs, the wool of which resembles fur, from Astrakhan in Russia" (OED). Such a coat would have been an expensive item. The photograph (fig. 14) showing Elizabeth wearing the coat was probably copied for the Ferriers in gratitude for the gift.

We were taken to Hamilton to give some lectures, while there we were the guests of Mr Sandford & Mrs Sandford [Sanford] & were Royally entertained. While there two dogs were sent from the East to Mr Sandfords & when they reached there although they were in a box [they] were so furious that the men did not dare to go near them to take them out.[36] Fortunately Mr Young was there & went to there relief. As soon as he saw the dogs he knew what was the matter, he immediately got some water & some food, & had no trouble. While there Mr & Mrs Sandford & the mission friends gave us a very handsome present a silver tea & coffee set. Which is now in the hands of our beloved son who is now a minister in Newtonbrook, Ontario, Canada.

While we were in Toronto we were cordially invited to senator John McDonalds [Macdonald's] for a week. A very happy one it was.[37] They did much to make us comfortable.

As soon as Mr Young was through with his engagements he was forced to leave me & go on [to Berens River] as it was getting late in the season and would be very uncomfortable travelling for me and the children as the winter season was closing in.[38] So again I was forced to travel alone, & yet not alone for those two dogs were left to my care as well as two Ministers Dr. Warner, Rev Mr Morrison & a Lady Teacher, Miss Batty. These with my dear

36 Elizabeth Young corrected her text from "a dog" to "two dogs." However, Egerton, in *My Dogs in the Northland* (New York: Fleming H. Revell, 1902), 184–90, told of receiving one rather agitated Newfoundland dog, called Rover II or Kimo, at Hamilton, shipped from Ottawa by its donor, the Reverend Dr. Mark.

37 Similarly, in *By Canoe and Dog-Train*, 256, Young wrote, "A very happy week was spent with my family at 'Oaklands,' Toronto, the beautiful residence of the Honourable Senator Macdonald, the Lay Treasurer of our Missionary Society." In fact, John Macdonald was not appointed to the Senate (by Sir John A. Macdonald) until 1887, although he was elected to the House of Commons in 1875: Michael Bliss, "Macdonald, John," *Dictionary of Canadian Biography* online. It was during the Youngs' visit with the Macdonalds that Eddie encountered the apple with "fish scales" in it.

38 In fact, Egerton left Ontario in early March 1874, doubtless taking a steamer to Duluth. His rail trip to Moorhead, Minnesota, was much delayed by snow, and he then had to travel 250 miles "in a stage on runners over the snowy prairies" (*By Canoe and Dog-Train*, 257).

children were my companions, so I was not alone, & yet another very uncomfortable companion seized the children, the whooping cough, first one would cough & run to me and then the other. So my hands, my heart, & my physical body was taxed to the limit. But in time we reached Winnipeg & there we found our dear loved one waiting for us.

Now we pushed soon on to our mission. There was much required to get ready for the winter. The mission house was new and there was much to be done. The little log hut Mr Young had lived in still had to be our habitation for ourselves & our precious children. The carpenters & Indians were pushing on as fast. Of course I had to cook & look after their food as well as take care of my children who still had their cough. We were glad to be able to help & do what we could to make & see things close up so that we could put things in some kind of a comfortable shape for the Winter. We did some painting and chinking up. For soon after going to that cold climate we sent for a webb of factory cotton seemed [seamed] it up tacked it at top & bottom of our living room walls, & then pasted newspapers all over that. Of course this made it much more liveable. Our fuel was not of the very best but such as it was we were thankful for. No maple, no beech, no coal, our wood soft Poplar, so through the very cold weather we had to be fuelling constantly to make it liveable at all. Until we got acclimated we were very uncomfortable I won't say unhappy for we were sure we were in the path of duty. So we worked & did the best we could to make ourselves comfortable, & went on with our work.

The little log hut that Mr Young lived in so long still had to be our habitation. One night it rained so hard that a large lump of mud & grass fell through unto the foot of our little one's cot. Had it been on her head it would have killed her but fortunately that was prevented.

The Church was to be built later on, but the school house, called the Tabernacle, was built & finished so that the services were carried on. The mission house was well on, and very habitable and a great improvement to the mud hut. We were now very comfortably settled.

This is where our dear Florence was born May the ninth, 1875, now as circumstances prevented our remaining any longer, Mr Young informed the Mission Rooms that he desired a change for my sake as the strain was too great.

So in the early part of the summer of 1876 we went to Port Perry. It was indeed a wonderful change.

While on the journey our babe Florence was taken with summer complaint so that every stopping place we called in a Dr but of no avail until we reached my mother's & the Dr there did much to relieve & place her on the way of recovery much to our delight.[39]

Can you fancy travelling over three thousand miles with three children and one seriously ill, & while on a flat bottomed steamer with the sick child in my arms [I] tripped over a hidden ring that is used for hawling in large bundles from shore, and so lamed myself I was unable to walk for days. I much needed help but being a poor missionarys wife, had to do without. Glad we were to get to a Dr that could give our darling relief, and at my mother's where we could be comfortable and rest. And get ready for our new circuit.

Here I was helped by my sister Clara, who went with me to Port-Perry to help me get settled, & here we met some very kind loving people, Mr & Mrs Aaron Ross & family & many others who were extremely kind and attentive to us.[40] It was a marvelous change from no stores, to be placed where we have shops of all kinds, Drs & nurses, & every convenience. The greatest trouble now, the money problem.

39 The "summer complaint" was acute diarrhea associated with summer heat and indigestion.

40 Clara married the Rosses' son William in September 1877; in her memoir of 1927, Elizabeth mentioned attending their fiftieth anniversary in September of that year.

13 Two Letters from the Reverend Enoch Wood
Regarding the Youngs' Appointment to Berens River

As the Youngs' assignment to Berens River drew near, issues and challenges arose that were to make Egerton uncertain about remaining in "the Indian work" — and indeed the Youngs did leave Berens River after only two years, having been expected to remain for at least three.

The first letter, addressed to Elizabeth, indicates that she (with Eddie, Lillian, and the two dogs in her charge) was staying with her husband's family, the William Youngs, at Trenton and reflects uncertainty over plans for her solo trip to rejoin Egerton in Manitoba. As her memoirs indicate, she and her children and the dogs did join the Saskatchewan party that left in July.

The second, addressed to Egerton's father, the Reverend William Young, takes up his son's concern about Elizabeth's health and, in a decidedly critical tone, Egerton's seeming ambivalence about continuing mission work in the northwest.

Toronto, June 24th 1874

Dear Mrs. Young,

Miss Wiggins will be free from her present engagement on the 15th July and will be ready to start in Aug. I presume early in the month.[41] I hope the party for the Saskatchewan Dt [District] will start by the middle of July at the latest: perhaps it would be more agreeable to you to wait for Miss W. than to go earlier. Ask Father Young to give me directions about the Dogs. I think they might accompany the first who go. Hoping your health will justify your taking this long journey, I am, D[ea]r sister, Affec[tionatel]y Yours in the Lord.

E. Wood.

Mrs. E. R. Young, Trenton

41 Miss Wiggins does not appear further in these records and so was not a fellow traveller. She may be Miss Charlotte Wiggins, who, by the 1890s, was active in the Ontario Women's Christian Temperance movement.

Toronto, July 31, 1874

My Dear Bro[ther],
Your son's wish to be retired from the work at Beren's River
as expressed in a letter dated on the 25th of June is founded
entirely upon the reported ill health of Mrs Young and the
prohibition to her joining him by some medical authority. The
decisions of the Committee of Consultation and Finance may
have strengthened that wish, but they had nothing to do with its
origin. Mrs. E. R. Young's strongly expressed wish to me to come
back to her beloved Ontario induced me to say, after the time
they had spent in the north, I think he did not intend to devote
himself to the Indian work I did not think he would be asked to
stay. He showed so much interest in this new mission that we
naturally looked to him to begin it, and thought he would put
in a term of three years: had we known their united opinion
about this, we should have made other arrangements. The Com^ee
[Committee] have treated your son with great consideration and
even liberality, and will regret the large expenditure incurred
by sending out a family for so short a period. There are so many
things involved in the dissatisfaction he has expressed to you I
cannot undertake to narrate them. This I will say, nothing has
been done but what you would have sanctioned yourself. He
Labored under an error as to the sum given for Beren's River, the
amount not being half of what he thought it was, but if it were
ten times more the Committee's duty is to say when and how
it shall be expended. I have always been interested in him and
his family, and yet from the time he left Hamilton on the 4th of
March, until the 25th of June in Winnipeg not a line was received
from him at this office. We know nothing of what he was doing,
and yet supposing he might have made a beginning Fifteen
Hundred Dollars had been forwarded for his use. The work is
the Lord's and He will take care of it.

    I am, Dear Bro[ther] Faith[full]y & Affec[tionatel]y Yours,
E. Wood
Rev. Wm. Young, Trenton

14 Letter from Little Mary to Egerton R. Young, 1887

This letter from Egerton Young's papers indicates that Little Mary returned to Rossville from Berens River and was still in touch with the Youngs eleven years after they left the Northwest.[42] It also documents that she was still making moccasins and doing beadwork for them and that she warmly remembered the two children she looked after during the Youngs' mission years. The letter was written for her, perhaps by Mr. Flett, who was to send it, together with the items she had made, to the Youngs, who were living in Brampton, Ontario, in 1887–88.

Rossville Mission

July 31st/87

My dear master,

I write these few lines to let you know that I send all the shoes that I made for yours and the beaded cap, I send [sent] these things with Rev. [John H.] Ruttan, the time that he went to Manitoba last winter, and now I send some beaded work again with Mr Flett that is for to use for the legings. Now this is all I done for you, and Please Sir. I would be very much thankful, if I see anything to pay me for my trouble making of these things.

This is all for the present. Please will you give my kind kiss to Sakastawokemaw and Lillie and kind respects to all of you. And may God bless you all.

I am yours very truly Servant

Little Mary

---

42 The Norway House treaty annuity lists show Mary Robinson as living there on her own from 1876 through 1887. In 1888, she was listed as "dead." Thanks to Anne Lindsay for retrieving this information.

15 Letter from Alex Kennedy, the Youngs' Dog Driver, to Egerton R. Young, 1890

In "A Missionary and His Son," E. Ryerson referred to Alex Kennedy as "my father's dog driver," which did appear to be his chief duty, although he was also described as "the man about the house," who sometimes speared sturgeon from the pond and helped in other ways. Originally from the St. Peter's Reserve, Red River, Kennedy achieved some notice in later life both as former Nile voyageur and as a dog driver, "the fastest runner in the North," making a one-hundred-mile trip from a Peace River post to Lesser Slave Lake in only twelve hours.[43] His letter indicates that he still fondly remembered the Youngs fourteen years after they parted at Berens River.

> Lesser Slave Lake, Peace River District HB Company
> January February 2nd 1890
>
> Dear Sir
> I have a Great Pleasure of writing you a Few lines of Remember
> you still I Cannot never Forget you where ever I have Been since at
> that Time you left us at Berens River soon after I and my Father
> and Mother went Down to Red River and Riman [remain?] since
> then and my self I am Been Traveling a Great Dale now I Pass in
> Canada in 1884 & 1885 I seen many a wonderful thing since Bouth
> in Europe and Africa and America I sopose I travel more than any
> Boys [??] I youse [used] to go to school [with] at Norway House.
> I Having been Here in this District & going on 3 years my time
> [w]ill Be out this Coming spring Back again to Winnipeg Manitoba.
> I was away down at Fort Chipewyan last Summer with late Senator

---

43 This feat was noted by Church of England clergyman Richard Young, in a circular letter describing a mission journey through the Athabasca–Peace River country, Diocese of Athabasca (Athabasca Landing, NWT: Mission Press, 1897).Kennedy was one of the Canadian "voyageurs" sent on the failed expedition to relieve Major-General C. G. Gordon at Khartoum, Sudan, in 1884–85, during the Mahdi uprising; he was listed among the boatmen as no. 94 on the nominal roll. C. P. Stacey, ed., *Records of the Nile Voyageurs 1884-1885* (Toronto: Champlain Society, 1959), 259. The ninety-one men recruited in Manitoba, both Aboriginal and white, were, Stacey observed, "by far the most literate": only seven made marks instead of signing their engagement forms (13).

Hardisty.[44] I am Carr[y]ing mail for HBCO since ever I Came out Here. I often wish to see Mrs Young I could never Forget the way she youse to Kindly Treat me she youse to treat me more than my mother even. I sopose Eady and Nellie [Lillie] Growing up Big I received a Bund[l]e of Picturs from Eddy when I was at Selkirk Manitoba

Late oul Chief Factor HBCO [Robert] Hamilton's son Max Hamilton is Here. He only Came Here 2 years ago and now is a Countant for the District its Him He told me He often told about you. I sopose you Have Forgotin your Dog Driver Now. I sopose oul Dog Jack Died Long now [?] of Dog Drivers in this Country yet.

This about all Kind [?] to you all

I am yours truly
Alex Kennedy

16 Elizabeth Bingham Young: Appreciations and Memories

Egerton R. Young, Dedication in *By Canoe and Dog-Train*, 1890
To the Faithful and Loving Wife
Who so cheerfully and uncomplainingly for years shared the hardships and toils of some of the most trying mission fields; whose courage never faltered, and whose zeal abated not, even when "in perils" oft, from hunger, bitter cold, and savage men; this volume is dedicated, by her affectionate husband.

"The Red Indian Missionary"
The following is an excerpt from an interview with Egerton Young, titled simply "Further Interview," that appeared in the *Bathurst Daily Argus* (New South Wales) on 21 June 1904, during the Youngs' travels in Australia.

---

44 Former HBC officer Richard Hardisty, appointed a senator early in 1888, died 15 October 1889 after a horse-and-buggy accident (Shirlee Anne Smith, "Hardisty, Richard," *Dictionary of Canadian Biography* online).

"Where was Mrs. Young while you were wandering about these trackless regions?" we naturally inquired. Mrs. Young, who was sitting by a cosy fire, as we put this question, looked up and smiled. It seemed impossible to realise that these two, looking so comfortable and unconcerned, had been through such extraordinary experiences. "My wife," replied Mr. Young, "was home missionary and I was the foreign missionary. While I was away Mrs. Young was in charge of the work at the Head mission at Norway House, which was about 400 miles from the city of Winnipeg. . . . So well did Mrs. Young attend to the school and look after the varied duties around that, when I returned after six weeks' travelling with my dogs preaching to the wandering tribes, the chiefs would meet me and, in their quiet, dignified way, would say, "Well, missionary, we are glad to see you back, but we did not miss you at all."

An Unusual Ballad, by E. Ryerson Young

December, Nineteen Twenty-Five. In Memory of December, Eighteen Sixty-Seven.

Yes, bring in the preacher and bring in his son;
For naught will be missed where a good deed's done.
Then loudly there rang the old school bell
And when all had been greeted,
And at table were seated,
In bounded Libbie, and Mary and Nell.

With shouts and with laughter, with health and bright eyes,
They entered; were silenced; but Love cried, "A prize!"
For back, in fast time, came the preacher's bright sonny;
And for Libbie, he brought a pretty white bunny
"Out of this," said the mother; "no vermin for me!"
And away went the lad and his bunny, pell mell.
But nothing could smother the love and the glee
Of those jolly ones, Libbie and Mary and Nell.

They drove the old horse in the tan-bark mill
And would sleigh-ride down the Bradford hill.
For work did not rob them of joy, love and play;
They could wash and could bake, make hats and be gay.
For quick were their fingers; nothing shirked, I can tell;
Aye, smart ones were they, Libbie and Mary and Nell.

The years came and went; they always hold sway.
The minister's son, to teach school, went away.
A Jim came for Mary and Nell took a Will;
Though many called Libbie, she held out still.
For love keeps its secret, like a clam in a shell;
And Libbie made hats for Mary and Nell.

From school to the pulpit, our hero ascended;
And was heralded wide, as someone right splendid.
Then offers were his of heiress's hands,
With preferment and riches, honors and lands;
But all of this glory to earth flatly fell,
When he thought of those bright ones, Libbie, and Mary and Nell.

Then back to the home where he met the school girls,
Where his heart leaped a-thrill at the sight of their curls;
And there our Ulysses found his brave Penelope,
Baffling the men and waiting in hope.
Then joy filled the days and loud rang the bell
As the last of them married, of Libbie and Mary and Nell.

This typescript was pasted on pp. 110–11 of a scrapbook kept by Grace Young Brown and inherited by her daughter, Elizabeth Brown, who gave it to Harcourt Brown in 1981. E. Ryerson Young, writing to his sister Grace in about 1933, noted of the "Unusual Ballad" that it "is *absolutely correct!!*" about their parents' early attachment.

In his 1962 memoir, E. Ryerson recorded a sequel to his father's original venture with rabbits. Soon after arriving at Norway House, Egerton made a try at raising rabbits in the attic, where the Youngs' predecessors, the Stringfellows, had kept their hens. "When mother had cleaned the hens out of the attic," he recalled, "father's love for rabbits revived, for they had been his hobby when a boy, and he thought the attic would be an ideal place to raise them. But the stars were on mother's side. She had not hesitated to protest against having animals in her home, and thought they were no better than hens. She reminded him of the time when they were in Bradford when he brought his first rabbit as a love gift to her. At the first sight of the rabbit, her mother had denounced him and said with all the forces she had, 'get that vermin out of here.' My mother was a pioneer's daughter, and when her father had cleared the trees away she had tried to raise a garden, but rabbits had made it almost impossible. Hence before grandmother's fury father with his rabbit fled."

"However," he continued, "in due course father managed to start his rabbit colony in the attic. The next day an Indian was sent to put some fish nets there and he threw it [them] up in the attic. When father went to see his flock the next morning he found the rabbits had caught their heads in the mesh and strangled themselves. After father had cleared away the dead rabbits, mother and the Indian woman thoroughly cleaned the attic and disinfected it and made it a desirable place where they could store the new things that were made for them by the Indian women." Presumably, the rather unsavoury end to the venture did little to increase Elizabeth's fondness for rabbits.

The Funeral Services for Elizabeth Bingham Young

Elizabeth Young died on 29 May 1934, aged ninety-one. As Newton Brown, the husband of Elizabeth's daughter Grace Amanda, recorded, the funeral oratory tested the Christian patience of the mourning relatives:

> The service was conducted by three ministers with the Rev. Ferguson a classmate of Ed's [E. Ryerson Young] in charge and he was the worst I ever heard. Over one hour at the house with the most fulsome talk about what Grandma had done as a girl — won a beauty contest in Bradford before she was married — and then ten minutes on her journey to the west in which he got his geography all mixed up. And slathers more on her wonderful family and then some straight evangelical preaching at the grandchildren and more

of the most banal talk I ever listened to. [The guests then drove to
Bowmanville for the burial.] Here at the church where Grandfather
used to preach 50 years ago . . . Ferguson went over the same stuff
that we had heard at the house. . . . One hour and a half — It was
awful — not a touching incident or phrase and such an opportunity
for a man to have made a beautiful inspiring address, but it was
not to be. . . . At the church Beth [Brown, daughter of Grace and
Newton Brown] got up and stalked out of the church after a
particularly insufferable bit of drivel — she had stood it for
40 minutes. But Ferguson . . . went on for 50 minutes more.[45]

Recollections from Harcourt Brown

On 5 September 1979, Harcourt Brown, Elizabeth Young's grandson, sent
a copy of the *Manitoba Pageant* issue (Autumn 1971) in which Egerton's
1873–74 letters to Elizabeth were published to Nigel Helme, the grandson
of Lillian Young Helme, in South Africa. What follows is an excerpt from
the accompanying letter:

Re "Your interest in our common ancestry": The E. R. Young letters
in the *Manitoba Pageant* fill a gap in the story, but only a small gap;
there is much more to be read about in the mss and old periodicals
of the Wesleyans of that day, and certainly room for a biography of
Egerton Young and his devoted wife, with whom I had the pleasure
of innumerable associations from earliest childhood as long as I
lived in Canada — up to 1929 — and thereafter, as we returned for
various occasions.

Jack Watson [Elizabeth Young's grandson] . . . described her
to me as the most methodist person you could imagine; he should
know, for she made her home with [his parents] Aunt Win and
Uncle Herb [Watson] from about 1915 to the end of her life in
1934. From her life in the Northwest she kept the habit of a cold

45 Newton Brown to his son Harcourt Brown, in New York City. Harcourt, who
was unable to attend the funeral, visited Toronto a few weeks later and delivered to
Victoria College library many books and other publications that his grandmother had
kept. Winnifred Young Watson probably supplied the "beauty contest" story: see the
introduction to Part I.

bath every morning, all year round; I recall that I had to clear a space on the shore of Lake of Bays when she came to spend part of a summer with us about 1921;[46] I moved rocks and smoothed the sand and when I came from the cottage where I slept to the house for breakfast I kept my eyes carefully averted from the small bit of beach where she bathed *au naturel.*

She loved her radio for church services; she sang the hymns in Cree from a small hymnbook. . . . She was generous to a fault, but no spendthrift; what she gave was worthwhile and usually treasured — I still have a fine Bible she gave me on May 30, 1916 [his sixteenth birthday], which I do not use for reference but keep in its pristine morocco binding.

She was a dynamic person, an organizer — she had to be, for E RY could get people working but his wife told them what to do and how to do it. I remember as a small boy of six or seven maybe eight — how the whole family rose at dawn in summer to cut the tremendous crop of sweet peas in the garden at Bradford [Algonquin Lodge] to count and package them for shipment by an early train to Toronto forty miles away for the morning market; there were several boxes every day, with bunches of flowers in fifties, I suppose; the director of operations was the same Elizabeth Bingham Young whose picture you recall. She ran the household at Bradford with tremendous energy; if one did not toe the line one heard about it with vigor. I don't remember being sloppily sentimental over her but I did have tremendous respect for her, and I have no single thought of anything but good about her. I may have disagreed with some of her views, but in retrospect I know now that I was wrong, and she was right; I could quote [George Bernard] Shaw and [Henrik] Ibsen, usually in the wrong places, but her silent disapproval was apparent and never led to an argument. . . . You have set free a flood of memories of a much-loved person, a grandmother to be proud of, to give us a heritage of courage and serenity and quiet breadth of sympathy and confidence.

---

46 Harcourt Brown's parents, Newton and Grace Young Brown, spent parts of several summers at a cottage on Lake of Bays in Muskoka, Ontario.

Index